SACRED TRUST?

Brian Mulroney and the
Conservative Party in Power

SACRED TRUST?

Brian Mulroney and the Conservative Party in Power

David Bercuson
J.L. Granatstein
W.R. Young

1986
Doubleday Canada Limited, Toronto, Ontario
Doubleday & Company, Inc., Garden City, New York

Copyright © 1986 by David Bercuson, J.L. Granatstein,
W.R. Young
All rights reserved

Cover design by David Shaw
Typesetting by Compeer Typographic Services
Printed in Canada by John Deyell Company

Canadian Cataloguing in Publication Data
Bercuson, David Jay, 1945-
   Sacred trust?

ISBN 0-385-25060-6

1. Canada — Politics and government — 1984-   .*
2. Progressive Conservative Party of Canada.
3. Mulroney, Brian, 1939-   . I. Granatstein, J. L., 1939-   .
II. Young, William Robert, 1947-   . III. Title.

FC630.B47 1986   320.971   C86-094037-2
F1034.2.B47 1986

Library of Congress CIP data applied for.

Contents

Preface

The authors of this book are historians of widely varying political hues who decided to apply the techniques of their craft to the events of the present. This may be a rash undertaking if only because very few of the preferred sources for historians are readily available to document the events of the first year and a half of the Mulroney government. On the other hand, the same methods of assessing historical evidence that are used to appraise the achievements of Sir John A. Macdonald or Mackenzie King, for example, can be applied to the public record of the current Progressive Conservative government and to the documents we have seen and the many interviews we have conducted. We know that some aspects of this snapshot of a government in its formative stages are better developed than others, and readers should understand that some pictures and events may be hidden in the shade or may not have made it into our camera's range. The people and issues that we have examined and analysed here were chosen because they interested us, because we had or could secure access to the evidence, and because their importance was so great they could not properly be omitted.

As this suggests, we have not attempted to cover every aspect of the government's record. Nor have we attempted to carry the story as near to the present as we might have wished. Our focus here is on the months from September 1984 to April 1986, and if that leaves some issues hanging in midair, as it regrettably does, we can only say that a cut-off point was inevitable in any book such as this.

This book could not even have been attempted without the help of the many men and women, bureaucrats and politicians, who gave us their time and cooperation (and cheerfully passed us on to their friends and colleagues) on the clear understanding that what they told us would be used without attribution. We are most grateful for their assistance.

We have also benefited greatly from the research work, stenographic skills, and talents as an appointments secretary of Leslie Morris. *Sacred Trust* could scarcely have been written without her help. We are also very grateful for the editing talents of Philippa Campsie of Doubleday who poked and prodded our prose into something approximating readability. We three are wholly responsible for any errors or omissions.

Spring 1986

D.J.B.
J.L.G.
W.R.Y.

SACRED TRUST?

Brian Mulroney and the
Conservative Party in Power

Chapter One
Introduction

The new government swept into power like a tidal wave. All across the country, the ministerial relics of the past government tumbled like tenpins, losing seats by huge margins to unknown Tories. Even in Quebec the Liberals were routed, their vaunted organization collapsing like a pricked balloon. Conservative organizers who had been watching the opinion polls in the days before the vote were stunned—the numbers had been there, but the result still exceeded their most optimistic projections. It was a triumph for the new leader, a victory on an unparalleled scale, an unquestionable mandate for change, and an opportunity to build a Tory era from the party's overwhelming strength in every region of English Canada and in Quebec.

That assessment of John Diefenbaker's victory in the general election of 1958 is also applicable to the triumph of Brian Mulroney in September 1984. Everything that Mulroney won in his election had been Diefenbaker's twenty-six years before. The Chief had then seen the dream of an enduring Conservative dynasty dissolve in party dissension and electoral defeat. Within four years, the great majority of 1958 withered into the minority government of 1962. By the next year, as his Cabinet tore itself to pieces over the nuclear arms controversy with the United States and prolonged economic difficulties, the indecisive and uncertain Diefenbaker was driven from power. Except for a brief interlude under Joe Clark in 1979-80, the Conservative party would not regain power until Mulroney did the trick. The ability to hold on to power by governing wisely has not been the hallmark of the Conservative party in the twentieth century.

Brian Mulroney could not be called a student of history, but he had a long record of participation in the politics of his party. As a student Tory in the Diefenbaker years, he had offered advice to the Chief and the party about Quebec, only to see most of it ignored. In the mid-1960s, he had worked closely with Davie Fulton of British Columbia, the most intellectual of Diefenbaker's ministers, and he and Joe Clark, a young Conservative from Alberta, had been important members in the group Fulton held in readiness for his leadership campaign whenever Diefenbaker finally succumbed to the long knives of his enemies. Fulton's ambitions went for naught in 1967 when the Tories chose Nova Scotia Premier Robert Stanfield as their leader. But Fulton's abilities as a talent spotter were certainly the best in the party: both Clark and Mulroney were leading contenders at the next leadership convention in 1976. Although Mulroney's campaign was brassier than Clark's, he was eliminated earlier and "Joe Who?" won the contest.

Mulroney was not a contented loser. Like John Diefenbaker, John Turner, and Jean Chrétien, to name only three, he chafed at serving those who had defeated him at party conventions. He refused to run for Parliament, he grumbled in the backrooms, and he kept his friends around him, ready to make another attempt for power if and when the new leader faltered. Although Clark led the party to a minority victory in 1979, his government was overthrown in 1980, a victim of overconfidence and the shrewd tactics of the Liberals. Pierre Trudeau was to reign for four more years. Although it took three years to topple Clark completely, that loss sealed his fate. And when the dust of the 1983 leadership convention settled, it was Brian Mulroney of Baie-Comeau (and Montreal) at the top of the greasy pole.

Who is this man? Born into modest circumstances as the son of an electrician, Mulroney was bilingual, Catholic, and ambitious. He made his way to St. Francis Xavier University in Antigonish, Nova Scotia, in 1955, a skinny sixteen-year-old who made friends with many of the movers and shakers at that small campus of about a thousand students and got himself deeply involved in politics as a student Conservative. His friends included Fred Doucet, Sam Wakim, Pat McAdam, and others, all of whom would later help get Mulroney the leadership of the party and the country.

After St. FX (where he wrote a senior honours essay on "The Politics of Quebec, 1933-58"), Mulroney went to the Faculté de droit at Université Laval in Quebec City in 1960. McGill was the usual place for an English-speaking Quebecker to learn the practice of law, but it was already clear that Mulroney was not restricted by the blinkers that had made English-speaking Quebeckers so hated by the French majority in the province. He was Irish and Catholic, for a start, and many of his Irish Catholic compatriots had learned to understand Quebec as well or better than any Québécois. Chubby Power, the long-serving, hard-drinking, and able Quebec City Liberal MP and Minister of National Defence (Air) during World War II, who had resigned from the Cabinet when Mackenzie King imposed conscription for overseas service in 1944, was just one example. Bryce Mackasey was another.

Mulroney had the nerve of a cat burglar and a powerful charm, dressed up (perhaps overdressed) with Irish blarney. He did not hesitate, for example, to call up major political figures to attend a conference on Quebec-Canada relations in 1961, to cajole companies for money, and to ingratiate himself with everyone with whom he dealt. He was good-looking, an almost handsome man whose looks improved as his face filled out and the tension between his large jaw and prominent nose eased. People liked to be with him, to bask in his regard and win his admiration. He had a quick mind and a sharp tongue, but he treated his friends unfailingly well. And in Quebec City during the Quiet Revolution he made more friends to add to the St. FX gang: Peter White, Michel Cogger, Jean Bazin, and Bernard Roy would all play major roles under Brian Mulroney in the future.

As a lawyer in Montreal with the firm of Howard, Cate, Ogilvy after his call to the bar in 1965, Mulroney built a good reputation as a negotiator of out-of-court settlements and as an arbitrator. He was a man who sought compromise and who could use an unstoppable flow of words to mask the differences between parties in a dispute. Through hard work and skilful bargaining, he made friends with top officials of the province's unions, with management figures, and with academics (he helped Concordia University's faculty resolve a dispute with their administration). He also kept up the connections he had forged as a student Tory with politicians in Quebec City and in Ottawa, carefully building ties of loyalty and friendship with those in power—and out. For example, until Robert Bourassa was defeated by the Parti Québécois in 1976, Mulroney was close to the Quebec premier, who appointed him a member of the royal commission headed by Mulroney's old Laval law professor, Robert Cliche, investigating corruption in the construction industry. Although virtually everyone else dismissed ''Boo-Boo'' Bourassa after his fall from power, Mulroney stayed on good terms with him. There was a warmth and a loyalty in Brian Mulroney that did him credit.

Well-off but far from rich, Mulroney eagerly accepted the post of president of the Iron Ore Company of Canada, an American subsidiary owned by the Hanna family interests of Cleveland, after his defeat at the 1976 convention. This was an opportunity to move up in the world and make some money, to settle into a better house with his young wife Mila and their children, and to get to know the captains of industry in the United States.

But there was a drawback to all this. As president, Mulroney had to follow orders from the parent company to shut down the company's operation at Schefferville, Quebec, in 1982, although the decision doomed the town. That was hard, and although Mulroney always claimed that he had secured a good deal for the displaced workers (who, in truth, did not protest much at the terms), clearly he had learned that power carries risks as well as benefits. Today's hero can still become tomorrow's villain.

Schefferville did not hurt Mulroney when he set out to wrest the party leadership from Joe Clark in 1983. Nor did it appear to damage his chances when he began the struggle to capture the prime ministership. He was helped by the extraordinary unpopularity of the Trudeau government at the beginning of 1984.

After almost sixteen years in office, Trudeau had become arrogant and his ministers governed as if they alone knew what was best for the country. Bereft of support in the West, Trudeau ran a central Canadian government that had antagonized the business community generally, Western business and the oil industry in particular, and hundreds of thousands of ordinary Canadians. And yet, without question, Trudeau remained the Liberals' trump card. He was the man who had beaten Lévesque during the 1980 referendum and saved the country from separatism, and he was still the most magnetic figure in Canadian politics, his face at sixty-five only slightly more lined than it had been at his accession in 1968. But Trudeau had stepped down and, after an unexciting convention in mid-1984, power and the prime ministership passed to John Turner.

As the aging fair-haired boy of the Liberal party, Turner had been Trudeau's finance minister until his huffy departure from the Cabinet in 1975. Then it was corporate law on Bay Street, daily lunches at Winston's, and a decade of waiting for Trudeau to depart. In the 1960s, Turner had seemed the very model of a modern Liberal, but upon his return to power, he quickly demonstrated that he had lost touch with the nation and with his party. The foolish decision to call a quick election, the devastating defeat he suffered in the nationally televised debates with the other party leaders, and the country's desire for real change all combined to topple him in the election of September.

So it was to be Mulroney who would have the chance to remodel the nation after the years of tight control under Trudeau. However, not even his firmest supporters would ever claim that Brian Mulroney was an intellectual with years of deep study of the problems of Canada or of the world behind him. His agenda for the future on the day he walked into office was simple: it was time for a change. In other words, he was no Pierre Trudeau. But what did he hope to achieve in power?

Mulroney's aims were not difficult to fathom. Although his supporters in the 1983 leadership struggle had tended to come from the right wing of the party (anti-abortion, anti-metric, pro capital punishment, pro balanced budgets, pro defence spending, and anti-universality in social programs), Mulroney was not a reactionary. His instincts tended toward the red Tory positions on most questions and he was, in many ways, not very different from Joe Clark, the man he had worked so hard to defeat. Like every politician, he was a creature of ambition, a man who sought power less for the sake of achieving great things with it, than for the sake of wielding it. He had gathered around him a group of friends who had proven themselves loyal and devoted and from whom he received the reassurance and praise he needed. He was less friendly to those with whom he had crossed swords in the past, although Mulroney's style was almost always glossed over with slap-on-the-back bonhomie (''Hiya Tommie, how are ya, boy?'' was his greeting to one MP in the House of Commons lobby). He had a tendency to let his words run ahead of his thoughts, a habit of exaggerating his own achievements, and a knack for downplaying his past positions. In private with friends, his descriptions of the men and women with whom he was forced to work were often vituperative and colourful. Mulroney, in other words, was a political animal, a man who would do whatever was necessary to stay in power. He was no Pierre Trudeau with, for example, clear views on how to resolve the conflict between separatism and federalism and to change the constitution, but he was not very different from Trudeau the patronage politician who had ruled Canada for sixteen years (nor from virtually every other prime minister Canada has had).

What Mulroney wanted to achieve was also fairly clear. On the political side, he wanted to make the Progressive Conservative party the new government party, Canada's natural majority party. That meant giving the party a solid, unshakeable base in Quebec, with roots in every community and in business and finance, not only in Montreal and Quebec City, but also in Rimouski and Rivière-du-Loup. To achieve that, he had to use the *deputés* that had been handed to him on September 4, 1984, as well as his friends throughout the province. He had to deal with the Parti Québécois government of René Lévesque and, after him, Pierre-Marc Johnson, and he had to do so cautiously enough to keep the support of *péquistes* who hated the federal Liberals. At the same time, he could not afford to antagonize English Quebeckers, who still viewed the separatists as traitors.

Mulroney also had to maintain links with the provincial Liberals, many of whom had voted for him and many of whom had also mistrusted Trudeau (and Turner), and with Robert Bourassa, who increasingly appeared to be the premier-in-waiting. If Mulroney could ensure a base in Quebec, he would be well on his way to creating a long-lived Tory regime.

Nor could he neglect the rest of the country. The West was perennially unhappy, its staple products such as wheat, lumber, and oil always at the mercy of swings in commodity prices or the tariffs of foreign competitors. The Maritimes, chronically depressed, had to be placated. Ontario was invariably critical and politically volatile, suspicious of the influence of the oil provinces on Mulroney's government. But if he could handle federal-provincial relations well, if he could damp down the flames of disagreement that Trudeau and his ministers had fanned, then Mulroney might be able to make his mark as a leader and as a political chief. His first priority had to be to negotiate agreements with Alberta on oil revenue and with Newfoundland on off-shore oil development. Premiers Lougheed and Peckford were not, however, the easiest of men to deal with.

On policy questions, Mulroney's platform as he ran for office was vague enough to permit almost anything once he was safely in power. He had promised to restore Canada's relations with the United States. The relationship had been damaged by Trudeau's contempt for some of the presidents with whom he dealt, by his sometimes capricious behaviour, by his National Energy Program, and by his end-of-regime peace initiative. Mulroney had said nothing favourable about free trade with the United States before September 4, but he gave ample indication that he sought American investment. Closer ties with Reagan's America could—and would—arouse fears that Mulroney would bind Canada too closely to Washington's chariot wheels. Mulroney had also made uncharacteristically clear and explicit promises in the area of defence: more money, more recruits for the forces, more assistance to Canada's alliances, and new uniforms to restore the morale that (old soldiers, sailors, and airmen still claimed) had been undermined by the unification of the armed forces almost two decades before.

Defence is expensive, however: the cost of a single ship today equals the entire federal budget of fifty years ago. Meanwhile, the federal deficit under Trudeau (most noticeably while John Turner was finance minister) had skyrocketed. Bay Street and St. James Street were unhappy about that and about the high taxes and interest rates necessary to support the cost of the deficit and the country's social spending. Mulroney had to get the deficit under control. Unfortunately for him, during the election campaign he had declared the preservation of the welfare state and the universality of social programs a ''sacred trust.'' How could the deficit be reduced if unemployment insurance, indexed old age pensions, family allowances, and other programs remained inviolate? Critics put the question differently: how could the deficit be reduced if companies in difficulty continued to be bailed out by federal funds? Even though that was not a fair comparison—bailouts eat up only a tiny fraction of the money spent on statutory programs—perceptions matter in politics.

Mulroney and his party also claimed to want to deregulate Canadian life. Under the Liberals (and under the Tory governments of R. B. Bennett and John Diefenbaker), the state had thrust its tentacles into virtually every aspect of Canadian life. Did Ottawa have to own airlines and aircraft companies? Did it really need inspectors to check almost every facet of commerce? Did it need a state-owned broadcasting corporation, a policy on Canadian culture, and programs to support academics, artists, and orchestras? Did energy have to be so tightly regulated? Liberals in the last years of the Trudeau regime had begun to consider those problems; unquestionably, however, more ministers in the Tory government thought that the answer to all or most of such questions was no.

The agenda of issues was a full one, but what Mulroney himself thought about most of them was unknown or, at best, unclear. This book will examine these questions and the difficulties that beset the men and women who tried to deal with them in the first year and a half of the Progressive Conservative government of Brian Mulroney.

Part One
Getting It Together

Chapter Two
The Arrival of the
Government-in-Waiting

On a sunny September day, a cavalcade of official cars pulled away from the Centre Block of the Parliament Buildings, swung past the War Memorial, drove along Sussex Drive, and entered the gates of Rideau Hall. As a matter of course, other Ottawa drivers caught in its path cursed quietly at the traffic holdup and then proceeded on their way. To live in the capital of Canada is regularly to confront these processions, a part of the bread-and-circuses that surround state occasions.

Although there were no great throngs in the street, this cortege did excite more interest than most. The cars dropping off passengers at Government House contained Brian Mulroney's choices for the Cabinet of the new Conservative government who were on their way to be sworn in. Across the city, the public servants gathered around their department's television sets and watched closely. The curtain was rising to reveal those who would govern the country for at least the next four years. The members of the new Cabinet, starting with the new prime minister, marched one by one to the front of the ballroom to take their oaths of office. Later, the forty Privy Councillors posed with the Governor General for the obligatory photograph. They then emerged from Rideau Hall to face the September sunlight and the forest of microphones.

The scene was all very ordered and gave few clues to the hectic months, even years, that had preceded it. Since June 1983, when the Conservative party had switched its leader from Joe Clark to Brian Mulroney, the Canadian political scene had changed significantly. When Mulroney took over the Tory leadership, the party was so high in the public opinion polls that it could go no higher—

11

the Conservatives could not even pick up the ten percentage points in the polls that normally follow a leadership convention. But Pierre Trudeau was still in office and the mandate of his Liberal government ran until 1985. Although all the pundits and the politicians were betting that Trudeau would retire before the coming election, no one knew just when he would choose to leave. Nine months after Mulroney's convention victory, on February 29, 1985, Trudeau made his decision, and in June the Liberal party anointed John Turner as its leader and the country's new prime minister. With the hoopla of the party contest behind him, Turner picked up support, and for the first time in months his party led the Conservatives. Deluded, as one senior Tory said, "by those wicked things" the polls, Turner called an election for September 4. He lost.

In the next two weeks, the Conservatives' years of hoping and planning were to be translated into action. Brian Mulroney had worked to make the Conservative party a government-in-waiting in image as well as in fact. The party and its leader had wanted to set the tone for the coming Tory epoch by a dignified and purposeful assumption of the reins of power. The cavalcade from the Centre Block to Rideau Hall was a very small part of it. The new government took office with a complete set of blueprints for power and probably the most intensive preparations ever undertaken by an incoming government in Canada's political history.

*　*　*

In June 1983, two weeks after he moved into the offices of the Leader of the Opposition, Brian Mulroney began preparations for the events of September 17, 1984. Although the Tories did have the advantage of having fairly recently organized a government—in 1979, when Joe Clark became prime minister—Mulroney was only too well aware that his party had very limited experience in government: nine months of office in the preceding twenty-one years. The new opposition leader asked Finlay MacDonald to study ways of assuming the reins of power. A longtime Conservative fundraiser from Nova Scotia, MacDonald had been campaign chairman during the 1972 election and later Robert Stanfield's principal assistant. He knew from this experience that a party in opposition is competent and confident only in limited areas. The party had to make up for its ignorance by finding the right people to help.

By early August, 1983, while Mulroney was getting himself elected to the House of Commons in a by-election in Nova Scotia's riding of Central Nova, MacDonald had finished his report and outlined his plans to the leader. During a retreat at Mont-Ste-Marie the following month, he presented it to the Conservative caucus.

The party accepted MacDonald's recommendation that four major teams would organize the transition. MacDonald coordinated the various groups and reported to Mulroney and to the caucus. Harvie Andre, an MP from Calgary, chaired the policy committee. Walter Baker—replaced on his death by Don Mazankowski—looked after the machinery of government, including an assessment of the senior public service. MacDonald worked on appointments and Peter White from the opposition leader's office took on the job of staffing ministers' offices.

The policy section of the takeover evaluation was merely shepherded by MacDonald's transition team; caucus committees developed the party's policy in specific areas. The Conservatives were determined to avoid coming to Parliament as Joe Clark's government had done, without a firm idea of a legislative program. They also wanted ministers to be able to take office with some understanding of their portfolios.

Information provided by the Liberal government aided the transition preparations by the caucus. Joe Clark's government had drawn up guidelines that permitted officials to brief opposition caucuses or party spokesmen. Pierre Trudeau had codified these guidelines in 1981 and sanctioned access to information on departmental organization, functions, and budgets as well as on the operation and content of new programs. Officials, however, could not disclose Cabinet confidences or express personal opinions without authorization from their minister. Requests were made to the minister concerned and then forwarded to the Clerk of the Privy Council. In addition to these briefings, the opposition could get information from ministers during question period, from written questions on the order paper, and from committee hearings and letters.

When MacDonald explained the guidelines to the caucus at

Mont-Ste-Marie, he provoked a flurry of interest. Many MPs had not known of the guidelines' existence and other caucus members, intimidated by the hitherto close relationship between the Prime Minister's Office and the Privy Council Office, had never asked for information. The caucus members asked the transition team to prepare most of the requests for information.

MacDonald engineered the introduction of Brian Mulroney to Gordon Osbaldeston, the Clerk of the Privy Council. The two of them hit it off and the senior mandarin undertook to fill many of the Conservatives' requests for information under the guidelines. At the same time, however, Osbaldeston was briefing the potential Liberal successors to Trudeau and knew that his office would be compromised in the eyes of any future prime minister if he did not act impartially and yet with loyalty to the government then in office. If there were any doubts about a request exceeding the guidelines' intent, Osbaldeston asked Prime Minister Trudeau for a final decision. No requests were denied.

The material that the caucus received was used to fashion Conservative policies. As a government-in-waiting, the Tory caucus had set up shadow Cabinet committees and a mirror of the priorities and planning committee, the major Cabinet body. A few of their studies gained national attention. The caucus worked out a policy for the humanization of Revenue Canada after a caucus task force chaired by the MP from Wellington-Dufferin-Simcoe, Perrin Beatty, travelled across the country to hear Canadians' complaints. The Tories had also reached an agreement in principle with Newfoundland about off-shore resources and had generally indicated their intention to dismantle the National Energy Program. Jim Hawkes, the MP for Calgary West, put together a report on technological change and job training. The caucus committees took the information provided to them by the Liberal government and worked to fit spending estimates for various programs into Conservative priorities. This exercise kept the fractious Tory MPs from wasting time on their notorious party vendettas.

At another gathering at Mont-Ste-Marie in the first week of April 1984, some of the Conservative policy platform was made public. This was all part of the strategy to reinforce the Conservatives' credibility as a government and to meet the criticism that the party lacked policy. Some of the proposals emerged in the style of white papers prepared by the government with provisions for consultation with interest groups and the provincial governments. They were later used as general campaign themes and to prepare the inch-thick campaign handbook. This catechism emphasized the continuing round of consultations with Canadians and made much of the differences between the Tories and the Liberal government.

Apart from the policy studies, the review of appointments by order-in-council was an essential task for MacDonald's transition team. Getting the Conservatives' own people into place on the various federal boards and commissions was seen as a top priority after the Clark government's experience. The party's morale had suffered in 1980 because Clark's office had moved too slowly; this had caused some resentment in the ranks, particularly when the party's defeat in the House in December 1979 left even Senate seats unfilled. The group looking after appointments identified the existing jobs and the terms that governed them and recommended that the party establish a committee in each region to identify prospective appointees. In effect, the team laid the foundation for future Tory patronage.

In approaching its third assignment—evaluating the senior public service—the transition team was divided. Those who worked in the opposition leader's office, like Charles McMillan, a policy adviser, did not expect that the upper echelons of the public service would hinder the work of incoming Tories. With one or two exceptions, the former ministers in the Clark government had generally felt well served by the senior bureaucrats. Caucus representatives, on the other hand, tended to believe that the bureaucracy might try to sabotage a Conservative government. Their feelings toward Michael Pitfield, former Clerk of the Privy Council, coloured the MPs' views of the entire public service. With some justification, the MPs concluded that since Pitfield and Trudeau had been joined at the hip, the Liberals had politicized the upper level of the bureaucracy and particularly the Privy Council Office. Despite his reputation as a hard-liner, Sinclair Stevens, the President of the Treasury Board in 1979-80, countered the caucus's fears by telling members that if a Conservative government automatically assumed that it was confronting a hostile public service, the Tories would be dead in the water from the outset.

By and large, the other members on the committee, while trying to ignore the MPs' concerns, remained sceptical of the public service, especially the senior levels. Afterwards, many members of the team claimed they were not involved in a witch hunt, but rather were searching for talented individuals who could be promoted. Despite dissent from some MPs, the transition team therefore decided to retain the existing bureaucrats, although no one dismissed the possibility of recruiting individuals from the private sector. As one of them put it, the true question was competence: "How to get new people in, get the better people up, and the clowns out."

The witch hunters, however, had not been put entirely out of business. Some of the planners were worried that if the Conservatives won only a few more seats than the Liberals, the civil service would not support the new government. With this in mind, some Conservatives sought to use the civil servants' briefings to the caucus as a way of flushing out anti-Tory bureaucrats. Erik Nielsen, the party's deputy leader, asked the MPs to write an evaluation of each senior public servant they met. This suggestion was opposed by other members of the transition team and by many of the MPs, who felt it unfair to judge an individual on the basis of a single meeting. Nielsen's request indicated, however, that powerful individuals in the Tory party wanted to take a more forceful approach to the bureaucracy.

If the Conservatives were to form a government, Mulroney would have to make a decision about the fate of the bureaucracy. At first, however, he appeared to waffle. In a speech in May 1984, he said that the Conservatives would make changes "within a sound budgetary framework . . . without any upheaval in the public service of Canada." In the next breath, however, the Conservative leader acknowledged that some senior bureaucrats would have to leave, some parts of the government would be abolished, and the relationship between individual ministers and their deputies would work themselves out over time. If they didn't, the deputies would be replaced.

As well as dealing with the bureaucracy, Mulroney's statement indicated the final concern of the transition team's work. They were evaluating the machinery of government and deciding on the type of organization over which the Conservatives wanted to preside. The object, of course, was to find the best means of turning their campaign commitments into legislation. The transition group looked at the organization of departments, the elimination of certain agencies, and the role of Cabinet committees. Its recommendations emphasized that policy should be developed by the political staff rather than by the bureaucrats. But, on the whole, the team accepted the existing organization of government. This, in effect, confirmed the decision not to rearrange radically the bureaucracy that would be giving them advice. They were relying on the determination of future Conservative ministers to bend the bureaucracy to their wills.

After MacDonald's groups presented their recommendations to Mulroney on March 17, 1984, the party leader acted with a combination of tact and good political horse sense. MacDonald had urged Mulroney to go outside the original group to implement the report because of the resistance that he and his colleagues had met from some Tory MPs. The MPs objected to the team as an elite club and resented taking orders from "staffers."

Mulroney solved the problem by using his corporate experience. He felt that his organization, the Tory party, should have, in addition to a chief executive officer (the party leader who gets policy advice), a chief operating officer—the deputy leader who implements the policy. In Mulroney's eyes, Erik Nielsen was the deputy leader in fact as well as in name. After the leader accepted MacDonald's report, getting the transition in shape, therefore, fell to Nielsen, who as an MP would not encounter the same resentment from the caucus. In early April 1984, Nielsen relinquished the Tory House leadership to devote his time to finalizing the transition arrangements.

Mulroney's idea looked good on paper, but it was not easy to carry out. Nielsen began operating in what one transition planner described as "Erik-style, Titanic-style—watertight compartments." Nielsen called in each worker separately to dole out assignments and to receive reports. In response to questions about how a particular task fit in with the party's requirements, he invariably replied that the individual did not need to know. As a result, most felt that they never understood the overall plan.

Nielsen's management techniques began to fragment the party. This became a serious problem once the election was called and the Conservatives had a limited time in which to set their final plans. Mulroney would instruct one person to do a job, unaware that someone else was supposed to be carrying it out. The Clerk of the Privy Council did not know which of two requests for the same information he should answer. Nielsen was out campaigning in his vast Yukon riding and was available only by radio phone. Pressured by members of MacDonald's group, the deputy leader finally agreed to give up the job of implementing the final transition plans.

The task fell to an unwilling Bill Neville, who had to take leave of absence from his job as vice-president of the Canadian Imperial Bank of Commerce. Neville had previously served Robert Stanfield as research director in the opposition leader's office; he had then taken on the job of head of the leader's office for Joe Clark, both in opposition and in government. He had the experience that most of the others lacked. The Conservatives promised him the full-time assistance of whomever he wanted. He chose Finlay Mac-Donald; William Jarvis, a former Clark minister; Hugh Hanson, a former Conservative aide; Graham Scott, a Toronto lawyer; and Carman Joynt of the consulting firm Touche Ross. Once Neville took over, things moved into high gear.

As a Conservative victory became increasingly probable, one of the more important tasks of the planners was assembling the staff for ministers' offices. Peter White, a member of the transition team, looked after the staffing procedure. His group had scouted across the country to compile a talent bank. Assuming that many of the Tory front-bench critics would be appointed to the new Cabinet, White interviewed them to ascertain their general and particular preferences. This included their choices for head of staff and for special assistants and policy advisers. White knew that he had to move quickly because prospective staff members had to be ready to leave other jobs and responsibilities.

White tried to attract candidates to head up the ministers' offices by raising the salary levels and providing other incentives. One such incentive, changing the title, was scoffed at by some of those in the party and by the press. Under a Conservative government, the head of a minister's office would bear the military designation of "chief of staff." This was to indicate a distinctly higher status than did the old appellation—"executive assistant."

By the time Mulroney announced his Cabinet, White's group had prepared a list of suitable staff members for every member of the government. The immediate task remained to match up the new ministers with their staff. Only about half the ministers had served as opposition critics and had had the opportunity to voice a preference. In the final assignment of places, the prime minister's advisers tried to place staff who had experience in government in the offices of ministers who did not. They also made an effort to give the strongest chiefs of staff to those whom they expected to be the weakest ministers. Finally, Peter White had to negotiate the choice of the chief of staff with each minister. If the new Cabinet appointee expressed a preference for someone not on the list, he would check out that person's curriculum vitae. Mulroney had told each of his prospective Cabinet members that as prime minister he would retain the right to veto their choices of staff members. On two or three occasions, he was advised to exercise this threat, but the minister usually backed down. One who did not was John Fraser, the Minister of Fisheries and Oceans, who stuck with his own nominee, Claude Boiselle.

Even more important than getting ministers off on the right track was making certain that a functioning Prime Minister's Office was ready to begin operations right after the election. Most of the staff from the office of the Leader of the Opposition in the South Block were ready to move down the street to suites in the Langevin Building where the prime minister had his offices. Some senior Tories and bureaucrats at the highest level wondered at Mulroney's wisdom in not casting about for new staff members and in planning to keep almost everyone who had worked with him during his time in opposition. When questioned about this, Mulroney said that he could train skills but that he could not train loyalty. For the Conservative leader, loyalty was the *sine qua non* he demanded of his colleagues. His staff agreed. In unison, they speak about answering a call from a friend. Most of them had worked on Mulroney's first leadership bid in 1976 and many had known the prime minister since his student days at St. Francis Xavier University or at Laval's law school.

Until the last minute, there was no unanimous agreement about the role or the structure of the Prime Minister's Office. During the election campaign, Peter White had written to Mulroney about the type of office that he thought should be established. His main recommendation was that the head of the office, the prime minister's principal secretary, should be the senior political adviser and administrator. The incumbent should not, White felt, take on the task of advising on policy. White also argued that the government should have a strong centralized policy unit in the PMO, because he thought that it was dangerous to build up strong sources of policy advice in the ministers' offices—the government thereby risked institutionalizing conflict between the ministers' offices and the PMO. White also felt that the Privy Council Office should not have the job of policy coordination that it had developed in the Trudeau years. His basic thesis was that no piece of paper should go to the prime minister until it had been seen by a political adviser in the PMO. (This advice was not followed to the degree that he recommended.)

Some of Mulroney's other advisers differed from White's point of view. They put forward the opinion that the role of the PMO's policy unit should be restricted to helping the government implement its election promises. As the government moved through its term, however, they felt that the role of policy development should diminish in the PMO and devolve onto the ministers and their advisers. Ultimately, the prime minister should limit his role to firefighting and working out long-term political strategy and goals. If the PMO retained the right to develop policy, it would be difficult to decide where to draw the line between the PMO and ministers' offices, the departments and the Privy Council Office.

* * *

The resolution of this issue, however, was put on the back burner following the massive election win on September 4. For the next thirteen days, public speculation focused on the membership of the new government. The guessing was uninformed, however, because Mulroney's cabinet building went on amidst the greatest secrecy. This veil prevented even those being interviewed for Cabinet posts from learning who their rivals and future colleagues would be. On September 6, Mulroney had a private meeting with his closest associates: Bill Neville, campaign director Norman Atkins, Jean Bazin, Erik Nielsen, Bill Jarvis, Hugh Hanson, Fred

Doucet, Charles McMillan, and Bill Fox. Newspapers reported on the meeting the following day. The prime minister-designate was furious. He cut down the number of his advisers by half to Atkins, Neville, Bazin, and Doucet. The obsession for secrecy became so great, Jeffrey Simpson reported, that Mulroney rotated unannounced between suites in four different Ottawa hotels. Reporters said that their normal sources had suddenly clammed up about what exactly was going on.

Behind this extraordinary furtiveness, Mulroney confronted the same problem that had faced all his predecessors in the process of forming a government: how could he reward supporters, appoint good ministers, and yet maintain a regional and ethnic balance in the Cabinet? Unlike previous prime ministers, however, Mulroney had an extra complication to deal with: what could he do with former party leader Joe Clark in order to keep the party united? One of Mulroney's strongest supporters, Sinclair Stevens, wanted the Department of External Affairs. So did Clark, and for a former prime minister it was the only Cabinet spot with enough prestige. Mulroney also had to decide how to treat Clark's supporters and the members of Clark's government, how to reward his own backers in the 1983 leadership contest, and how to deal with rivals within a province.

On September 17, when Prime Minister Mulroney unveiled his Cabinet, it was to general acclaim. Mulroney had dealt admirably with the regional conundrum without offending any area. Western Canada had gone from having a single elected representative in Cabinet in the previous government to having thirteen members in charge of some of the most powerful departments. Yukon MP Erik Nielsen continued as deputy leader with the title of Deputy Prime Minister. Among the Alberta contingent, Joe Clark had his coveted prize; Don Mazankowski took over his former portfolio, the Department of Transport; Calgary's Harvie Andre became the Minister of Supply and Services. Manitoba had four ministers: Jake Epp in the Department of National Health and Welfare; Jack Murta, Minister of State for Multiculturalism; Duff Roblin, Government Leader in the Senate; and Charles Mayer, who would be responsible for the Canadian Wheat Board. From Saskatchewan, William McKnight went into the Department of Labour, and Ray Hnatyshyn became Government House Leader. British Columbians moved into the departments of Fisheries and Oceans (John Fraser); Energy, Mines and Resources (Pat Carney); and Science and Technology (Tom Siddon). The West was well represented, but the other regions could not complain of neglect. Ontario supplied eleven ministers, mainly in the economic portfolios. They were Michael Wilson (Finance), Flora MacDonald (Employment and Immigration), George Hees (Veterans' Affairs), Sinclair Stevens (Regional Industrial Expansion), John Wise (Agriculture), David Crombie (Indian Affairs and Northern Development), Perrin Beatty (National Revenue), Otto Jelinek (Fitness and Amateur Sport), Walter McLean (Secretary of State), and James Kelleher (International Trade).

The eleven-member Quebec contingent was reduced from Pierre Trudeau's last Cabinet (Trudeau had chosen fifteen Québécois for his thirty-six-person Cabinet). Since most of the new ministers were also neophyte MPs, they held junior portfolios. Consumer and Corporate Affairs went to Michel Côté, External Relations to Monique Vézina, Environment to Suzanne Blais-Grenier, Youth to Andrée Champagne, Small Business to André Bissonnette, Minister of State for Transport to Benoît Bouchard, and Mines to Robert Layton. The best of them, it was expected, would be promoted in subsequent Cabinet shuffles. Apart from the prime minister, the senior Quebec ministers were Marcel Masse, the Minister of Communications; Robert de Cotret, the President of the Treasury Board; and Roch LaSalle, the Minister of Public Works. There was some complaining that Quebec did not have more senior ministers connected with industrial and regional development.

From the east, John Crosbie of Newfoundland became Minister of Justice; Elmer MacKay and Robert Coates from Nova Scotia took over as Solicitor General and Minister of National Defence, respectively; Prince Edward Islander Tom McMillan became the Minister of State for Tourism; and Gerald Merrithew from New Brunswick was chosen Minister of State for Forestry.

In general, the need for unity overcame the desire to settle grudges and Mulroney also acted to bridge internal party schisms. George Hees's presence symbolized the end of the party feuding from the Diefenbaker era. Joe Clark's position speeded up the process of healing from the 1983 leadership campaign. In addition, sixteen ministers from the 1980 government were among the chosen. There was new blood too—twenty-three new ministers, not including the prime minister. The moderate wing of the party was there (Flora MacDonald, David Crombie, and Walter McLean), as were the right wingers (Robert Coates, Otto Jelinek, and Sinclair Stevens). The six women ministers formed the largest number in Canadian history; moreover, Mulroney had not put them in the traditional jobs of health, culture, and consumer affairs.

Reservations about the new Cabinet were minor. The only one of any consequence concerned the number of portfolios—John Turner had cut his Cabinet back to twenty-nine. But Turner did not have the whopping majority accorded to Mulroney, who had to satisfy 211 members of Parliament. By doling out parliamentary secretaryships to match each minister, he was able to give positions to eighty Conservative MPs. The other quibbles concerned individual omissions—a predictable feature of cabinet making. Why was James McGrath left out? Why was Gerald Merrithew of New Brunswick, and not Frank Oberle of British Columbia, named as Minister of Forestry?

Brian Mulroney had demonstrated two of the characteristics which some of those who worked with him closely perceived as his guiding forces. The first of these was his belief in civility. He thought that various elements within the Tory party—and the country—could and should discuss issues until they reached agreement on a solution. To achieve this purpose, the prime minister was willing to take risks and to expose himself to charges of delay and indecisiveness. The second was that he desperately sought to make the Tory party a lasting government. A close adviser commented that for Mulroney, every action or decision must ''go through that prism.''

His cabinet making demonstrated that Mulroney had learned from the history of the internal wranglings of the Tories, and that he was a good politician. As one senior mandarin pointed out, Brian Mulroney applied his energy and capacity if something had a political value to him and if he could relate it to the body of political knowledge that he had accumulated. Putting together a good Cabinet fit both these criteria. But was this good enough to satisfy most people, who expect a prime minister to display more than average acumen across a broad range of questions?

It might have been smoke and mirrors, but Mulroney quickly expressed his concern that his Cabinet not bear the smudge of scandal. Part of the reason for this stemmed from the Tory reputation for incompetence that Mulroney had inherited from John Diefenbaker and Joe Clark. In an interview with Allan Fotheringham, published in mid-December 1984, the prime minister commented that he would fire a minister for "anything that violated the public trust or anything that displayed a degree of malice toward the Canadian people or . . . that offended the sense of propriety and dignity of our institutions." He insisted that all of the ministers in his Cabinet conform to regulations on divestiture or disclosure that had originally been established by Pierre Trudeau. His guidelines on conflict of interest were made available in September 1985; they stated that non-personal property, farms, and interests in businesses for which the shares were not traded publicly must be disclosed, and either put into a blind trust or sold. Those in a blind trust were under the control of independent administrators. It all looked good on paper.

From the very start, observers watched to see how the rambunctious Tories would pull together to run the country. Joe Clark's behaviour in particular was scrutinized—a lot of blood had been spilled in the past and there were expectations that more would follow. Many nasty contests between Conservative nominees during the election could be traced to battles between the two factions in the party. As Clark's staff commented, Mulroney needed Clark in a minority situation but not with the huge majority that he had gained. But by giving Clark responsibility for foreign affairs, the prime minister showed that he must have felt a little guilty about his treatment of the former prime minister. Fortunately for all those concerned, Clark's general approach to foreign policy was close to Mulroney's and this prevented many problems from cropping up.

There were, however, immediate tensions between Clark and James Kelleher, the trade minister, who reported through the Department of External Affairs. The lawyer from Sault Ste. Marie resented his status as a junior minister. He was a protégé of Sinclair Stevens and had no previous connections with Clark. In the first months of the government, there was some talk of moving the responsibility for trade out of the orbit of External Affairs but Mulroney decided against this. On the other hand, Clark quickly captured the respect and admiration of Monique Vézina, the other junior minister, who looked after international aid and relations with francophone Africa. An ardent Quebec nationalist, Vézina respected Clark's efforts to learn French and to understand the political realities of French Canada.

Erik Nielsen, the Deputy Prime Minister, ran the same type of shop in office that he had as the leader of the transition team. As one of his colleagues puts it, Nielsen said nothing either to his staff or to the Cabinet. His role evolved into that of "the tough cop." Nielsen, however, quickly captured the respect of highly placed officials in the Privy Council Office. They cited the difference between the public man who equated politics with war and the shy private man. He established a reputation as a totally honest minister. As a member of the government, he became the "fixer" who sought no credit for himself. He was put on all Cabinet committees and given charge of communications—not the most felicitous assignment for a dour, silent man.

Sinclair Stevens provoked a contradictory reaction. Initially, senior public servants who dealt with him found him to be a more complex individual than they had expected. What impressed them was his populist position with regard to the poor, his unorthodoxy, and the fact that he had clout. "If anyone talked to Stevens," commented one of his associates, "I don't think he would go away thinking he was a bad human being." Despite his emphasis on the need for change during the campaign, Stevens revealed himself to be a pragmatist during his first days in office. As the President of the Treasury Board in 1979-80, he was realistic enough to know that miracles don't happen overnight.

Michael Wilson's chemistry mixed well with that of the Department of Finance. His career in Toronto's financial community and his time as finance critic gave him from the beginning the appearance of feeling comfortable as Minister of Finance. In the department, he impressed the senior public servants as having groomed himself for years to be a minister. But Wilson did not have the same clout in the government that his Liberal predecessor, Marc Lalonde, had wielded in Trudeau's Cabinet. Traditionally, the Minister of Finance ranked high on the list of precedence and would have spent many years both in the House of Commons and in the Cabinet before assuming this responsibility. First elected in 1979, Wilson's main strength came from the confidence that he enjoyed among the business community and the resulting confidence of the prime minister in his finance minister. It was generally agreed that ''Moose'' Wilson began his ministerial career with an image of unremitting sincerity.

In the Department of National Health and Welfare, Jake Epp quickly proved himself to his public servants. A workaholic, he absorbed information quickly because he had been opposition critic for the department. He was happy, relaxed, and easy to get along with. Combined with this, he had strong views about limiting the role of the state to that of aiding the disadvantaged who could not help themselves. He believed in the party system and was loyal to his leader. He never undercut the Cabinet even though he disagreed with some of its decisions. In November 1984, when Michael Wilson proposed that the country had to bite the bullet and to cut back on some of the statutory payments for social programs, Epp agreed with this approach. He was not a red Tory—in fact, his later disagreement with Wilson about de-indexing old age pensions was based on his belief that it was a political mistake, and not on philosophical differences.

Energy minister Pat Carney had been opposition critic for energy and she knew her stuff. One of her officials said ''she's tougher than nails, but it's nice to work for a minister who delivers for her department.'' There is no better way to build up the team spirit. The department and the minister began working on parallel tracks although most journalists had been predicting fireworks.

Many felt that Don Mazankowski was the best-informed minister ever to have been appointed to the transport portfolio. He had had a lengthy tutorial as a Tory critic, member of the transport committee, and former minister. ''Maz,'' most of those who worked with him believed, would be a minister who never got his prime minister into trouble. A careful man, he proposed to consult with all those whose interests were at stake before making any major shift in policy. As decisive as he was well-informed, his appointment was welcomed in the department and in the transportation industry.

* * *

It is not only politicians who prepare for transitions in government. In the summer of 1984, the bureaucracy was updating the sacred scrolls they call ''briefing books,'' which would be presented to every member of the Cabinet of an incoming administration. These information manuals contain descriptions of the department's organization and programs. For most of the deputy ministers, supervising the preparation for the post-election briefings of their new ministers was relatively easy. After all, they had finished such an exercise three months earlier when John Turner took over the government. The increased contact between the civil service and the caucus in the previous months had also eased the task somewhat. Nonetheless, a few wanted to gain additional information about the Conservatives' plans. Since senior mandarins did not automatically have access to the Tories' campaign material, they tried to get copies from their contacts in the Conservative campaign organization.

By far the most crucial meeting was that between the Clerk of the Privy Council and the post-election prime minister. Gordon Osbaldeston had arrived in the PCO after a nine-month stint as Under-Secretary of State for External Affairs. His predecessor as clerk, Michael Pitfield, had been disliked by many of the higher bureaucrats and before his departure had become ineffective because of the isolation that this imposed. When Osbaldeston took over, it was common speculation that Trudeau was about to take his leave and that the new clerk would become a bridge between the Trudeau years and the future.

The planners in Osbaldeston's Privy Council Office shared the Conservatives' desire to effect a smooth change of government. It was only common sense for the PCO to try to avoid any mistakes that could be held against the Canadian public service. Osbaldeston worked to avoid the situation that had arisen in 1957 when the Conservatives assumed office. The new prime minister, John Diefenbaker, had viewed the Clerk of the Privy Council, R. B. Bryce, as something of a mole, because he had held the job during the previous Liberal government. Bryce, however, tried to overcome the problem by his openness and hard work. Nonetheless, Diefenbaker and some of his ministers never quite got over their suspicion of the bureaucracy as a whole. Consequently, in 1984 the Conservative transition planners knew what would be in the briefing books prepared for Brian Mulroney—partly because of the Clark experience and partly because they were told by the PCO.

Everyone in the public service knew that whether Turner or Mulroney won the election, change was in the air. In some departments, the more prescient deputies carried their preparations further than simply drafting an outline of existing programs to present to the new government. Senior public servants in the Department of National Health and Welfare, for example, began to study ways to reduce departmental staff. So that they would not affect the outcome of the election, the bureaucrats kept the exercise a secret from the current minister, Monique Bégin, who had announced her retirement from politics. The Canadian Broadcasting Corporation also worked on a reduction exercise called ''Plan A'' before the election was called. In the Department of Finance, the senior planners had concluded that with either John Turner or Brian Mulroney as prime minister, the government would take a more conservative tack and call for reduced expenditures. In May 1984, senior officials in Finance started to look at ways of getting the deficit under control. In this case, the Liberal minister, Marc Lalonde, knew that the officials were carrying out the study. When Wilson took over, the officials had a briefing book ready setting out concerns about the deficit and the options for the government.

Despite most bureaucrats' intentions to act as impartial advisers, the seeds of potential conflict between the Tories and the bureaucracy were planted in the days before the election. None of the Conservatives questioned the prime minister's prerogative of dismissing deputy ministers. The transition advisers also agreed that no deputy should have to preside over the dismantling of programs identified with him. Moreover, in conducting their so-called talent search, the Tories had found that the only way to break up the logjam to the top for many public servants was by sweeping away the current holders of top-level positions. If thirty deputy ministers were let go, said one senior Conservative, ''There would be pain in some Ottawa homes but wild parties in others and speculation everywhere about who was moving up.'' Hardliners among Mulroney's advisers had overcome those who advocated a more easygoing approach to the bureaucracy. Confidential notice was given to the Privy Council Office that ten to fifteen deputy ministers would be on the street before a new Conservative Cabinet had left Rideau Hall. Gordon Osbaldeston geared up to save the public service from such a blow but at the same time, the PCO began to draw up the necessary documents to effect this change.

The recommendation for the dismissals leaked out, and exaggerated news stories predicted a wholesale cleanout. Finlay MacDonald immediately advised the prime minister not to follow the advice on the proposed firings and Erik Nielsen declared that the Conservatives would not carry out a witch hunt. Mulroney asked for another review of the situation.

In the days immediately following the massive Conservative victory, the pendulum swung in the other direction. On September 6, Osbaldeston met with the prime minister-designate. They rapidly consolidated a relationship based on mutual respect. The prime minister decided to trust his senior adviser from the public service. Before the Cabinet was formed, Marshall (Mickey) Cohen, the deputy minister of finance, spent some time with Mulroney and gave him the department's ideas on policy options for tackling the deficit. As the former deputy minister of energy, Cohen had helped to establish the National Energy Program, the *bête noire* of the Conservatives, and the deputy was a possible candidate for an immediate dismissal. But he impressed Mulroney with his grasp of the issues and his capacity to present options upon request. The final decision was made after the election when Mulroney met with Osbaldeston and Bill Neville to discuss the senior bureaucracy. At this stage, the neophyte prime minister rejected the advice of those who wanted a purge and decided to put off major changes in the upper level of the public service.

Once Mulroney had taken this decision, those who had been calling for the bureaucrats' heads denied that they had even considered a purge. Instead, the Progressive Conservative caucus became the scapegoat, blamed by the prime minister's advisers for any pressure to fire senior public servants.

Despite this hitch, the Conservatives had achieved their aim of turning the government-in-waiting into an administration. The transition planners' work was paying off. The new government was armed with a set of policy directions and the clout to make them stick. The staffing of ministers' offices was proceeding and the PMO was already in operation. The Tories had deferred any plans to clean out the bureaucracy which, in any case, had no choice but to place itself at the government's disposal. To inaugurate the new Tory era, it remained for Brian Mulroney and his Cabinet to pull the levers of power and move the vast resources at their disposal to achieve their ends.

Chapter Three
Style or Structure?

Most tourists to Ottawa climb up Parliament Hill and many of them visit the East Block, that great stone pile, which has been carefully restored to its original ornate Victorian splendour. The public can view the refurbished corridors, rooms, and furniture that were once at the service of the prime minister and his colleagues when they gathered in Cabinet to deal with the nation's business. The rooms in the East Block provide an impressive but wonderfully anachronistic scene.

For several years, however, the real locus of power has lain across the street in the Langevin Block. This edifice, the first government structure erected after Confederation, had been vacated by the Department of External Affairs a decade before; then it fell victim to the whitepainters. The Department of Public Works ripped out the marble fireplaces that had graced most of the offices and installed wall-to-wall deep blue wool carpets (which bore a remarkable resemblance to the synthetic indoor-outdoor variety) to prepare the space for its new tenants. At this point, the Langevin Block became one of the best-known addresses in the capital. At the top of the grand central staircase, on the second floor in the north-west corner, Prime Minister Pierre Trudeau had his office. The Clerk of the Privy Council and Secretary to the Cabinet, Michael Pitfield, was ensconced above him. Their staffs occupied the rest of the building.

After Brian Mulroney took over, most of his staff still shared the Langevin Block with the Privy Council Office but Mulroney himself eschewed regular use of that building. He took himself off with a couple of staff members and secretaries to the prime minister's smaller suite located in the Centre Block on the Hill itself. In a way, this switch by Mulroney and the Conservatives symbolized their rejection of the trappings and structures associated with their Liberal predecessors. It affected their planning for the transition, especially once they set about bending the machinery of government to their own purposes.

The spectre that most haunted the Conservatives was that of Pierre Trudeau, the man who relished controversy but whose serene demeanour left critics frothing at the mouth in frustration. This attitude, the Tories believed, had infected the Cabinet and had led to unnecessary quarrelling with the provinces, impaired relations with the United States, and alienated most Canadians from their government.

Conservatives also loved to hate the men surrounding Trudeau. James Coutts, who had served as the prime minister's principal secretary, had been the keeper of the Liberal coalition, the greaser-of-the-wheels, and general facilitator for the Liberals. The Conservatives suffered from his schemes, which embodied behind-the-scenes political conniving at its wiliest. There was also Michael Pitfield, former Clerk of the Privy Council, the *éminence grise* who ran the secretariats that serviced the Cabinet committees and set the style—"management by objective"—that shaped the bureaucracy. With Pitfield at the helm, any ambitious manager in the public service had his easel, grease pencil, and flow charts ready at the drop of a memo. To the Tories, Pitfield had committed the cardinal sin of giving the PCO a role in setting policy. Since the PCO coordinated the work of the Cabinet, this meant that the ministers and their departments had to toe the line so that the government would present a common front under scrutiny in the House of Commons or in the press.

The Conservatives made a serious and fundamental error by equating Trudeau and his associates' style with the structure over which they had presided. This was particularly the case when the new government confronted the complicated interrelationship of the Prime Minister's Office, the Privy Council Office, and the various departments.

At the same time, the Conservatives did not seem to realize that part of the system they so detested was now no longer in existence and that other parts had not changed quickly enough to fill the void. As a senior bureaucrat who had worked for both Liberal and Conservative governments remarked: "The structure to a substantial degree determines policy." The Trudeau regime had given the impression that the prime minister had garnered too much authority and that individual ministers had lost power as a result of the Cabinet committee system and the policy coordination that had accrued to the PCO. It was commonly accepted that the structure stifled both creativity and initiative.

In order to restore this lost capacity, Brian Mulroney's Conservatives determined to modify the system while implementing their own programs. Bureaucrats would keep to their station in life—providing information and not making policy. Although the Cabinet committees and the PCO secretariats remained on the organizational chart, the Conservatives did not intend to use them.

Nevertheless, the Tories failed to replace the old structure with anything that would coordinate the conflicting interests that are always present in Cabinet and in rival departments of government. *Faute de mieux*, the prime minister and his entourage became the de facto coordinators. Everything ended up on Mulroney's desk. He not only failed to take full advantage of the Cabinet committee system, but he appointed no replacements for the PCO's policy coordinators. At times, he desperately seemed to need an alter ego like Jim Coutts to handle political crises. The Tories were out of shape as far as governing was concerned. In general terms, observed one senior officer at National Defence Headquarters, "You would have thought they were coming in with a whole thought-out blueprint—all the signals were there to give us hope. But the fact of the matter is, just learning to use the tools of government has been a learning experience for them."

* * *

Having rejected Trudeau's approach, it was only natural that Brian Mulroney should use his own business experience as his guide. Those who work in his office claim that this corporate style helped to overcome certain problems, citing his experience as a labour arbitrator and corporation president as a combination to be valued in running the country. His years as a labour lawyer, they said, made him aware of nuances that others missed and helped him to develop a shrewd sense of political implications when sorting through the options before him. His staff also felt that he gave ministers a fair hearing and assisted the inexperienced when they presented cases in Cabinet. If a minister was having a language problem, the prime minister would intervene to make certain that everyone understood. Mulroney and the people around him really believed that if they worked to avoid picking fights à la Trudeau, they would thereby develop a cooperative style with the result that a great many problems would go away of their own accord. They thought that this would clear the way for economic growth and better federal-provincial relations. But when their efforts to get along did not substantially alter any positions, especially with regard to federal-provincial contacts, the prime minister was taken aback.

He forgot that whereas a labour arbitrator merely helps others reach an agreement, a prime minister must make decisions that affect his own future. Mulroney disliked confrontation and was uncomfortable when forced to make a choice. One observer was heard to remark that he had seen the prime minister actually try to make a decision by reading the ticker tape off the Canadian Press wire or by watching the television news. But it should be said that Mulroney's desire to form a consensus and to compromise could be useful at times. The Bonn Summit is a good case in point. Mulroney quickly grasped the dimension of the issues—particularly the political problems—and tried to bridge the gap between Presidents Mitterand and Reagan.

Despite this early success, upper-level mandarins felt that the prime minister had erred by trying to run the show as if he were a corporation president. This group of observers noted that Mulroney treated Cabinet meetings as an unnecessary distraction. One who attended noted that Mulroney had been a political maverick for so long that he had forgotten the importance of teamwork. Mulroney also had to learn not to think aloud and to study his briefings more carefully. Although Pierre Trudeau might have made decisions autocratically, he had at least allowed his ministers to talk in Cabinet—often until they had exhausted both themselves and their listeners.

His self-image as a board chairman with a commitment to consensus led Mulroney to believe that he could set the broad directions for his colleagues and that everything would then fall into place without his getting mixed up in the minutiae of detail. At the same time, Mulroney did not encourage questioning. "If he says we'll move the mountain, no one asks what the cost will be," commented one former PCO official, who went on to say: "Reality has shown you can't do that. You have to go through the drudgery of going through these documents. You need to have gone through the details before you make the broad generalizations of where you want to go."

Mulroney's involvement in the energy deal seems to confirm that view. Before Pat Carney went out west to negotiate with the provincial energy ministers in March 1985, she met with the prime minister. Mulroney knew what was going on, but he did not get involved in the details and gave Carney no specific instructions, said one participant. After she reached an agreement, she called Mulroney. The prime minister did not ask what the deal was but was heard to exclaim: "You're terrific."

The government's model for communicating with the public was that of the boardroom—again a method that Mulroney readily understood. He prescribed that the Cabinet should behave like the members of a company's board of directors and not talk to the media individually to explain corporation policy or behaviour. As the Conservatives took over the reins of government, the normal channels and sources of information open to the press were thereby closed off. The shutout was part of the strategy to show ministers, their staffs, the bureaucracy, and the press that from now on there would be one single voice and one boss. Minimal contact with the press also provided a way to avoid errors. The prime minister's press scrums outside the House of Commons allowed for the maximum manipulation of the forty-five-second clips for the evening news that so preoccupied the television reporters.

Despite carping from the press, the Tories' restrictions on information worked as well in the first months of the government as they had in opposition. After his swearing-in, Mulroney declined to call a press conference and Erik Nielsen advised the new ministers to avoid talking to the press. The *Globe and Mail* reported that one of them had remarked: "Erik said we'd be out on our ear if anybody was caught talking to you." All announcements were to be made through the PMO and were limited to written press releases, which allowed no opportunity for amplification. For example, on September 21, Peter Elzinga, the Conservative party president, stated in a news interview that the Tories would launch probes to investigate problems with the Canadian way of life. Elzinga refused to elaborate on his statement and spokesmen for the prime minister either said that they knew nothing about it or else failed to return journalists' telephone calls altogether.

After Michael Wilson's financial statement in the first week of November, some of the new ministers and their staffs and deputies went too far in their desire to please. In fact, the government was manipulating the news in order to impress upon the country the fact that the cupboard was bare. The "fear of Erik" was very strong and, by this time, his wariness of open communication had become legendary. Every Conservative minister was calling the PMO for approval prior to contacts with the press. But the interdiction went well beyond the ministers. Nielsen also forbade civil servants to discuss the effect of expenditures on the various departments and programs. Then a leak from the Department of External Affairs indicated that the government had cancelled the Liberal patronage appointment of Bryce Mackasey as ambassador to Portugal and planned to replace him with former Speaker of the House Lloyd Francis. Joe Clark reacted to the leak by prohibiting all except authorized personnel at External Affairs from expressing personal opinions about government policies, even in the context of social conversation. In sheer defiance, this order was sent to the press.

The press wailed loudly and succeeded in manoeuvring Mulroney into a position in which he was obliged to make a decision. Reporters claimed that Mulroney was breaking an election promise. In Kingston on August 12, 1984, Mulroney had made a campaign speech that strongly condemned secrecy in government. He had raked John Turner over the coals for not opening the Petro-Canada books to the Auditor General, Kenneth Dye. (Dye had gone to court to pry information from the Liberals about the public corporation's takeover of Petrofina. On November 19, Minister of Justice John Crosbie told reporters that the Cabinet system would crumble if the information about the Petrofina takeover was released.)

The question of secrecy sorely exercised senior officials in the

PCO who felt that the prime minister did not understand the absolute necessity for Cabinet confidentiality. Every Privy Councillor takes an oath of secrecy. Moreover, the Access to Information Act, which came into force in July 1983, protected Cabinet documents from disclosure. Faced with the ruckus over secrecy, Mulroney's initial impulse was to conciliate and to give way. The PCO dug in its heels, however, until Mulroney backed down.

The government groped for weasel-words that would allow it to give in gracefully. Mulroney tried to re-establish his reputation for civility by saying that he was reviewing the guidelines governing relations between the public service and the press. On November 23, he announced that public servants were free to talk to the press if the matter concerned factual information about programs and policies. Mulroney had, in fact, reverted to the position on openness that Joe Clark had established in 1979. At the same time, Mulroney removed the responsibility for Cabinet communications from Erik Nielsen's purview, giving it to a new Cabinet committee consisting of Don Mazankowski, Perrin Beatty, and Ray Hnatyshyn, all of whom tended to favour far greater access than Nielsen had tolerated. Nonetheless, the government had not abandoned its efforts to manage the press. The new rules forbade off-the-record briefings, except in special circumstances. Deputy ministers had to appoint primary spokesmen to respond to inquiries. By making all pronouncements on the record, the government hoped to be able to control leaks.

The press and the Public Service Alliance called the guidelines a threat to freedom of expression. The opposition parties claimed that the guidelines were preventing them from getting the briefings they needed—briefings that had been provided to the Conservatives when they were out of power. Even Mulroney had to admit that the guidelines restricted public servants from discussing the impact of policy changes. This meant, for example, that no predictions about the loss of jobs stemming from a particular economic measure could be made. This particular skirmish with the press provided ample proof that the practices of corporate communications could not be applied to government operations.

Those who were on the spot and had observed Mulroney in action, had explanations for his behaviour. To avoid confrontations, Mulroney always made political considerations his first priority. Policy followed. This was a complete reversal from Trudeau's practice—for him, political strategy almost always followed a policy decision. Others attributed Mulroney's desire to run the show to a fear that giving up control of the political agenda would damage the Conservatives' chance to stay in office for more than one term. The combination of these tendencies led Mulroney to get mixed up in too many questions at once. Unlike Pierre Trudeau, Mulroney did not use the existing structures of government to limit his own activities to a few important issues that he could master thoroughly. Mulroney's reluctance to cut back was demonstrated particularly when it came to questions affecting Quebec—the prime minister clung to the accepted wisdom that the Tories had to retain their strong position in Quebec in order to extend their government's tenure beyond four years.

* * *

The other main element of the new style of government could be expressed in a single word—consultation. "This is a government that is in touch," declared Government House Leader Ray Hnatyshyn after being sworn in. The first few of Mulroney's decisions were, claimed Allan Gregg, the chief Tory pollster, based on highly sophisticated polls that showed what Canadians wanted. By the end of September, this had prompted efforts to re-establish a special relationship with the United States, which included the prime minister's quick visit to Ronald Reagan and the transformation of the Foreign Investment Review Agency into Investment Canada, a body set up to attract foreign capital. The government moved to create 70,000 winter jobs by adding $430 million to various employment programs and imposed a temporary freeze on hiring and discretionary spending throughout the public service. The money-losing sports lottery was wound up and the Canadian Unity Information Office, believed to be a Liberal propaganda machine, was eliminated. Energy Minister Pat Carney began her negotiations with the Newfoundland government in order to settle the ownership of off-shore resources.

The consultative style also fitted in very well with those of Mulroney's advisers who took a pragmatic approach to government. Charles McMillan, for example, argued that the election victory had not given the party a mandate for a right-wing policy agenda. These advisers felt that the nature of the Canadian federation required a middle-of-the-road approach. The election of a Conservative government did not mean that the Canadian public wanted to dismantle the apparatus of the state.

The PMO claimed that consultation would put the Conservative ministers in charge of the policy-making process. The intent was to put questions out for public discussion, letting ministers stand back before making a decision. But after issues like the universality of social programs blew up into major rows, the government came to realize, or so one observer noted, that it could not allow major issues to be debated without some prior discussion to decide what the desired end result should be. That way the public discussion could be guided in the proper directions.

By the time Parliament reconvened on January 21, 1985, after the Christmas holidays, the Conservatives had only the Investment Canada bill to point to as their own. But the Conservative government had promised action (or at least discussion papers) in many areas. There would be economic consultations with the provincial premiers in February. Pat Carney was in the middle of her energy negotiations and was, in effect, testing the Tories' commitment to better relations between the federal government and the provinces. John Crosbie was ready to introduce a new divorce act and amendments to the Criminal Code that would toughen penalties for drunk driving.

On February 1, 1985, Mulroney took up the "consultation" theme in a news conference in Ottawa. He admitted that it left the government open to being "scorched," but he denied that using discussion papers to stimulate debate on trade, training, housing, justice, benefits to the elderly, and child assistance was a sign of weakness. He claimed instead that it was part of his plan to build a consensus around proposed changes. "I don't think that it diminished my virility not to be out shouting at people and abusing them." It was, he said, part of the Conservatives' mandate to mend fences and he insisted that a climate for economic growth was not possible without cooperation with the provinces and economic interest groups.

Conservative advisers justified the delays by arguing that the legislative process is really the outcome of consultation and policy development. Since they were starting from scratch, there was no reason for them to have a lot of bills ready for Parliament. They also commented that Mulroney did not want to invent a lot of bills just to keep parliamentarians busy. Wilson's economic statement of November 1984, they pointed out, took time to work its way through the legislative system. They believed that the government should not introduce legislation until it was completely ready and that it would keep its neck out of the wringer by not moving precipitately. It was bad strategy, they said, to take action in one area to avoid pressure in another. Furthermore, they felt that the days of activist government were over and they explained that they were struggling to establish the degree to which the role of government should be cut back.

The high point of the consultation process was the economic summit in March 1985. The meeting of business and union leaders and interest groups fulfilled one of Mulroney's campaign promises. But, said one of its organizers, the preparatory work had not been done and there was no script. The consensus that the Cabinet thought the meeting would produce failed to materialize.

The economic summit was not written off as completely useless, however. There were two processes at work: the formal televised summit, which was disappointing and predictable, and the workshops, which were livelier. The participants were given the opportunity to talk to people that they would not normally be able to speak to. Some of them emerged with a different perspective. As an exercise in consultation, however, it had mixed results, because the government did not quite know how to use all the information it had gathered.

The consultation process may in fact have been the reason for delaying legislation, but it also revealed that the government did not have a real grip on the levers of power. A senior bureaucrat remarked that behind all the activity there was no very strong ideological orientation or vision.

* * *

During the Trudeau years, the prime minister had used the Cabinet committee system to cope with the complex variety of matters that needed collective judgement. Routine questions slowly but surely wound their way to a decision. Unless a hitch developed, they did not come to the notice of the full Cabinet.

One solution to some of Mulroney's early problems would have been to use the Cabinet system to build a consensus around problems and thereby lighten his own load. Gordon Osbaldeston, the Clerk of the Privy Council, advised him to do this, but the Conservatives came into office with a predisposition to simplify the machinery of government. They knew that many of Trudeau's ministers chafed at the constant meetings of Cabinet and its committees. In their view, Cabinet committees vetting and modifying ministers' work stifled their energy and impeded their efforts to do their jobs and run their departments. Because it took so long to gain approval for any initiative, the Trudeau government was often slow to respond to crises.

Despite the general dislike of the structure, the Conservatives retained much of the Cabinet committee system that Trudeau had instituted. It was the only logical way to set up work for a body too large to make decisions efficiently. Without the committees, the government could not have handled its annual workload: more than 300 meetings of Cabinet and its committees, 900 departmental submissions, 750 recorded decisions, 4000 orders-in-council, and 6000 Treasury Board decisions.

Under Michael Pitfield's influence, Cabinet committees took on great importance in the system of government. Prime ministers had set up committees on an ad hoc basis for decades, but with the exception of the Cabinet War Committee during World War II, their decisions were not substituted for those of Cabinet as a whole. For Pitfield, however, they were one means of making the system of government more rational. Trudeau accepted Pitfield's recommendation and set up nine Cabinet committees. Some dealt with policy—economic or social, for example—and others looked after operations or overall coordination. Ad hoc committees were created for special situations. During the short-lived Clark regime, the committees gained the authority to supervise spending in their respective areas.

The idea behind the committee system was to prevent a strong minister from overriding ill-informed or weaker colleagues. Policy options produced by departmental civil servants and endorsed by the sponsoring minister would go before a Cabinet committee in which ministers with related interests would discuss the issue and come forward with a recommendation, which would then go to full Cabinet for ratification. Normally, the full Cabinet would not debate a committee decision unless a minister requested further discussion. As one senior public servant pointed out, the system allowed Trudeau the freedom to involve himself intensely wherever he wished, while other business was dealt with routinely.

John Turner, as a result of his experiences in Trudeau's Cabinet, showed great distaste for the committee system. First appointed to Pearson's Cabinet in 1965, Turner was more at home with the style of this earlier period whereby strong ministers could get things done without having to navigate a proposal through the unending labyrinth of meetings. When he took over the prime ministership from Pierre Trudeau, Turner immediately moved to simplify the structure of government. He did away with the Cabinet committees on communications, labour relations, and Western affairs. He also cut back the size of the Cabinet to twenty-nine.

Turner, in fact, stole some of Brian Mulroney's thunder. During the election campaign, Mulroney signalled his own intention to reduce the complexity of the Cabinet committee structure. Once in office, he confirmed Turner's elimination of the three committees, and added foreign and defence policy to the list.

By simplifying the committee structure, Mulroney greatly increased the importance of the priorities and planning committee, which he saw as analogous to a company's board of directors. As in the Trudeau period, its fifteen members became a de facto inner Cabinet which exercised the power to decide for the whole group. (During his last period in office, Trudeau had endowed the committee with the power to issue decisions.) The priorities and planning committee was also the government's strategy body, with representatives from the PMO in attendance.

Membership in the priorities and planning committee was an indication of power. Naturally, Mulroney and Nielsen were chairman and alternate chairman, respectively. Other places on the committee were occupied by the heads of other Cabinet committees—Sinclair Stevens of the economic and regional development committee, Jake Epp of the social development committee, Robert de Cotret of the government operations committee, and Ray Hnatyshyn of the House planning committee. Mulroney also selected important regional ministers, including John Fraser of British Columbia, Robert Coates of Nova Scotia, and Marcel Masse of Quebec, to mention a few. Michael Wilson was there because of his position on all Cabinet committees concerned with spending. Ministers whose political advice the prime minister wanted on major issues—for example, Flora MacDonald, Joe Clark, John Crosbie, Don Mazankowski, and Pat Carney—were also on the committee.

Of the other Cabinet committees, that of the Treasury Board had the final say on government spending. Generally, it was the place where various ministers' plans were made to fit the available fiscal resources. Most plans were pared down to suit the chairman, Robert de Cotret, or the vice-chairman, Michael Wilson, who had to enforce the Cabinet's financial priorities.

The Cabinet committee on economic and regional development supervised between 15 and 20 percent of all government spending. Apart from its chairman, Sinclair Stevens, and vice-chairman, Pat Carney, ministers from economic departments such as transport, fisheries, forestry, and international trade sat on the committee. The chairman and members of the committee had to ensure that the government's economic priorities would be met.

But industrial development strategy could be stretched any way the committee wished; most of this money in the ''economic envelope'' could be distributed at the discretion of the committee.

Its freedom of action—and potential for abuse—was not a characteristic of the other important Cabinet committee, the committee on social development. Most social programs (family allowances and pensions, for example) are statutory. The monies allocated for these programs—almost 45 percent of the federal budget—allowed for little discretionary spending. But any changes in social programs had to go through this committee, making it a centre of debate.

Mulroney's simplified committee system was sound in theory but did not work very well in practice. The prime minister's involvement in every question made the committees redundant and this was known and understood. The priorities and planning committee did not spend much time on the tasks that its name suggested. The ministers, as well as the prime minister, showed their inexperience by using the committee to discuss every question that came before the Cabinet or other committees. This caused tremendous problems by creating a backlog of items to be discussed. The committee also spent extra hours discussing foreign affairs. The other committees also had limited success. Ministers in charge of big spending departments do not make effective keepers of the purse. Often their departments have to give up funds to high-priority projects, but the ministers' inclinations are usually to defend their own departments' budgets.

Sinclair Stevens was not very popular as chairman of the committee on economic and regional development. Both his Cabinet colleagues and the PCO objected to his disregard for the rules. Ministers had to give notice of an item seven days in advance, and four days before a meeting they had to submit a document for distribution to the committee members. But Stevens would frequently arrive with a proposal in his briefcase and expect the other ministers to discuss it and to give him a decision on the spot. This particularly irritated Pat Carney, the vice-chairman of the committee.

The committee on social development was not much use during the debate over universal social programs, which eventually erupted in November 1984. After this, however, it began to reflect the very careful approach of its chairman, Jake Epp. Epp decided to use his committee more effectively and to take more time over fewer issues. The government operations committee under Robert de Cotret became something of a dead letter and met infrequently.

By the spring of 1986, Mulroney's plan to simplify the Cabinet system had been ditched; the Conservative Cabinet structures began to make Trudeau's committee system look simple. Erik Nielsen "mishandled" communications in the first few months and a Cabinet committee on communications, chaired by Perrin Beatty, was quickly set up. Finally, Mulroney re-established the foreign and defence policy committee and instructed the Cabinet and the chairmen of other Cabinet committees not to bring a matter to the priorities and planning committee until it had gone through the proper committee channels. The Cabinet dealt with many issues on an ad hoc basis and new Cabinet steering groups, sub-committees, task forces, and work groups (all roses by other names) sprang up to deal with crises or criticism.

In the fall and winter of 1985, the lack of coordination of the

Cabinet's work became evident in the ministerial agendas, which were crammed with Cabinet meetings. In one week, for instance, free trade was discussed in the foreign affairs and defence committee, the trade sub-committee of the priorities and planning committee, and the economic and regional development committee; then it went before the priorities and planning committee, a joint meeting of the foreign and defence policy and economic development committees, and, finally, to the full Cabinet.

These marathons were necessary because the prime minister would not give responsibility for coordinating policy on this question to any single Cabinet body. Instead of clearing the decks and devoting his time to chairing a group to work out a trade deal with the United States, he proceeded to distance himself from the discussions. He put Joe Clark in charge of the Cabinet sub-committee on trade. This left Mulroney completely free on the question. With responsibility in other hands, Mulroney could disclaim responsibility for any details and then pull the rug out from under Clark when he wanted to. It might be a smart move to protect his political flank, but it was not the way to use the Cabinet to coordinate and to orchestrate important economic and foreign issues.

* * *

The trouble with the Cabinet committees was related to the Conservatives' attitude to the bureaucrats and particularly to those in the prime minister's own department, the Privy Council Office. There, a secretariat headed by an assistant secretary to the Cabinet was assigned to each important Cabinet committee to facilitate its work. In theory, the secretariats fed information to the Cabinet committees to allow them to debate and resolve issues. Under the Liberals, however, this function grew until the secretariat had the capacity to coordinate and, in a sense, control the information upon which the committee based a decision. The PCO could make recommendations in addition to coordinating policy. This bureaucratic influence was compounded by a system of committees of deputy ministers that mirrored every major Cabinet body. To give the senior officials even greater input, the ministers brought officials, or even sent them as their substitutes, to the Cabinet committees. Again, there were complaints that the officials dominated the Cabinet committees' discussions. In many cases, a minister would present a document and then public servants would answer questions from the other ministers. Responses from the experts who had prepared the submissions in the first place intimidated the ministers, who felt that their legitimate queries often received short shrift.

The Conservatives were determined to have none of this. They believed that as politicians they had a closer and more accurate reading of public needs than the civil service. They felt that in the Liberal government, many ministers—especially those with no expertise in their departmental jurisdiction—were the captives not just of the departments but also of the central agencies.

But by the time they were in a position to change the structures that reduced the politicians' power, many of these objectionable features had disappeared. When he took over as Trudeau's last secretary to the Cabinet, Gordon Osbaldeston shared the philosophy of Gordon Robertson, who had held the position when Trudeau came to power. Osbaldeston felt that the PCO should get involved in policy only as a last resort, should remain apolitical, and should function as a mailbox for the ministers and their deputies. If the Secretary to the Cabinet supervised policy formulation and analysis, however, a neutral role would be impossible. Accordingly, Osbaldeston set about reforming the machinery of government. He arranged the devolution of power from the PCO and restored the policy analysis functions of the departments. In order to reduce the centralized power which had built up in his own shop, he began in 1982 to move out many of these who had served in the priorities and planning secretariat.

The brief alliance of Osbaldeston and John Turner reduced the bureaucrats' powers of coordination even further. They abolished the ministries of state for social and economic development, which had coordinated policy and spending for the individual departments within their spheres. The two also abolished the mirror committees of deputy ministers, which had coordinated strategy in advance of a Cabinet committee meeting. When the Conservatives took office, Mulroney gave the *coup de grâce* to any structures that could coordinate policy. He forbade most officials to attend Cabinet committee meetings and showed the government's determination to politicize the structure by increasing the number of ministerial staff allowed to attend. The agenda items both for committees and for the full Cabinet were initiated by the ministers, who presented and defended their plans before their peers. Because there was no central clearing house for information, the various departments strengthened the teams that briefed their minister for meetings. The briefers tried to make up for their inability to find out the positions of other departments and ministers at Cabinet committee meetings by developing informal networks throughout the government.

During the first year in office of the Conservative government, the PCO engaged in an operation to hold on to the powers it still possessed. Some members of the secretariats felt that Osbaldeston, despite his assistance to Mulroney during the transition, had trouble with what they called the "political interface." In short, Osbaldeston was not Mulroney's man.

The PCO secretariats tried to make themselves useful by devising a new format for Cabinet documents; these were simplified and "politicized" by eliminating much of the bureaucratic and technical language. A three-page synopsis at the beginning of each Cabinet submission was designed to allow a minister to gain an appreciation of a document without having to plough through the full submission. The PCO retained certain powers by virtue of its writing up the reports of Cabinet committees and Cabinet decisions (CRs and RDs, in Ottawa lingo).

For their part, many of the prime minister's advisers did not appreciate that this transformation had taken place. Even after eighteen months in the PMO, one of the staff members remarked that the PCO would love to continue with its policy functions. While the PMO appeared oblivious to the change in the structure, the bureaucrats certainly noticed. Even after fourteen months, some were still unsure of the government's priorities.

Without the PCO to analyse and coordinate policy, it became a case of sink or swim for individual ministers. One of the prime minister's staff tried to sum up the success of the Cabinet by pointing out that ministers fit a pattern. After several months, Perrin Beatty, the Minister of National Revenue, and Pat Carney, the Minister of Energy, Mines and Resources, had impressed both the prime minister and the public not only as two of the best ministers but also as the two with the best policies. The reform of the tax collecting practices of the Department of National Revenue and the plans to dismantle the National Energy Program had been the result of the Tories' work in opposition. The ministers who had the most trouble were those who were weak and had weak policies—Suzanne Blais-Grenier, with her lack of of commitment to environmental issues, was a prime example. In between were strong ministers who had policy difficulties—like Marcel Masse, who had ditched the Conservative caucus's cultural policy but who seemed to have trouble developing an alternative.

It was, however, not just a question of a clearly defined policy that could carry the day, but also of the alliances between ministers and bureaucrats in particular departments. The senior officers of the Department of Finance cooperated with Michael Wilson and quickly filled the void that had resulted from the reduced power of the central agencies. The finance mandarins harked back to the days before Pitfield had clipped their wings and moved much of their influence to the PCO. The Wilson-mandarin alliance gained great power because the government had no policy coordination unit to say them nay.

Even before the election in September, the senior public servants in the department had planned most of what became Michael Wilson's November economic statement. The minister and his bureaucrats shared such a common point of view that it is difficult to say who persuaded whom. The bureaucrats in the Department of Finance led the pack in trying to put restraints on universal social benefits and the old age security system. The department wanted to orchestrate the debate on this issue and after it was over felt that if Mulroney, Epp, and Wilson had been more cohesive, "They could have cut through the crap that we [sic] took from Turner and Broadbent." But, claimed the same official, "We haven't quit." He concluded by commenting that "Mike has championed effectively what we wanted him to champion." The arrogance of this statement was worthy of Pitfield's PCO at its worst.

One highly placed veteran who had served in both regimes—and who believed that the PCO should not formulate policy—did not like the new system any better than the old. The new-found power of the Department of Finance, he concluded, meant that the department would set its mark on social policy, which would become a leftover of macroeconomic policy. This, he believed, meant that the government would never get a coherent social policy.

Some other ministers were convinced that Wilson was taking his cue from departmental officials, and felt that the government risked recommending policies that were politically unsound. It took a strong personality like Pat Carney to hold her ground. Since one way to get the deficit under control is not to reduce revenue, Wilson, on the advice of Mickey Cohen, his deputy, hesitated to lower taxes on the oil industry. Carney, who was determined to dismantle the National Energy Program, told Wilson that they had to arrive at a political solution that incorporated a party point of view acceptable to both sides. With the support of her own department and her staff, Carney went to Wilson for what one participant described as "full and frank discussions— eyeball to eyeball," and the taxes were cut.

* * *

In the absence of an apparatus to coordinate the government's activities and with Mulroney's penchant for trying to keep on top of everything that was going on, it was hardly surprising that his office became larger and even more powerful than those of his predecessors. The opposition hounded the government about this in late February 1985, and demanded to know why Mulroney allowed his own staff to grow when the government was forcing all other areas to cut back. The government estimates revealed the extent of the expansion and Mulroney's plans to increase his staff from ninety to 120 and to spend $6.7 million rather than the $4.4 million that had sustained Pierre Trudeau's operations. Mulroney provided no real answer to this but claimed that the elimination of some of the Cabinet committees and the two central agencies (the ministries of state for social and economic development) had forced his office to take on some of the coordinating role.

Some members of the prime minister's staff did not like the excuses made by their boss. They felt that he should have simply acknowledged that he needed extra help. When Pierre Trudeau had taken over in 1968, he too had presided over an increase in the size of his office. A new prime minister comes into power with a certain distrust of the advisers of the previous regime—whether of the same party or not—and wants to bring in his own people. At the same time, he wants to put his stamp on government policy and coordination. Most of Mulroney's staff believed that the bulge in staff was temporary and that it would ease off after some time in government. Some felt that the PMO was still too small to perform all the functions that it had to undertake as a result of the shrinkage of the PCO.

The principal secretary's job in the PMO took some time to fill. Just before the election there had been no senior francophone on staff in the Leader of the Opposition's office and it was logical that the principal secretary be from Quebec. The choice boiled down to a list of three, all classmates and friends of the prime minister: Lucien Bouchard, Jean Bazin, and Bernard Roy. Bouchard refused to consider the job because as a former *péquiste*, he felt that his presence would embarrass the prime minister; Bazin would not take on the job for personal reasons. That left Bernard Roy, who also turned it down at first. But he was the choice of both Mulroney and the election campaign chairman, Norman Atkins, and they broke down his resistance.

Of all the people who ended up working for Mulroney, Roy's character wins the most praise both from politicians and from bureaucrats. He had proven his loyalty to the leader—he had even been best man at Mulroney's wedding. To many, he was the golden boy with decency, honesty, and ability to spare. Although he possessed leadership qualities, he was not perceived as a political operator. Roy could deal with the PCO, give the prime minister advice, and tone down Mulroney's wilder impulses.

At the same time, however, Roy enjoyed dealing only with particular issues. With the exception of Quebec, he was not reputed to be particularly interested in politics or policy. Some senior Tories, PMO staff, and bureaucrats felt that this lack of political experience and instincts was a handicap. He had run only one campaign in his life—the 1984 general election in Quebec. Perhaps wrongly assuming that there was enough political acumen in the office, he took no interest in day-to-day politics. There was the general view that the prime minister needed someone strong to work in tandem with Roy—someone who knew everyone in the party, who would stay up all night if necessary to coddle recalcitrant individuals, to make certain that the right calls were returned, and that important correspondence was answered promptly. They also needed someone to keep the troops in line. Others felt that Roy was handicapped because he did not have a vision of what he wanted to achieve and therefore could not direct the PMO and the government to accomplish things. Among the rest of the prime minister's chief advisers there seemed to be no defined pecking order. Fred Doucet, who had been a St. Francis Xavier University bureaucrat before serving as Mulroney's chief of staff in opposition, generally appropriated the areas of federal-provincial relations and foreign policy—especially the relations with the United States. He also did a fair amount of Mulroney's political work and acted as a conduit of information for the Tory party. Charles McMillan, formerly a professor of administrative studies at York University, had a heavy bias toward domestic economic issues. Geoff Norquay, previously the research director for the Canadian Council on Social Development and later head of the Tory caucus's research team, looked after social policy. Peter White, a businessman from London, Ontario, looked after appointments that fell within the prime minister's responsibilities. This meant that in addition to the executives and boards of crown corporations and agencies, he was in charge of the order-in-council appointments.

They all wrote some speeches and did Mulroney's briefings for the priorities and planning committee within their areas of responsibility. The senior staff all presumed upon their long friendship with the prime minister to gain access to him. They also did not hesitate to provide advice on questions that fell outside their own bailiwicks. Because he rarely went to the Langevin Building, the prime minister regularly saw only those who had offices with him in the Centre Block. By the spring of 1986, these were Bill Pristanski, his executive assistant; his personal secretary; Fred Doucet; and Geoff Norquay. The press secretary, Bill Fox, also saw him quite often.

Every Monday morning, the legislative assistant and others met to discuss current and anticipated issues. There was a daily meeting to brief the prime minister and to prepare him with explanations for the press and for the House of Commons. There was, commented one participant, "no clear-cut mechanical way or methodology that you can adopt in a system like this. If it's empirical, it's only in the sense that it's unpredictable."

Many criticized the service that Mulroney received from his advisers in the PMO. Because the staff treated everything as equally important, they forced the prime minister to overextend himself, running from one crisis to the next. In part, this resulted from their belief, one Mulroney himself shared, that politics was of the highest importance. Charles McMillan and Fred Doucet made it clear to senior bureaucrats that the prime minister did not like "unpleasant conversations." They left the impression that bad news should be kept from him. The prime minister did not, the bureaucrats believed, need political advisers like Doucet and McMillan because he was a political animal himself. (Peter White was seen as a special case. He had some ideas about the bureaucracy that senior public servants found objectionable, but they thought of him as "straight up" and a worthy opponent.)

Doucet and McMillan also came under attack for the quality of their policy advice. Fred Doucet was seen as a man who made commitments without understanding much about the intricacies of a subject. In the first months of 1986, his involvement in the abolition of generic drugs in Canada was often cited as an example of this, in that his position did not take into account the provinces' responsibilities in the area of health, nor did he reckon the ultimate cost to the provinces and to consumers.

Charles McMillan was accused by some senior public servants of trying to take over the policy functions that rightfully belonged to the departments. Furthermore, he simply did not understand that Osbaldeston had moved much of the policy functions out of the PCO. As a result, his work in economic policy "infuriated the departments" and involved him in feuds between bureaucrats and ministers.

The role of the PMO itself during the first year of the new government was very much that of firefighting and lurching from one crisis to another. Many of the senior staff members reported that they had to tell ministers to stop calling the PMO for advice on matters within their own competence to decide. But because the government had no other central agency to coordinate its policies and political approaches, the ministers' reaction had been an understandable one.

They had learned from Michael Wilson's experience with the debate over universal social legislation that followed his economic statement in November 1984. Wilson had taken his statement as given and expected that his colleagues had accepted it. But as soon as he understood the political cost after the opposition had launched its assault, Mulroney pulled the rug out from under Wilson by declaring yet again that social benefits were "a sacred trust." Senior public servants felt that the prime minister had not done his homework and studied the implications of Wilson's proposals.

Had the prime minister had a well-functioning office or had the PCO been allowed an aggressive role, the differing interpretations would have been settled behind closed doors before Wilson rose to his feet in the House of Commons. After eighteen months in office, some of the PMO staff admitted that they were naive about how easy their jobs would be and shared the prime minister's skittishness about incurring criticism. With the previous troubles in mind, Osbaldeston sat down with the prime minister and went through the spring 1985 budget, line by line, to make certain that he understood and approved what it contained.

Many in the party also tended to blame the prime minister's advisers for the resignation of the Minister of Communications, Marcel Masse, on September 25, 1985. It had been a bad week. Fisheries minister John Fraser had left the Cabinet two days earlier as a result of his countermanding the departmental inspection service and ordering the release of tainted tuna. The last thing that the Conservatives needed was another scandal to fuel attacks on the government. On September 25, the RCMP had arrived at Masse's constituency office in Thetford Mines and seized documents for an investigation into spending violations in the minister's election campaign. With a full schedule that day, Mulroney went about his work and then came back from lunch ten minutes before question period to find that Masse was resigning. If the right people had been in charge, claims one Conservative adviser, the Minister of Communications would have told the Speaker that he would resign only if a charge were laid. But by the time Mulroney heard of it, it was too late to change Masse's mind. "Where," asked one adviser, "was the principal secretary all that morning?" There was no way that the Liberals, particularly Jim Coutts, he ruefully noted, would have let it happen. "Why did no one sit down with Masse," complained another, "talk to him, and convince him not to go?" (Somewhat ironically, Masse's action eventually rebounded in the government's favour. Mulroney kept Masse's portfolio vacant until after the investigation and, once cleared, Masse rejoined the Cabinet on November 30. Mulroney then pointed out that other MPs were being investigated and that candidates from all parties had suffered because of the the 1974 Election Expenses Act.)

Over time, there was a change in the balance of power among the PMO's advisers. Geoff Norquay, to some observers, greatly increased the efficiency of the prime minister when he displaced McMillan as chief policy adviser. Elements of policy coordination and advice did make their appearance in the PMO after the reconstitution of the foreign and defence policy committee in September 1985. The PMO's foreign policy advisers monitored its agenda, attended its meetings, and tracked the issues, both in committee and in the priorities and planning committee, if necessary. The three-part system involving advice from the department, the PMO, and the PCO was re-establishing itself. Bob Fowler, the secretary of the Cabinet committee on foreign and defence policy, would present options, give a historical explanation and make recommendations. The PMO position was to provide an overview so that Mulroney could manipulate an issue.

* * *

The ministers' staffs took on the same outline as the Prime Minister's Office in terms of functions and attitudes. In general, ministers' staffs that had provided little policy advice during the Liberal years were enlarged and strengthened by the appointees recruited by Peter White of the PMO.

Up until the late 1950s, ministers had functioned with very small staffs. Before then, the bulk of the work lay on the shoulders of what were called secretaries but were usually women who wrote speeches and correspondence and looked after political matters to a small extent. Only in the late Diefenbaker and early Pearson years did the "executive assistant" make his appearance. The Liberals used these jobs to train the young political elite that they hoped to develop. Indeed, many of the executive assistants of the 1960s became the MPs, ministers, and deputy ministers of the 1980s.

One of the chief errors of Joe Clark's government was hiring the wrong people for many ministers' offices. They took most of the MPs' assistants or researchers from the Tory party offices— many of them underpaid, underqualified, and undertrained. Clark's ministers often bore the consequences of having political staff too easily bamboozled by the public service.

There is a striking uniformity about the new Tory political elite. Like the Liberals who preceded them, they are almost all in their thirties and forties, they are well-educated and somewhat pragmatic. Not surprisingly, their political outlook is conservative and most have earned their political spurs in one or more of the leadership campaigns of Mulroney or his rivals or worked for a time as researchers for the Conservative caucus.

Their presence also serves as an informal but important political network linking the departments at the top. They maintain friendships with their counterparts in other departments and they are in constant contact with the PMO. The chiefs of staff meet regularly every Wednesday as a "kiddies' cabinet" to consolidate their links and approaches to various issues.

Like the prime minister's advisers, they consider it their job to formulate the questions for the bureaucracy to answer. Many of the staffs set the political agendas for the top level of the bureaucracy. They then work with the bureaucracy to ensure that policy options are developed that meet the political objectives of their ministers.

Policy operations in the ministers' offices had not been Peter White's intention when he began the process of selecting assistants. Originally, White had not planned to bring in staffs with policy expertise because he wanted the Prime Minister's Office to retain the function of analysing and coordinating the government's policies. White's plans were pre-empted by the desire of some ministers to hire strong policy advisers and halted altogether by the criticism over the size of the PMO in February 1985. The question remained: would the absence of a strong central unit in the PMO leave the ministers open to errors?

Obviously, some ministers were not well served. Fifty percent of the bright young Tory chiefs of staff were gone by the end of the first year. Jake Epp's office, however, typified the best of the new system. Epp decided that he needed strong policy advisers because he felt it only natural after twenty years of Liberal rule that the public servants would not be familiar with the new government's approach. His chief of staff, Russ Wunker, did not become involved in policy development and looked after the administrative side of things. Policy was left to Ian Shugart, who had three staff members under him. In one sense, this group represented the extreme in terms of providing policy advice. In an unusual departure from normal practice, Shugart toured the provinces with senior bureaucrats to assess provincial reaction to the Liberals' Canada Health Act, which had prohibited doctors from extra billing. He also kept in touch with the PMO as Epp's alter ego for the Cabinet committee on social development.

In some instances, the marriage of the senior bureaucracy and the new political staff worked well and to the advantage of the Conservative government as a whole. Perhaps the prime example of this was the relationship of Pat Carney's assistants with Paul Tellier, the deputy minister. Some of the goodwill could be attributed to the strong background in energy policy of Carney's two key staff members, Harry Near and Steve Probyn. This allowed them to speak easily with the public servants and to translate the political requirements into terms that had relevance to the system. In their own words, Carney's staff were ''awed'' that the bureaucrats were so open to change. The staff also greased the wheels with good humour and encouraged informal contacts with the department. Papers associated with the staff's work went to the deputy minister's office and he was informed about all events.

In some cases, however, the ''we-versus-they'' attitude caused considerable trouble. When the ministers ignored the public service expertise, the result was half-baked or flawed Cabinet presentations that other ministers would rip to shreds. Almost from his swearing-in, Robert Coates suffered as Minister of National Defence. His staff had aroused the distrust and animosity of the bureaucrats and suffered for it. John Fraser, the Minister of Fisheries and Oceans, came into office with the idea that he had to keep his bureaucrats in line and told them that they should take requests from his chief of staff as though they came from Fraser directly.

* * *

A determination to enforce their will on the public service was one of the reasons that Fraser and his staff got into trouble in the fall of 1985. On September 17, *the fifth estate* revealed that Canadians had been eating rotten tuna. The CBC television program reported that the Minister of Fisheries and Oceans had overruled his department's inspectors and authorized the release of cans of tuna that the inspectors had declared unfit for human consumption. For the next few days, the media was full of charges and countercharges as the government tried to defend itself. The day after the revelation, the prime minister stood up for Fraser. He denied any suggestions that Fraser should leave the Cabinet "given the assurance by the minister and other colleagues that there was no evidence of any kind of threat to health or safety." As on other occasions, Mulroney had to eat crow. Following a meeting of the priorities and planning committee the next day, the minister announced that he had authorized the recall of all the questionable tuna. There was, affirmed Fraser, no question of his resignation over the affair. The prime minister then called the minister's actions " a reasonable and appropriate response" that had dealt with the situation. In the next breath, he told reporters that it was "pretty damned obvious" that the questionable fish should never had been put on grocery store shelves.

Fraser complicated matters when he stated that the PMO had known about the tuna weeks before the story broke. He contradicted the prime minister on this (Mulroney had claimed that his first awareness had come after the television show) Fraser also cast doubt on the prime minister's claim that he—not the Minister of Fisheries—had ordered the tuna withdrawn from sale.

The skein grew even more tangled as the details of Fraser's decision to overrule his civil servants became public. The fisheries inspectors had been complaining about the tuna from the Star-Kist plant in St. Andrews, New Brunswick, since 1982. The smell, taste, and texture had caused them to reject such a large percentage of the plant's output that the company had told the minister that the inspectors were going to put them out of business. The company threatened to close down the plant in the spring of 1985. Premier Richard Hatfield became involved and pressured the minister to save the 400 jobs in his province and to change inspection procedures. Fraser accepted Hatfield's suggestion that a provincial laboratory test the fish. He even went to St. Andrews and tried some himself. After this, he released the tuna for public consumption even though the final results from the New Brunswick laboratory were not ready. Canadian armed forces cooks had refused to serve the fish and the relief coordinator for Ethiopian famine aid, David MacDonald, had turned down the tuna as a contribution.

Fraser quit the Cabinet on September 23. Thereafter, the focus of the controversy shifted to Mulroney, who had to defend himself from allegations that he had known of the scandal in advance. Mulroney did admit that his office had discussed the question prior to the public airing, but denied personal knowledge. Apparently, Fraser's staff had asked Ian Anderson, Mulroney's deputy principal secretary, what to do about the potential trouble. Anderson and the PMO's caucus liaison officer, Pat MacAdam, had alerted Fraser's chief of staff, Claude Boiselle, about the issue and he had replied that his boss had acted within his power in releasing the fish. Then Fred McCain, the MP for Carleton-Charlotte, where the plant was located, told reporters that he had raised the matter of the tuna in caucus prior to the public furor. Although McCain changed his story after a chat with PMO officials, his initial claim challenged Mulroney's veracity yet again.

The Star-Kist tale rattled around in the press for another month. Allegations and countercharges emanated from the company, the unions involved, MPs, and the government. Mulroney claimed the last word when he told a reporter with the *New York Times*, "When it was brought to my attention—bang! Immediately the minister's resignation was secured." The claims of who knew which details and when are almost impossible to verify.

What can be said, however, is that there was a classic mix-up resulting from the failure to communicate between the minister, his chief of staff, the PMO, and the PCO. Determined to show the bureaucrats who was boss, Fraser and his chief of staff had challenged the inspectors' rulings in the first instance. Even the dep-

uty minister of fisheries, Art May, had written a letter to Fraser
that defended the inspectors and noted that "according to internationally recognized standards," the fish were unfit for human
consumption. It seems that Fraser and Boiselle did not listen to the
deputy as he outlined the risk that the decision had created. Three
months later, the deputy was moved out of the department. According to the PCO, May should have gone there to warn the clerk of
Fraser's error. As a deputy minister, May had a responsibility to
the prime minister, who appointed him, as well as to his minister.
As for Anderson and MacAdam of the Prime Minister's Office,
they too should have gone to the PCO for advice on what the
consequences of overruling the inspectors might be. Insiders generally excuse the prime minister. As one of them said: "Politically, he's too smart to put smelly tuna on the market." The fiasco
in the government's handling of the case, however, provided a
prime demonstration of the dangers that the Mulroney government was risking.

*　*　*

In August 1985, Paul Tellier left the Department of Energy, Mines
and Resources. On the day of his departure, Pat Carney's staff
wore black armbands. His success in that department had convinced the prime minister to appoint Tellier to replace Gordon
Osbaldeston, the retiring Clerk of the Privy Council. Tellier's
promotion sent out contradictory signals. In his first stint in government in 1967, Tellier had served as an assistant to Jean-Luc
Pépin, a Liberal Cabinet minister. He moved to the PCO in 1968 to
work on constitutional reform. After spending two years as deputy secretary to the Quebec cabinet, he returned to Ottawa in 1972
to work for Pierre Trudeau's government. Four years later, after
René Lévesque won power in Quebec, Tellier set up one of the
most powerful policy coordinating bodies in the PCO to devise
federal strategies to counter the rise of separatism in Quebec.
Tellier's office was always cluttered with flow charts, the symbols
of Pitfield's style of management.

To many Conservatives, Tellier had too close an identification
with the *ancien régime*. Joe Clark had moved him to the Department of Indian and Northern Affairs in 1980. Later he had gone to

the Department of Energy, Mines and Resources, where the National Energy Program had originated. One of Brian Mulroney's first decisions in September 1984 was to disband the hated Canadian Unity Information Office that Tellier had headed earlier in his career. Obviously, when the Conservatives took over in 1984, Tellier was one of those expected to leave the government.

But he stayed and quickly became one of the most respected deputies. At a Cabinet meeting, Mulroney cited Tellier's relationship with Pat Carney as a model for all the deputies. The prime minister's staff thought him the perfect foil for a minister. When asked to set about a task, he did not question the task but efficiently presented options for carrying out the job.

As soon as he moved into the clerk's office in the Langevin Block, the prognostications were that Tellier would strengthen the weakened PCO. Given his background, Tellier seemed likely to increase the coordination of government activity. Tellier was seen as Mulroney's man and quickly established the reputation of having a very close relationship with the prime minister.

By the spring of 1986, there was evidence that coordinating functions were making their reappearance in both the PMO and the PCO. Shortly after Tellier's appointment, Mulroney laid down the law to his ministers about using the Cabinet committee system properly. Matters that had not reached a preliminary conclusion were not to be brought to the priorities and planning committee. The PMO finally set up an organized system of briefing the chiefs of staff of the Cabinet's activities, thus complementing the informal network that the ministers' staffs had established.

In the PCO, new functions were accruing to the Cabinet committee on communications, which was given the authority to review committee recommendations before they were sent forward to the priorities and planning committee for final approval. In essence, this imposed a new layer on the Cabinet system and was intended to prevent some of the public relations fiascos that the government had encountered. In addition to this, the PCO was picking up new responsibilities. Tellier had Wednesday morning breakfast meetings with all the deputy ministers. The committees of senior public servants began reappearing (usually with new names) and bureaucrats began displacing ministers' assistants at Cabinet committee meetings. The creation of a new position, an assistant secretary to the Cabinet for regulatory affairs, was announced in mid-March 1986. These changes were ironic, given Mulroney's initial style and the commitment of the Conservative government to eliminating many of the structures associated with the Trudeau years. The exigencies of governing were starting to turn the clock back.

Chapter Four
The Business Side of Politics:
Consolidating the
Conservative Empire

From the day that the Conservatives won their massive election victory in September 1984, Brian Mulroney directed his party never to forget the election that lay four years in the future. The new prime minister had an enduring preoccupation with making the Conservatives the natural governing party—as the Liberals had been from 1935 to 1957 and again from 1963 to 1984. To build loyalty to the party, Mulroney's office set in motion a well-organized and pre-planned patronage operation that would guarantee that party supporters received their long-denied share of the thousands of government appointments and contracts. But patronage is a messy business, and problems quickly arose.

* * *

When he served as the national organizer of the Liberal party in the 1930s, Norman Lambert referred to patronage as "the business side of politics," and regretted that it was carried out behind closed doors. No matter what the euphemism, patronage greases the wheels of politics. It is still conducted behind closed doors. Everyone knows those aspects that have given the idea of patronage its sleazy connotations—kickbacks, firing of public servants, and contracts to relatives and friends, even though most of these abuses have been tempered in Canada. Legislation guarantees security of tenure to public servants, governs the awarding of most contracts, and allows for independent auditing of the government's books. Political parties must now submit lists of their

61

contributors and the 1983 Access to Information Act has exposed government contracts to public scrutiny.

At the same time, governments keep certain important positions open to be filled with individuals who share the political sympathies or outlook of the ruling political party. This applies across the board—the New Democrats differ not a whit from the Liberals, Conservatives, or Socreds. Further down the ladder are the contracts given for government advertising services to any agency of correct political views. And then there are the legal tasks which are distributed across the country. Is one respectable law firm any better at drawing up routine legal documents than another? The argument runs that those who have sacrificed their time to aid a party that has achieved power deserve these small plums which may not even compensate for their efforts. On this level, patronage—or perhaps the hope of patronage—is the glue that holds together most political organizations and certainly all of Canada's parties.

Patronage positions can cement thousands to whatever federal party is in power. When the Conservatives took over in 1984, there were something like 3500 positions that could be filled at the discretion of the Cabinet—governor-in-council appointments—and 10,000 spots that could be filled by the ministers. The range covered prestigious jobs such as the Senate or heads of certain crown corporations and agencies, down to the wharfingers, the keepers of the local dock.

In its last years, the Trudeau government had a system for reconciling conflicting interests. At regular intervals, the Prime Minister's Office and the Privy Council Office—involved by virtue of the senior appointments secretariat—circulated a list of upcoming vacancies broken down by province. This notice went to key party workers in each province and to the ministers concerned. Under the chairmanship of the chief political minister for each province, the ministers met to discuss proposed appointments. This system tended to create czars within the Cabinet and caused considerable dissension and fragmentation as ministers fought to get their own appointees, or those of the MPs in their particular area, put in the vacant positions.

After September 4, 1984, Brian Mulroney's patronage activities came under considerable scrutiny as a result of a legacy of publicity from the election campaign. Pierre Trudeau left office with a flurry of about 150 order-in-council appointments to supporters who had served him. As if this did not exercise the press enough, John Turner confirmed a further round of high-level appointments—seventeen of them Liberal MPs—on July 9, the day he called the election. This batch went to the Senate, the bench, the diplomatic corps, and the boards of important federal agencies. The cynical self-interest of the selections was epitomized in the public mind by the choice of Bryce Mackasey, a Trudeau loyalist, who had fallen from grace and had already received the chairmanship of Air Canada in 1978. Joe Clark had fired Mackasey from this spot in 1979. When he received an ambassadorial nomination, Mackasey was a central witness in a fraud trial in Montreal.

Mulroney's response was scathing and he immediately promised that, if elected, he would clean up the system and subject high-level positions to parliamentary review. But the Tory leader could only take the high road before the general public, not the party faithful. His line to party workers was that he would appoint Grits and New Democrats, "but not until there isn't a single breathing Tory left." Then the Conservative leader immediately blotted his copybook before the general public by an off-the-cuff remark to reporters on his campaign airplane, "There's no whore like an old whore," he joked about Bryce Mackasey. While this comment may have cast the Tory leader in a bad light, he recouped any losses during the second televised debate among the party leaders on July 25 by chastising Turner (who claimed that as prime minister, he had "had no option" but to make the appointments as a result of an agreement with Pierre Trudeau). With patronage so much in the spotlight during the election campaign, Mulroney's every move was guaranteed to gain publicity.

Notwithstanding the furor during the election campaign, the Conservatives had always recognized that patronage was a natural tool of the party that it would be madness to ignore. They operated on the assumption that if the party organizers and workers did not feel that the government of the day was looking after its own, then the party and the government would quickly be in trouble. As one of them put it, "Ninety per cent of governor-in-council appointments net the recipient $3000 per year and a couple of trips to Ottawa. They are nothing, but you get that person to sit on a board and you have a friend.''

The Tories had their patronage machine ready to roll even before they moved into their government offices. As part of the exercise in transition planning, Finlay MacDonald had studied the terms of the order-in-council appointments to identify those that a Conservative government could fill. Individuals seeking appointments had begun sending their résumés to the leader's office. Mulroney staffer Peter White also collected the names of everyone working on the 1984 campaign. After the election, this work made any conscious compilation of a list unnecessary.

The transition team also recommended that the Conservative government not exercise its right to fire all the order-in-council Liberal appointees. The planners knew that the government's every move would be scrutinized for the first few months. According to one of them, they worked on the ''5 a.m. theory.'' He explained it as getting a squeaky-clean reputation for being out of bed at 5 a.m. for the first few months in office, so that they could sleep in for the rest of their lives. Accordingly, the team wanted the Liberal appointees replaced as their terms of office expired.

The theory explains Mulroney's announcement three weeks after taking office that he had chosen the former Ontario leader of the New Democrats, Stephen Lewis, as ambassador to the United Nations. It was a brilliant stroke. It seemed to suggest that the new government would be completely impartial in its choice of appointees. At the same time, the appointment snatched away one of the NDP's brightest lights and briefly stifled criticism from the left.

On October 24, two weeks after cancelling Mackasey's appointment, the Conservatives named the defeated Liberal MP and former Speaker of the House, Lloyd Francis, to take the diplomatic posting in Portugal. This took the wind out of the sails of the Liberals, who could not fault it because Trudeau had appointed other former speakers to diplomatic posts.

Other early appointments also could not be criticized. These included the choice of former Tory MP and civic do-gooder, Jean Pigott, as chairman of the National Capital Commission; the appointment of peace activist and former MP Douglas Roche as ambassador for disarmament; and the choice of Allan Lawrence, Solicitor General in Clark's government, as chairman of the Canadian section of the Permanent Joint Board on Defence. In late December, Justice Minister John Crosbie announced that the federal government would consult with the provinces before appointing federal judges. This settled a long-standing tiff with the government of Saskatchewan and reinforced the consultation with the Canadian Bar Association that had been going on for years.

* * *

But the operation of patronage was dictated, in part, by the Conservative party itself. Party members were determined to have a voice in the decisions because they wanted to make certain that their supporters were rewarded. Mulroney hated the idea of political ministers being responsible for the appointments in a group of ridings in their region. Former Liberal minister André Ouellet was Mulroney's bad example for the self-interested manner in which he had controlled patronage appointments in Quebec. Mulroney felt that powerful regional ministers in the Liberal government had been so arrogant that they had disrupted internal party unity. It was also good political sense for Mulroney to prevent ministers building up independent power bases and to give the party some input over patronage. With a centralized operation under trusted staff members, the prime minister would know exactly what was going on.

The centralized system was in place a few days after the election. In the Privy Council Office, a unit called the senior personnel secretariat looked after the processing of the appointments. The Tories' lists were in the care of Peter White in the PMO. While the Clark government was in power, White's predecessor, Jean Pigott, had compiled the "yellow books" of pending vacancies, but White had everything put into a computer. The PMO began working with four months notice for a vacant position, but since the House of Commons was going to be reviewing the appointments as of the spring of 1986, the PMO changed the advance warning to six months. The PMO claimed to have a detailed profile of every position to which they could make an appointment. White checked the formal criteria for appointment and then generated a checklist of personal qualities that the position required.

The names were then fed into a party system that the Tories hoped would minimize conflict and trouble over potential appointments. The prime minister himself retained control over the most important spots—senators, some ambassadors, and lieutenant-governors. On December 21, he appointed three senators. These did not provoke any controversy in the press—so inured had journalists and the public become to the use of the Senate as a reward for bagmen and warhorses.

Other appointments went through several stages of party review procedure. The Conservatives set up a National Advisory Committee chaired by Erik Nielsen. On it were the head of the PC Canada Fund (to represent the interests of the party bagmen), the caucus chairman (to make certain that the MPs were not forgotten), and the head of the Tory women's organization. The committee met in Ottawa once a month to vet and recommend candidates for important national positions.

At the next level there were advisory committees for every province, each with a chairman chosen before the election by the prime minister-designate. Mulroney chose one minister from each province (two each from Ontario and Quebec) to sit on the provincial committee (called a PAC in Tory language). One MP from each provincial caucus attended, along with prominent provincial organizers and fundraisers. The rationale for this was that those active in local Tory circles would know the names that should be put forward. Accordingly, the PAC was responsible for collecting names for upcoming appointments. Some of the ministers on the PAC attended every meeting; others sent substitutes. Despite the intention that the system would stifle any attempts to create fiefdoms controlled by powerful ministers, it did not always work that way. Public Works Minister Roch LaSalle and Communications Minister Marcel Masse, the two Cabinet members on the committee for Quebec, immediately began a struggle for the control of the committee operations in that province.

The committees were slow to get under way but the tempo rapidly speeded up. Every month, White's computer spat out a list of upcoming vacancies in each province and the PAC received a list of dates for submitting the names of nominees. Members of

Parliament were given advance notice of forthcoming vacancies and were asked to submit names. The PAC was then responsible for selecting one name to recommend to the government to fill the vacancy. The committees tended to put forward two or three alternatives but were told that they had to come up with one name to recommend. Naturally, there were disputes but, on the whole, the organizers felt that the system worked well. Occasionally, a minister would put forward a candidate within his or her own departmental competence and steal a march on the committee. In this operation, the PMO acted mainly as a post office box for the PACs and the National Advisory Committee.

* * *

After their auspicious start, the Conservatives proceeded relatively cautiously for the latter part of 1984 and there was little protest. But the replacements proceeded inexorably. By making some of the changes over the Christmas holidays when Parliament was not sitting, the government kept opposition criticism to a minimum. For example, on December 21, Mulroney named eleven new directors of the national oil company, Petro-Canada, nine of whom were long-time active members of the Tory party. Of the others, one was a Conservative sympathizer and the other a Liberal friend of the prime minister. Fifty-one other positions were handed out, mostly to the Tory faithful, as gifts on Christmas Eve. The appointments included membership on the boards of the Canadian Broadcasting Corporation, the National Museums of Canada, the National Energy Board, the National Parole Board, and smaller agencies. Next was the New Year's list of federal Queen's Counsel—when both Conservatives and Liberals were appointed. In early February 1985, the prime minister named the former Ontario attorney general, Roy McMurtry, to replace the Liberal Donald Jamieson as High Commissioner to the United Kingdom. This post had long been a political appointment although Jamieson had served as Trudeau's Secretary of State for External Affairs and, on paper, appeared more qualified than McMurtry.

It was commonly thought that the Conservatives would continue to replace the Liberal appointees with their own party supporters but would leave high-profile Liberal incumbents in their jobs unless they wanted to send out a particular message. The dismissal of Joel Bell, the president of the Canada Development Investment Corporation, on November 2, was a case in point. This was to pass the word to the private sector that the Tory government remained committed to privatization. But in areas less scrutinized by the press, the Tories moved more precipitately and more ruthlessly. Special federal prosecutors who dealt with drug cases, all Tories, were being appointed as quickly as the Conservative MPs could submit names to the Department of Justice. In Ontario alone, over 500 lawyers were named to handle these cases and Canada Mortgage and Housing Corporation business.

There were some notable squeals at the occasional dismissal, such as the dumping of Geraldine Copps from a $46,000-a-year job as a citizenship court judge in Hamilton. Mrs. Copps, the wife of a well-regarded and incapacitated former mayor of Hamilton and mother of the vociferous Sheila, MP for Hamilton East, was fired despite lobbying from non-partisan groups on her behalf. Secretary of State Walter McLean added fuel to the fire when he told reporters to check the record of her daughter's comments about the government.

On paper, the system should have kept going on a relatively low-key level and, given the fact that patronage will never completely disappear, should have produced suitable candidates for the various positions that opened up. Naturally, there was some carping, but not very much. The prime minister invited it by his aggressive defence of choices. Moreover, ministerial use of government jets provided at least one story a month to reporters willing to send in access to information requests. Mulroney made the situation slightly ridiculous by calling the government's Jetstars the ''sacred instruments of travel'' in justifying his ministers' trips.

But the Tories were in too much of a hurry. They tried to cram into one year what the Grits had done in twenty. Senior officials from the PCO offered advice about the impact of certain appointments and cautioned against moving too quickly. In reply, the PMO and Mulroney himself said that the pressure from the party was too great to resist. Throughout January and February 1985, the lists of appointments lengthened and the press printed stories of positions processed so quickly that some nominees had not even received the official notification of their new status when they read about it in the newspapers. As the Liberals had before them, the Conservatives announced their appointments on Friday afternoon, too late for questions in the House or the Friday papers. By the following Monday, they assumed, no one would bother to make a fuss.

In March there were ninety-five appointees. The Friday slaughters continued when the Tories moved ruthlessly and asked for mass resignations, such as that of the entire board of directors of Air Canada. Naturally, Conservatives replaced them. This followed the similar move when the entire board of Via Rail was shown the door except for the president, Pierre Franche. First on the list of new members was the former premier of Newfoundland, Frank Moores. Then there was Fernand Roberge, the manager of the Ritz Carlton Hotel in Montreal and a member of the provincial patronage advisory committee. The Conservatives also tried to cover some of their tracks by appointing the respected former editor of the *Globe and Mail*, Richard Doyle, to the Senate the following week. But this went for naught when, in early April, Flora MacDonald, the Minister of Employment and Immigration, fired Florence Bird, a former senator, from the refugee status advisory committee. The respected head of the Pearson era's Royal Commission on the Status of Women, Bird had hired MacDonald, then at odds with Tory leader John Diefenbaker, to help write her commission report.

The cat was among the pigeons. Unanimously, the press began to howl about pork-barrelling and called the appointments the creation of an "instant Senate." The opposition referred to the appointees as "hacks, flacks, and bagmen." The identification of many of the new appointees with the prime minister set him up as the target for the assaults from all sides. Even his defence, based on the 5 a.m. theory, did not deflect the attack. Then it was revealed that Frank Moores had personally lobbied the government on behalf of a European firm trying to persuade Air Canada to purchase their product. Moores resigned after it became known in the summer of 1985 that he had served as a consultant to Wardair and Nordair, two of Air Canada's competitors.

Although the Tories defended their appointments at the time, a few months later even some in the PMO felt that they had failed to gauge the public sentiment properly. They admitted that firing the Air Canada board had been a mistake. They also conceded that they had erred in announcing all the appointments at once without statements giving the new nominees' qualifications. Stories circulated around Ottawa that the Minister of Transport, Don Mazankowski, had prepared a list of experts to sit on the boards, but that these had been rejected by the prime minister, who appointed partisan Conservatives instead.

Apparently Mulroney had given in to pressure from the party and had overruled his own staff who claimed that they had not intended to fire the order-in-council appointees. There also had been tension between ministers, who felt that they should have more say, and the party organization's committees. Because the Conservatives wanted to give all order-in-council appointments a fixed term, they decided that where they wanted to replace individuals, they would ask for resignations rather than fire the holders of the positions.

But the dam had broken and the orders-in-council flowed at an increasing pace. The press relished publishing the weekly listing of new appointees. Arts organizations condemned appointments to the national cultural agencies. The choice of Montreal Tory Joan Price Winser for a consul-generalship in Los Angeles was the first of a non-elected party worker to a diplomatic post. This added insult to injury in a department already suffering from low morale as a result of political appointees (by the end of the summer of 1985, 20 percent of the heads of posts abroad were estimated to be political appointees). In early July, the appointment of Lucien Bouchard, one of Mulroney's law school classmates, to head the embassy in Paris, rekindled the criticism. After all, as journalist Jeffrey Simpson commented, Canadians had often looked down their noses at the American choice of political bagmen unschooled in diplomatic practice.

The Conservatives tried to mount a defence. The Minister of Supply and Services, Harvie Andre, claimed, ''Everyone uses their friends. If you're buying a car or a house, you say, 'Gee, we can get it wholesale here.' It's part of the human experience.'' The Conservatives also pulled back a little. After dismissing Betty Hewes, one year into her term as chairman of Canadian National Railways, the Tories replaced her by Maurice Leclair, the company's president and a career administrator. Also, during each later round, a token Liberal or non-partisan candidate was reappointed. The Conservatives were not too bothered by the publicity over their appointments which they saw as a "thirty-second wonder."

Officials throughout the government were pleased that the government's job creation programs set up by Flora MacDonald tended to erase certain elements of patronage. They reflected the views the Tories had expressed while they were in opposition and got away from make-work projects. They felt that the grants did not have the constituency approach to job-training as had the programs set up by the Liberals. Under the *ancien régime*, getting money for the riding had depended on whether the MP belonged to the government party. The Department of Finance felt that this change in approach was nothing short of a revolution. As one of them said, "You get more bang for your buck."

There was, however, one riding where this did not apply. Grants and subsidies flowed like a torrent into Mulroney's constituency. In late March 1985, Mulroney announced $6.7 million in public works contracts to improve ports and airports in Manicouagan. The announcement was made just before a prime ministerial visit. Then, in mid-June, Mulroney announced that a new $50 million maximum-security prison would be built at Port-Cartier, also in Manicouagan. Less than a month later, Mulroney flew from hamlet to hamlet to announce the construction of a $25-million road along the north shore of the St. Lawrence to link the isolated communities. A month later, the residents received a $1.9 million grant to create jobs. This was, he claimed, all part of the long climb back to prosperity for the disadvantaged region.

* * *

Senior Conservatives felt that their reputation for special treatment and nepotism was far more damaging in the long term than their patronage appointments. Giving a relative a job was something that the public particularly opposed.

The first sensational case of political favouritism was spread over the newspapers for weeks. On September 25, the RCMP had found a plastic bag containing marijuana in the suitcase of the premier of New Brunswick, Richard Hatfield. They had searched his luggage as he was about to board a plane with Queen Elizabeth. While the premier was under investigation but before any charges were laid, Elmer MacKay, the federal minister in charge of law enforcement and the RCMP, met Hatfield in the Chateau Laurier Hotel in Ottawa. On October 26, Hatfield was charged, but he was later acquitted on January 29, 1985. The story of his meeting with Solicitor General MacKay did not surface until early February; it immediately provoked claims of impropriety and preferential treatment. Unconvincingly, MacKay claimed that he had not known the reason for Hatfield's request for a meeting and said that he felt he should always see a provincial premier at the latter's request.

Other controversies quickly followed. Many of the complaints arose over the handling of government advertising. Right after the election, the Conservatives terminated the contracts of the Liberal appointees who had managed the government's advertising and hired Tories to do the job. All government advertising contracts fell under the supervision of the group that reported to the Minister of Supply and Services, Harvie Andre. Like their predecessors, the government compiled a list of advertising firms with the technical capacity and political affiliation to handle the jobs.

In early January 1985, the first fuss occurred over the awarding of a contract to a group to serve as "agency of record" and to handle the supervision of $60 million worth of government advertising. Naturally, the two principals, Peter Simpson and Roger Nantel, were Conservatives. Nantel got himself in trouble by telling reporters that he would give part of the profits back to the Conservative party. Another adman, Peter Swain, admitted that he had refused to go along with the deal because it involved raising contributions. Immediately, Jerry Lampert, the national director of the party, questioned the statement. Nantel, a friend of Mulroney's, denied any plan to kick back money. Harvie Andre claimed that the issue was a tempest in a teapot over a possible $100,000 yearly profit. Although the Liberals cried foul, they had set up the system in the first place. The fuss died down.

In mid-April, the press focused attention on the connection between Michael Wilson and the vice-president of the Lawson Murray agency, Doug Robson. The adman was the president of Wilson's riding association in Etobicoke, had served as his chief of staff in 1979, and had set up the administrative side of Wilson's ministerial office in 1984. Robson's firm received an untendered contract to advertise government bonds three weeks after he had left Ottawa. Andre's press spokesman, Perry Miele, replied that the advertising management group had assigned contracts to agencies based on their capabilities. Wilson's office denied any knowledge of the contract. Two days later, the newspapers were full of the family connection—Wilson's brother-in-law was the president of the firm.

Despite denials by Wilson and Murray, charges of nepotism flew. Ed Broadbent, leader of the NDP, demanded an explanation from the prime minister as well as firm guidelines to stop abuses. Mulroney's election promises about patronage came back to haunt him. It is one thing for a relative of a Cabinet minister to win a contract by submitting a winning bid, pointed out Broadbent, ''It is quite another matter to obtain a government contract, be related to a minister, and not have to go through the tendering process at all.'' Citing Mulroney's conflict of interest rules, John Turner called for Wilson's resignation.

During an unedifying display in the House, Mulroney threw back countercharges and noted that Lawson Murray had withdrawn from the contract before the publicity had started. He vociferously defended his minister's integrity. In the midst of the controversy, Sheila Copps got a measure of revenge for the treatment of her mother by producing documents that showed that the prime minister had remained on the books as the director of a moribund company for a few months after taking office.

The opposition sensed the political utility of the nepotism issue even though the furor died down a bit when Harvie Andre promised guidelines to regulate advertising contracts—with certain hedges that still gave Tories the best chance at the deal. The Liberal ''rat pack''—Don Boudria of Glengarry-Prescott-Russell, Sheila Copps of Hamilton East, and John Nunziata of York South-Weston—began their PAW awards (Patronage Award of the Week). During the first week of May, they gave the award to Joe Clark's brother and sister-in-law. The Tories had made Peter Clark the lawyer for the 1988 Winter Olympics in Calgary and appointed Marcia, his wife, a temporary member of the Parole Board.

Then in June, John Crosbie had to employ all his Newfoundland gift of the gab to defend his family. The law firms of his two sons, both lawyers in St. John's, had received legal work given out by the Department of Justice, John Crosbie's bailiwick. When the storm hit the House on June 4, even the staunchest defender of the Cabinet, Erik Nielsen, obliquely admitted that Crosbie might have gone too far in stretching Mulroney's conflict of interest guidelines, which forbade preferential treatment of relatives. The following day, the Minister of Justice created an uproar in the House when he attacked the opposition as "cowardly, despicable, and dastardly" for slurs on his family. "Quiet down, baby!" he yelled across the aisle at Sheila Copps. While maintaining that he had appointed the law firms because of their competence, he also told the House that Mulroney had refused the offer of his resignation from the Cabinet and that his sons' firms had withdrawn as the government's legal agents.

The Crosbie family made the news twice more during the summer. A week after the initial attack, Crosbie furiously defended his brother, Andrew, who had declared bankruptcy. Mulroney upheld his minister's right to come to the side of his beleaguered family members. Two months later, the question of Crosbie's sons arose again when it was revealed that they had been reappointed as legal agents. Three weeks after the first resignation, the firms had received new business, this time for the Federal Business Development Bank. Moreover, the *Globe and Mail* obtained a letter indicating that the appointments originated directly in the Department of Justice. Liberal justice critic Robert Kaplan demanded Crosbie's resignation for yet again violating Mulroney's own conflict of interest guidelines. Crosbie replied, irrelevantly, that if his sons had worked for a large Toronto law firm, no criticism would have been made.

Following the brouhaha over Crosbie's sons, Peter White recommended to Mulroney that the government formally prohibit any practice that might appear nepotistic. The fuss, White felt, reflected the office's lack of centralized control over many government patronage operations. Although the major contracts were scrutinized, some of the small ones escaped. As one PMO staff member commented, "It's impossible. It's the little ones that get us, not the biggies."

During the summer recess, there were hints that White's advice would result in action as part of the government's new strategy to demonstrate a stronger hand on the helm during the autumn session of Parliament. The priorities and planning committee of the Cabinet piously took commercial flights to their meeting in Vancouver in mid-August.

Then, on September 9, two days after the *Globe and Mail* revealed that $200,000 worth of government legal work had followed the prime minister's friend Sam Wakim to a Toronto firm, Mulroney announced tougher conflict of interest rules. "Many of these steps are long overdue," he stated, "and heaven knows this government has had cause to regret their absence." He issued an outright ban on ministers hiring their own family members and the hiring of colleagues' families without impartial tendering. The rules also prohibited ministers from dealing with their former departments for two years. John Turner pointed out that the announcement was timed to draw attention away from the collapsing Canadian Commercial Bank. NDP leader Ed Broadbent remarked that the rules would prove useless if they were not enforced. For families maybe, but for friends, likely not. The choice of Sam Wakim for the legal work of the Export Development Corporation all but eclipsed the new conflict of interest guidelines.

Mulroney's new guidelines, however, extended beyond Cabinet members. They also applied to officials and ministerial staffs. The disclosure of assets applied to public servants, as did the prohibition on working in an allied area after leaving the bureaucracy. The most important change was the announcement that the government would experiment with committees of Parliament reviewing senior order-in-council appointments. The committees would not be able to veto appointments, but Mulroney implied that the government would likely withdraw a nomination if the scrutiny proved embarrassing. The prime minister also announced that lobbyists must register and declare their list of clients. The prime minister's actions, however, fell far short of the recommendations of the task force on parliamentary reform led by St. John's MP James McGrath. The committee recommended that Parliament have a veto over certain appointments and that review should include some regulatory bodies such as the Canadian Transport Commission, among others.

From September 1985, the contests over patronage contracts proved yet again that the issue would continue to plague the government. The flood of appointments continued—145 in the two weeks following September 26. Nor did the fuss over contracts abate. At the end of the year, Frank Moores made it into the papers again by signing a contract with Petro-Canada, a crown corporation, for his firm Government Consultants International to lobby the federal government.

On December 19, Mulroney's promised action to monitor consultants appeared stalled in its tracks—sent to a committee for study. Nonetheless, following the renewed controversy surrounding Moores, Mulroney ordered all crown corporations to cancel contracts with consulting firms to lobby the government on their behalf. Then in the spring of 1986, the first parliamentary review of a senior appointment took place. Gérard Veilleux, the government's choice as secretary of the Treasury Board, was due to appear. The meeting was cancelled due to lack of a quorum.

* * *

By the spring of 1986, the Conservatives were beginning to master the "business side of politics." At the same time, their initial spate of patronage appointments left many observers wondering whether this would prove yet another lull before a continuing gale. Mulroney's guidelines had irritated many public servants who felt that they should not be constrained in the same manner as political figures. The government contracts kept filling the pages of the newspapers, which had not relaxed their watchful gaze where Tory shenanigans might be concerned. The Tory faithful seemed to be quiescent and happy with the plums that were being tossed in their direction.

The Conservatives, however, were far less successful in building up a solid base in Quebec, the second part of their long-term strategy. There were reportedly power struggles going on between various factions of the Quebec party, partly over patronage, and one MP left the party to sit as an independent. Because of the illness of Roch LaSalle, the struggle to be the Quebec strongman was resolved in favour of Marcel Masse. And Robert Bourassa, as shrewd a politician as Mulroney, was firmly in power in Quebec City. Signs of the rot that had helped destroy John Diefenbaker twenty-five years before were already apparent in Mulroney's Quebec ranks.

Chapter Five
Le p'tit gars de Baie-Comeau

The key to Conservative party strategy was Quebec. With Brian Mulroney as leader, the party for the first time in its history had a fluently bilingual, Roman Catholic, native-born Quebecker at its head. Mulroney was of Irish origin, of course, but the Irish in Quebec had long had the status of "honorary" French Canadians. Mulroney was in a unique position to establish the Tories in Quebec on a firm base.

But there was a historic record of mistrust to overcome. Sir John A. Macdonald, with his shrewd sense of politics and people, had established the Conservatives in Quebec after 1867 but, by hanging Louis Riel in 1885, Macdonald had forfeited much trust. Ten years later, Wilfrid Laurier led the Liberals to power and created the entrenched *rouge* support in French Canada that persisted into the 1980s. In 1958, John Diefenbaker had received the backing of the Union Nationale machine and had stunned the country (and the Grits) by taking fifty seats. Those winnings evaporated quickly, however, as the Chief had eventually alienated French Canada. From 1963 to 1984 the Liberals had the safest of bastions in French Canada, support that was bolstered by Pierre Trudeau's personality and politics. In the 1980 election, Trudeau had held Joe Clark's Tories down to 12 percent of the popular vote and one seat in the province.

But Trudeau's successor, Toronto's John Turner, albeit fluent (if rusty) in French and for years an MP for a Montreal constituency, was no native Quebecker. Nor was he attuned to the attitudes and mores of post-referendum Quebec. Turner had the support of most of the Quebec Liberal machine, but he tried to distance himself from his predecessor, something that he believed required him to hold out the promise of softer policies on bilingualism to Manitoba, for example. If he was hated in English Canada, Trudeau was still a heroic figure in Quebec and his bilingualism policy had massive support.

But Trudeau was gone. The choice for 1984, therefore, was between Turner and Mulroney. Out of conviction and calculation both, Mulroney had led his party to a position of firm support for the rights of Manitoba's francophones, a difficult task, considering the bigotry of some in the Tory party. Mulroney's stand won him respect in Quebec. So too did his colloquial French, especially when it was compared to Turner's slightly stumbling efforts. Moreover, Liberal leader Robert Bourassa, a personal friend of Brian Mulroney, had declared his neutrality in the federal election. It soon became clear that this meant that provincial Liberal organizers could work for the Tories without fear, and there were estimates that up to 30 percent were doing so. By the summer of 1984, Tories were beginning to hope that Mulroney might take twenty seats in Quebec, a triumph considering the party's still nonexistent organization there. Even so, Liberal party polls in Quebec, taken just after Turner's convention victory, showed a lead of thirty-nine points for their party. Mulroney was honest and blunt about those polls: "If we don't win seats in Quebec, we're dead."

By August, the Tory leader's strong and well-orchestrated campaign had made gains in Quebec and all across the country. With 38 percent support in Quebec and Turner only 6 percent ahead, Tory strategists translated the figures into at least thirty seats. In Roberval, a constituency where the Tory candidate had drawn 1.49 percent of the vote in 1980, Mulroney filled the hall with enthusiastic supporters. Shrewdly, Mulroney promised to stop the war between Quebec City and Ottawa and to cooperate with the Quebec government. That implicit promise of a new agenda helped to make Mulroney's party a home for every shade of nationalist opinion. There was room in the Conservative party for anyone who had reason to dislike the Liberals and/or John Turner. In his own riding of Manicouagan, Mulroney promised to make the development of the north shore of the St. Lawrence a priority of his government. His own seat was far from sure, but the promises held out hope for every area that had received little, despite long records of supporting Grits. By the last week in August, the rout was on, and the Quebec Tories told everyone, "*Ne manquez pas le bateau.*" This promise of patronage rewards had an authentic ring to it. The smug and complacent Liberal machine proved unable to counter the floodtide and Quebec gave its native son fifty-eight seats. It was a revolution in Canadian politics, or so it seemed.

Mulroney's goal was to institutionalize this revolution. Although there were some strong representatives elected in Quebec such as Robert de Cotret and Marcel Masse, most of the new MPs were politically green. Who else, after all, would have been so foolish as to run for the *bleus*? Even so, the prime minister gave ten of his fellow Quebec MPs ministerial responsibility, made another eight parliamentary secretaries, and named eleven more to House committee chairmanships or vice-chairmanships. Thirty of the fifty-eight Tories in the House received rewards. Nonetheless, it would fall to Mulroney himself, aided by the creator of the party machine in Quebec, Bernard Roy, head of the Prime Minister's Office, to handle Quebec.

The first task was to decide how to deal with René Lévesque's Parti Québécois government. Since the referendum in 1980 and the provincial election that followed it, the Parti Québécois had lost ground to the Liberals as party supporters questioned the wisdom of the independence issue, particularly in the prevailing economic atmosphere of hard times. Lévesque suffered a string of by-election defeats. Massive change was imminent.

In such circumstances, Mulroney had to decide whether to wait until electoral change had taken place to try to resolve Quebec's status in Confederation and in the constitution (from which it had been virtually excluded in 1981-82). In November, he said that the constitutional accord was incomplete so long as Quebec opposed it, a half-proffered olive branch. Lévesque was willing to talk, but Mulroney soon said, "I wouldn't anticipate that there would be any negotiations on the constitution." The federal position, it seemed clear, was to bide its time and wait for Lévesque and the Parti Québécois to disappear from the scene. After Lévesque urged his compatriots to put independence behind them, the Parti Québécois cabinet was wracked by defections. For Lévesque, the survival of whose regime depended on settling matters with Ottawa, Mulroney's coolness was not good enough. Lévesque and Mulroney met in Quebec City on December 6, but all the Quebec premier received was an unstoppable flow of honeyed phrases from the prime minister. Clearly, the federal leader had no intention of holding serious negotiations until after a provincial election. Lévesque had backed himself into a corner by proposing a major change in Parti Québécois strategy before he had a commitment from Ottawa. All he could cling to was Mulroney's willingness to negotiate Quebec's right to opt out of federal programs and to receive full compensation. That was not much when set against the prime minister's earlier adamant refusals to countenance any such arrangement. After a second meeting in March, Lévesque was no further ahead.

If that was viewed as encouraging by Robert Bourassa and the provincial Liberals, it probably was. So too was Mulroney's opposition to efforts to create a provincial Conservative party. (A ragtag group of Tories did set up a provincial party, but they produced nothing but embarrassment in the December 1985 election.) Bourassa was delighted: a Tory party would only split the federalist vote in Quebec, he said. And with the March 1985 polls showing the Liberals twenty points ahead of the Parti Québécois, power seemed guaranteed to drop into Bourassa's hands once more.

On May 17, 1985, Lévesque took his last shot at resolving the constitutional impasse. In a major address he called for recognition of the existence of the people of Quebec, for exemption from all but the "democratic rights" sections of the Charter of Rights and Freedoms, a veto over or financial compensation for changes to the constitution, and a significant new division of powers. Although the *Globe and Mail* quickly labelled the package a challenge to Ottawa's claim to represent all the country, the prime minister was equally quick to concede that Quebec was a "distinct society." That was true and it cost nothing to give it away, but Mulroney had not budged an inch on Lévesque's other demands. Checked once more, Lévesque finally announced his departure on June 21. At the beginning of October, by an unprecedented popular vote among its members, the Parti Québécois selected a successor, Pierre-Marc Johnson, the son of the Union Nationale Premier of the 1960s, Daniel Johnson.

Despite Mulroney's tactical victory on the question of the Constitution, his base in the province was disintegrating. The province's ministers, as new to federal politics as the MPs, were unsure how to act. Only Masse, LaSalle, de Cotret, and, to some extent, Benoît Bouchard, the Secretary of State, had made any impact. The polls in the summer of 1985 demonstrated ominous signs of a decline in Tory support in Quebec. After a meeting with the Quebec caucus, Mulroney put Roch LaSalle, his public works minister and a long-time party warhorse, in charge of a new organization committee that would "put the government's message across to voters." As Quebec's economy continued to stagnate, the Tories stuck to public relations.

The real test of the caucus's power lay in what it could deliver to Quebec. One possibility was a $300 million plant to be built by Hyundai, the Korean automaker. Quebec was one of four provinces to bid on the plant. Johnson had called a provincial election for December 2. Mulroney's ministers seemed to be everywhere in the province to announce grants and programs that, critics charged, could only help the incumbent Parti Québécois government. All eyes were fixed on the Korean automaker, because its decision involved millions in Canadian subsidies and duty remissions. On November 15, Premier Johnson announced that the plant would be located in Bromont, Quebec. As Graham Fraser noted in the *Globe and Mail*, many were beginning to wonder if Mulroney "isn't trying to buy himself a political party, if not a government in Quebec." Despite Mulroney's denials, Ottawa was obviously lending its support to Johnson.

That was a bungle. The Parti Québécois lost the election on December 2, 1985, and the new premier, Robert Bourassa, although a friend of Mulroney's, owed little to the prime minister after the federal government's election intervention. A nascent alliance between the new Liberal premiers of Ontario and Quebec to oppose free trade with the United States also threatened the central Canadian base Mulroney had so successfully created.

With amazing speed, Canadian politics had reversed direction in 1985. Ontario and Quebec were in new hands, and the Tories, cock of the walk in September 1984, were suddenly in difficulty in central Canada. And nowhere was the change more dramatic than in Quebec. "Look, I'm no fool," one Quebec Tory MP said in December. "If there were an election tomorrow, we'd probably get ten seats [in the province]." After the Montreal refinery affair that blew up later that month, that estimate seemed optimistic, and in February 1986, opinion polls showed the Tories with only 23 percent support in Quebec.

* * *

Every region of Canada was feeling the pinch of unemployment. Jobs, particularly those with a high technological component, are scarce commodities, and no government—federal, provincial, or municipal—can sit by and allow employment to disappear. At the same time, there is traditionally a close relationship between politicians in Quebec and their constituents, a relationship that dates back to a time when the *deputé* was expected to struggle for his *comté* in Ottawa to ensure that his people got their fair share of patronage jobs. Paternalism, some might call it, and paternal it was.

At the beginning of the government's term of office, the new MPs had to demonstrate that they could look after their constituents as well as their predecessors had. After Brian Mulroney became prime minister, the desire to show Quebec that *les bleus* cared had special importance. If the Tories were to turn their massive support in the election into a permanent Tory base, if Mulroney was not to see his majority disappear the way Diefenbaker's had done a generation earlier, then Quebec had to be looked after.

It is always hard to assist declining industries in depressed areas. Business decisions tend to be made to maximize profits, not to help governments hold their support. Other provinces and regions always have competing claims, individuals have their own hopes and aims, and politicians can be as prickly as any category of humankind. The struggle over the Gulf refinery in east-end Montreal showed the complexity of the problems that faced Mulroney and his government in dealing with Quebec, its politicians, and multinational business.

Early in December 1985, Ultramar Canada purchased Gulf Canada's holding in the eastern part of the country. Included in the deal were 675 service stations in Quebec and the Maritimes, a deal that made Ultramar the leading gas company in Quebec. The deal was to close on January 8, 1986—after Gulf had completed the shutdown of its Montreal refinery at a cost of $25 million. The Montreal plant, run by 450 employees and with a capacity of 75,000 barrels a day, was said to be redundant because Ultramar could supply its stations in the province from its newer and more efficient Quebec City refinery. If the Gulf refinery closed—the fourth shutdown out of six refineries originally located in east-end Montreal—the losses of jobs would be only marginally lessened by Ultramar, which agreed to keep on ninety Gulf workers.

Ultramar's president said that the owners of Gulf, the Reichmann family of Toronto (through their Olympia and York Developments Ltd.), had "tried every way possible to find a buyer for Gulf Canada's eastern assets who would keep the refinery open. It was in their interest to do so because of the cost of the refinery shutdown." But the only competing bid for Gulf's holdings, one from Gaz Metropolitain of Montreal, offered less than Ultramar.

Up to that point, Ottawa's involvement had been minimal. A few days after the sale, Robert de Cotret, the President of the Treasury Board, told representatives of the Montreal refinery's workers that the sale was a private transaction between two companies. There was a certain embarrassment about de Cotret's disclaimer, largely because it was made at a press conference announcing the formation of a blue-ribbon committee to study ways to bolster Montreal's sagging economy. But because Ultramar was British-owned, Ottawa's Investment Canada had to approve the decision to shut down the refinery, a decision that was made and approved within two weeks or so of the transaction. Sinclair Stevens, the Minister of Regional Industrial Expansion, said that Investment Canada had determined that the deal was beneficial to Canada because it would provide security of employment for Gulf's 880 workers and, he added, because Ultramar would invest $125 million over five years to improve its operations.

But a government report prepared by the Combines Investigation Branch of the Department of Consumer and Corporate Affairs had demonstrated only a week before that Quebec motorists collectively paid from $300 to $500 million a year more than they should for gasoline because of insufficient refinery capacity in the province. Prices at the pump were three to five cents a litre higher in Quebec than in Ontario and that was troublesome. The Quebec National Assembly unanimously adopted a motion condemning the sale. Then, on December 30, three Tory MPs, including the Minister of State for Transport, Suzanne Blais-Grenier, signed a petition calling on the prime minister to reverse the decision made by "the office of the Ontario minister Sinclair Stevens." "I can't keep silent in a situation so important for workers, for the east end of Montreal, and for the petroleum industry in Quebec," Blais-Grenier said, also adding that her colleagues were too hasty in approving the deal. The oil companies had employed "pressure and blackmail on various ministers" to ensure that Ottawa would not intervene. "Threats [like those] of Ultramar and Shell should not happen in a democratic society," she said.

But in a parliamentary democracy, a minister should also not criticize Cabinet decisions and on December 31, Blais-Grenier resigned, her departure coming just before it could be demanded by the prime minister. She was the fourth Mulroney Cabinet member to go in fifteen months in power, but the first to get only a twenty-word letter without any expression of regret at her departure.

Blais-Grenier was, to be blunt, no loss to the government. A first-time MP with graduate degrees in economics, sociology, and social work, she had been handed the plum job of environment minister in September 1984, and almost instantly found herself at odds with conservationists and the environmental lobby. Her comments downgrading the danger posed by PCBs, for example, had provoked sharp denunciations from frightened Canadians. So too had her planned reduction of $3.8 million in the budget of the Canadian Wildlife Service and her willingness to allow logging in national parks. Moreover, she proved blunder-prone in the House, and in August 1985, Mulroney moved her to the junior portfolio in Transport. But Blais-Grenier's problems dogged her still. A $64,000 expense claim for two European trips (only nominally on government business) drew sharply critical comment in Parliament and in the press.

With only a minimal chance of surviving the next Cabinet shuffle, the general view was that Blais-Grenier had left on a point of principle to avoid forced relegation to the back benches. She had resigned, her letter to the prime minister said, because "The real influence of ministers from Quebec in the Cabinet's decision-making process seems to me insufficient," a curious remark, since Mulroney himself was a Quebecker. Even so, the resignation—and the grumbling from other Quebec MPs, some of whom had been talking of crossing the floor of the Commons even before the Ultramar affair—highlighted the government's problems with the Montreal refinery, with its Quebec party, and with the province generally. After Blais-Grenier's departure, Montreal in particular was even more underrepresented in the ministry. Only Mines Minister Robert Layton remained to represent the city and he was an unknown member in an unimportant portfolio and an anglophone to boot.

The critical nature of the Quebec problem became clear early in the new year. Opinion polls showed the Liberals well ahead in the province—in LaPrairie, south of Montreal, the Grits gained 25 percent in three months to ride comfortably 16 percent ahead of the Conservatives. So bad was the situation that a plan to put Marcel Prud'homme, a Montreal Liberal MP, into the Senate and open a seat for Bernard Roy, the head of the PMO, had to be abandoned. Opinion sampling had demonstrated that the Tories could not win Prud'homme's riding—or any other—in Montreal. The newspapers were full of rumours that "at least five" Quebec MPs had begun to talk to the Liberals about joining their party. There was "a feeling of panic" in the Tory ranks, one Liberal MP commented. The Montreal refinery workers, turning off the taps and preparing to shut down their livelihoods, twisted the knife a little more. "Mulroney pretends he hears the problems of the Québécois," the plant local's president said, "but he is just working where the big guns are, and that's Ontario."

The prime minister put the best face possible on the Gulf affair. "I want my MPs to speak out on issues," he said. "I want them to be independent. The fact that a Conservative MP speaks out on an issue vital for Montreal is not a sign of weakness." But Mulroney weakened the force of his pieties when he claimed that not a single MP had expressed "discontent" with the government's decision, a claim quickly and easily challenged by reporters, who fired back the names of the dissenters.

The Gulf issue caused general discontent to coalesce. There was, as Graham Fraser of the *Globe and Mail*, noted, a "common front." "Every now and then, like a lunar eclipse, different interests in Quebec pull together on a single issue, and a difficult, complicated question becomes transformed into a piece of popular mythology. The result can be political dynamite." It was all true: the Gulf refinery had made Quebeckers of all stripes concerned about jobs, concerned about Ontario's power in Confederation, concerned about the Mulroney government's weaknesses, and concerned about the high prices they had to pay for gasoline. "Brian Mulroney's whole election victory strategy was based on not outraging Quebec," Fraser noted. "Now, his government has annoyed almost everyone."

* * *

Brian Mulroney's efforts to reintegrate Quebec into Canada (and to keep the province firmly within Tory ranks) had their international dimension as well. For years, ever since a confrontation at an educational conference of French-speaking countries in Gabon in 1968, involving Pierre Trudeau's federal government, Daniel Johnson's Quebec, and a meddling France, Canada had been unable to work out a method of securing provincial representation at international conferences. This impaired the effectiveness of La Francophonie, the loosely knit organization of French-speaking countries and a kind of parallel to the British Commonwealth. Under the Trudeau government, Canada refused to participate if Quebec had "national" status, and France would not allow La Francophonie to meet if Quebec were not represented. Eager to show that he was sensitive to Quebec's aspirations, Mulroney was determined to give Canada a chance "to balance our external activities" and to help the country develop an "enviable diplomatic network" that would include the francophone nations.

Negotiations with René Lévesque and then with Pierre-Marc Johnson's Parti Québécois government began in 1985 on this issue. By early November, with the election campaign under way in Quebec and with a meeting of La Francophonie scheduled for February 1986 in Paris, an agreement was reached. Quebec would have a special, but not independent, status within the Canadian delegation, sitting behind a placard labelled "Canada-Quebec." Provincial representatives could take a direct part in discussions on culture and education, areas under provincial jurisdiction; but only the federal representatives could participate on economic questions and international affairs. As "interested observers," the Quebec representatives could discuss such questions with the Canadian representatives before speeches or interventions at the conference were made. Johnson was delighted at the agreement, particularly because he had achieved something that his father, Daniel, had been unable to manage. He called it a breakthrough that let him represent "the Quebec people" abroad. Mulroney, already under fire for intervening in the election on Johnson's behalf, denied that he had given this right to the *péquiste* premier. "I have maintained impeccable neutrality as a Quebecker and a Canadian," he said, convincing no one. More to the point, perhaps, Mulroney had made a radical departure from the policy of Pierre Trudeau, who held that "Canada speaks with one voice internationally. Quebeckers speak through the voice of the federal government when it comes to international affairs."

But Mulroney was nothing if not cunning. Although Premier Johnson claimed that Ottawa had agreed to exclude the officially bilingual province, New Brunswick, from participation at the Paris summit, Mulroney insisted that Premier Hatfield's government was as entitled to representation as Quebec's. "There aren't two kinds of francophones—first-class and second-class," the prime minister stated, sounding very much like Pierre Trudeau. Johnson called the inclusion of his neighbours "a gesture hostile to Quebec."

The Paris meetings were set for February 17 to 19, 1986, but the squabbling between Ottawa and Quebec City did not cease when Robert Bourassa's Liberals drove the Parti Québécois from power. Every bit as keen on the summit as Johnson, Bourassa called it "a precedent and a breakthrough." But there were still difficulties. In Quebec, Gil Rémillard, the new Minister of International Relations and, ironically, a former adviser to Mulroney, said that his premier would address the opening session. To Mulroney, however, the matter was beyond dispute: "If the leader of a national government is invited, I presume that means me."

One of Bourassa's advisers then changed tack and noted that

since the opening would be only a brief, formal session, it was proper that Mulroney should speak. "But, if the French government changes its approach, and ten or fifteen leaders should speak, it would be normal for Mr. Bourassa to speak." Mulroney was equally firm about protocol at the meetings. "You can be sure that Mr. Hatfield and Mr. Bourassa—anytime they want to speak— all they'll have to do is to nudge me and ask me, say that they'd like to say something. You can be sure that I'll want to hear their voices." Although the Quebec press complained that Bourassa had been outmanoeuvered, the premier himself said he had insisted on speaking at the closing session to help Quebec in its bid to host the next meeting of the organization. In fact, the premier was named rapporteur, charged with wrapping up the discussions and summarizing them.

The Paris meetings opened with full French panoply, including flashing swords and mounted musicians, at the Palace of Versailles. But there was to be little peace between the warring Canadian factions. Under as much pressure as Bourassa to have a large profile at the summit, Mulroney led off by hailing Canada's domestic "reconciliation," symbolized by "the presence of the Premier of Quebec here beside me." The harmony turned to confusion when Bourassa proposed a "new Marshall plan" to distribute the European Economic Community's surplus foodstuffs to Africa. It was a good idea, although it hadn't the slightest prospect of being implemented. But it violated the agreement between Ottawa and Quebec that forbade the provinces from making international proposals of their own without federal consent. Smooth, slippery, and self-satisfied, Bourassa blandly observed that he had not told Mulroney what he was going to say although he had informed him that he wished to speak on agriculture. "I was assuming for commonsense reasons that the federal government would have no objection . . . " It was Bourassa at his shrewdest and most politically opportunistic.

The initial federal response was one of stunned confusion. Mulroney was furious at the way his generous gesture (too generous, many had warned) had exploded. Junior ministers scrambled to put the best face possible on Bourassa's defiant intervention. Bernard Roy, Mulroney's chief of staff, finally spoke for his man. "It would be untrue to tell you that we didn't wonder about it . . . [but] there was no gesture made consciously to test the limits,'' as *Le Devoir* had reported. More convincing were the prime minister's own remarks. Mulroney, a man known to harbour grudges, was blunt at the end of the meetings: ''Do it to me once, blind side me once, and you've got a problem.''

This squabble between Quebec and Ottawa, so reminiscent of the difficulties during the Pearson and Trudeau years, diminished Canadian prestige at the Paris summit. There were agreements on numerous technical and cultural areas on such subjects as scholarships, data banks, television and computer technology, and the like. Quebec was selected as the site of the next meeting in 1987 (with a carefully worked out plan between the two Canadian capitals on sharing arrangements). But the contretemps had demonstrated that the tension between Quebec City and Ottawa was, if not permanent, at least inevitable. Quebec's drive for international recognition had not ceased and, indeed, thanks to Mulroney's decision to allow Quebec a role, the province's aims had taken a leap forward. There were difficulties for a novice prime minister at every corner, and Robert Bourassa, determined to demonstrate that he was no one's satrap now, had won the opening rounds on points. The Quebecker had called the summit ''a diplomatic triumph,'' and so it was—for Quebec.

Part Two
Right Turns and U-Turns

Chapter Six
A Sacred Trust

On June 19, 1985, Brian Mulroney had one of the most important confrontations of his short parliamentary career. The federal budget announced in the House of Commons by Finance Minister Michael Wilson on May 23 had taken a step toward removing inflation protection from Canadians receiving Old Age Security, also known as the old age pension. As part of his campaign to cut federal expenditures in the fight against continuing high deficits, Wilson had proposed that the practice of raising the value of the pensions to match increases in the cost of living (indexing) be stopped. Beginning in January 1986, the OAS would be increased only if inflation exceeded 3 percent.

Canada's senior citizens were incensed by the move and they, together with the opposition parties, the press, the unions, and even business leaders, accused the government of breaking a promise not to tamper with Canada's social programs. In the weeks following the budget speech, opposition to de-indexing mounted across the country; Mulroney, Wilson, and other Cabinet ministers were hard pressed to defend themselves. The climax to the demonstrations came on June 19, a drizzly morning, outside the Parliament Buildings in Ottawa, where a small group of senior citizens gathered to voice their displeasure. They set up a loudspeaker and played a tape of a Mulroney election speech in which he promised to protect old age pensions. Just before noon Mulroney emerged from the building and was confronted by 63-year-old Solange Denis of Ottawa. "You lied to us," Denis told the prime minister, "You made us vote for you, then, goodbye Charlie Brown . . . If you do anything [to the pensions] you won't get back in three years." "I'm listening to you, madame," Mulroney answered. "Well, madame is damned angry," Denis replied.

* * *

In the heat of the 1984 election campaign, Liberals and New Democrats had accused the Tories of secretly planning wholesale changes to Canada's social security programs. They claimed that Mulroney would do in Canada what Social Credit Premier Bill Bennett had done in British Columbia: slash social programs and cut government services drastically in the name of fiscal restraint. Mulroney's advisers knew that this was an area in which he and his party would be vulnerable, because many voters believed that the Conservatives were dominated by right-wing types who disapproved of social welfare and espoused policies similar to those of Ronald Reagan. This was not true: the Tories had strongly supported the Canada Health Act, for example, passed in the spring of 1984 in an effort to ban extra billing and hospital user fees, and they had either accepted or supported every other major piece of social welfare legislation adopted since World War II. Nevertheless, the perception remained. Because of this persistent belief, Mulroney insisted that Canada's social welfare system was "a sacred trust not to be tampered with." He promised that although the Tories favoured a policy of fiscal restraint, they would maintain the welfare state. Mulroney offered a bargain to Canadian voters. "Elect me," Mulroney declared, "and I will preserve your social programs." The voters accepted.

In 1981 and 1982, the Canadian economy had been plunged into near-depression. Even when the United States began to make a strong recovery (apparently in response to President Ronald Reagan's economic policies), Canada continued to languish in the economic doldrums. The inflation rate fell below 10 percent by the end of 1983, but unemployment remained high and productivity stayed low. Businessmen, economists, and Conservative politicians claimed that Canada had to get its massive budgetary deficit under control before the economy could recover. The deficit had been growing dramatically since the early 1970s. In 1971-72 it had reached almost $1 billion for the first time in Canadian history; ten years later it stood at $14.5 billion. When the Canadian economy went into recession in 1982, the Trudeau Liberals were unprepared for the severity of the economic downturn. Tax revenues fell as Canadians lost their jobs, corporations cut back production, and farmers and businesses went bankrupt. At the same time, however, the demand for government services in the form of welfare payments and unemployment insurance increased sharply. The Liberals tried to spend their way out of the mess, with the result that the deficit increased from about $14.5 billion in 1981-82 to almost $32 billion two years later—the largest increase in Canadian history.

When governments overspend, they must make up the difference by borrowing, usually by issuing bonds. These bonds, together with other government loans, constitute the public debt upon which interest must be paid regularly. In Canada in 1983-84, the gross public debt stood at close to $200 billion dollars. Almost 25 cents of every dollar spent by Ottawa went to pay interest on the debt.

As the deficit grows, so too does the amount the government needs to pay interest on its loans. More and more of the taxes paid by Canadians are not spent on programs or services but on debt charges. The government is forced to compete with private borrowers in the securities markets and this forces interest rates up. If Ottawa could cut its deficits, the federal government could decrease the public debt, use its revenues more efficiently, lower taxes, drive down interest rates, and restore confidence in the Canadian economy. Or so the conventional theory goes.

Mulroney and the Tories agreed with this theory and promised deficit reduction and job creation in their 1984 election campaign. But although deficit reduction is simple in theory, it is much harder to achieve in practice because governments, for the most part, spend most of their money on statutory programs—programs such as Old Age Security, family allowances, and medicare—that have been established by law and that must be financed to a certain level in order for the government to meet its obligations. In promising to treat these programs as a ''sacred trust,'' Mulroney was announcing that his government would preserve the Canadian welfare state while reducing the national debt. That was a tall order which brought the concepts of fiscal and social responsibility into constant conflict.

The Canadian welfare state began with Old Age Pensions, first introduced in 1927 and payable to any Canadian over the age of seventy who could pass a means test. The pension paid in 1927 was $1 per day. In those days, the capitalist virtues of thrift, hard work, and self-reliance were subscribed to by one and all; it was part of the basic faith that those who were talented and hard-working would eventually enjoy the fruits of their success. The poor, most Canadians believed, were basically indolent, ignorant, or immoral and they deserved little better than Christian charity from their social and economic betters.

That attitude changed during the Depression. For almost ten years the Canadian economy was gripped by the worst economic slump of the past century. Suddenly, it seemed, almost everyone was out of work. Canadians no longer believed that the poor were poor because they deserved to be. Voters began to demand that the government take a more active economic role to ensure that a disaster such as the Depression did not happen again.

During World War II, the government began to comply with this demand. The baby bonus, or family allowance, was introduced at the end of World War II to distribute wealth throughout society to ease the transition from a war economy to a peace economy and to undercut union demands for high postwar wage increases. Because it was not viewed as a welfare measure (that is, designed to help only the poor), it was given to every Canadian mother and was the first universal social program in Canada (means tests for old age pensioners were not abolished until 1951). It became the yardstick by which "universality" was defined—a program in which the benefits were equally distributed to all members of the target group regardless of income or economic standing.

The welfare state was fully in place by the time Pierre Elliott Trudeau became prime minister in 1968. The Canada Pension Plan had become law (1966), as had a national medicare scheme (1968). In 1966 a Guaranteed Income Supplement (based on income) was introduced for old people who had only the old age pension to rely upon. The poor and the unemployed could count on unemployment insurance and the Canada Assistance Plan.

By 1985 social programs accounted for more than 40 percent of the federal budget (most of this was paid over to the provinces for them to administer), and Canada ranked 11th in the world in per capita social and educational spending. Canada's medical care and social security programs are among the most generous in the world and allow Canadians to enjoy a high level of health and income security. These programs are more than just a safety net for the poor. But can Canada afford them? As the boom years of the 1960s faded, the question was asked more and more often.

It was Trudeau's Liberals who first tried to come to grips with the problem. In November 1970 the Trudeau government published a white paper entitled *Income Security for Canadians*, which was intended to reallocate income security dollars to Canadians who needed them most, thereby ending universality. The process involved allowing family allowances and old age pensions to wither away through inflation. They would be replaced with a Family Income Security Plan (FISP), a kind of guaranteed annual income paid, on a sliding scale, to Canadian families whose earnings fell below a predetermined level. In 1971 the government limited the Old Age Security (OAS) to $80 per month and increased the Guaranteed Income Supplement (GIS). FISP should have been introduced in 1972 but the legislation was not ready when the session was ended by Trudeau's election call. The election killed the plan: the Liberals formed a minority government dependent on NDP support and the NDP strongly opposed ending universal programs such as OAS and Family Allowances. FISP died, the OAS was fully indexed, and the $80 per month limit was lifted. Since then, old age pensions in Canada have been partly universal (the OAS) and partly not (the GIS).

Although the Tories did little to put the Canadian welfare system into place, they have accepted it as a political necessity from the beginning. They voted in favour of both family allowances in the 1940s and medicare in the 1960s. Conservative Prime Minister John Diefenbaker was largely responsible for the implementation of national hospitalization insurance in the late 1950s. Since achieving power in September 1984, the Conservatives have not wavered in the enforcement of the Canada Health Act of 1984, which imposes financial penalties on provinces that allow extra billing by doctors or that allow hospitals to charge user fees.

Health Minister Jake Epp has been far less abrasive than his predecessor, Monique Bégin, in forcing the provinces to toe the line on medicare, but he has been no less firm.

* * *

Although Liberals and Conservatives have shared basic views on the Canadian welfare state for over forty years, bureaucrats in the departments of Finance and of Health and Welfare believed that Trudeau's departure from the political scene was going to bring major shifts in public policy. The massive overspending that marked the last two years of the Trudeau regime simply could not continue. And since social programs account for more than 40 percent of the federal budget, a major re-examination of social welfare spending was considered a certainty.

In May 1984, senior public servants in the finance department launched two parallel studies in preparation for the expected policy changes. The first outlined obstacles to economic growth and the other suggested ways of attacking the deficit. By September a comprehensive document had been produced. This document was used by deputy minister Mickey Cohen to brief both Mulroney and Wilson immediately after the election. It formed the basis for the major policy statement later issued by Wilson. The document expressed departmental concerns about the deficit and suggested options for dealing with the situation.

In the Department of National Health and Welfare, studies were also being prepared to see how the department would react to directives to cut its services by different percentages. Since senior bureaucrats feared that the outcome of the election could be affected if word of the review was to leak out, the minister—Monique Bégin—was not told. As one senior department member later put it: "It had become pretty evident that the whole fiscal position of the government was up for review and possible retrenchment. It was hard to see how social policy would be immune." In contrast to the practice in the Department of Finance, however, the studies were not immediately brought forward to the new minister after the election. They only reached Jake Epp's desk in November after the Treasury Board and the Department of Finance had started to suggest ways in which social programming might be cut.

These preparations eased the transition of power that took place after September 1984. So too did the approaches of the two new ministers to the senior personnel in their departments and to the task of policy review that lay before them. Both Michael Wilson and Jake Epp had solid backgrounds in their respective fields and fit into their new ministries with remarkably little friction. They shared basic assumptions about the role of government and have, from the beginning, generally agreed on the future policy direction of the government—even though in some quarters Wilson is considered a conservative, and Epp a red Tory. It was also clear to both men that the departments they inherited were not nearly as dominated by Trudeau-style philosophies as many Tory backbenchers had charged.

Despite his red-Tory label, Jake Epp is a fundamentally conservative man. He was born in 1939 in the Mennonite community of Steinbach, Manitoba. Both his father and his father-in law were Mennonite ministers, but Epp eventually left the Mennonite Church to join the Evangelical Free Churches of Canada. His new church is not a bastion of far right-wing ideas, as are some similar institutions in the United States, but it is "definitely conservative," according to Pastor Lloyd Peters, its spiritual leader. Epp takes his religion seriously. He has been a strong opponent of abortion on demand and he fought to have a reference to God included in the preamble to the new constitution. He is a workaholic—it is reported that he gets about five hours sleep a night—and a strong believer in free enterprise and self-reliance.

Whatever Epp believes in private, however, he is not dogmatic. He has strongly defended medicare, for example, because he believes that the Conservatives must preserve it or sacrifice the party's credibility. He distinguishes between the basic social programs that constitute the social safety net (for example, medicare) and other social reform programs that were put into place in more prosperous times. In the words of one senior policy adviser: "Epp considers the social safety net untouchable, but not the other programs, which he thinks should be open to question because of society's reduced ability to pay for them." It is unclear which "other" programs Epp has in mind.

Epp is a powerful and able minister. He was the Tory critic on health and welfare for several years before heading the department and he did his homework well. He knows the department and he immediately impressed his senior bureaucrats with his thorough knowledge of both the programs and the departmental structure. He is a member of the Cabinet's priorities and planning committee, head of its important social development committee, and political boss of the Conservative party in Manitoba. He has displayed a high degree of competence since taking over the department and clearly qualifies as one of the most successful of Mulroney's ministers.

Not so Michael Wilson, who (like every finance minister) has been regularly and harshly criticized in his first eighteen months in office. Wilson was bound to be the scapegoat in a government that put deficit reduction and job creation at the centre of its political program. But when he was sworn in to his portfolio in the early weeks of the new government, few observers could have foreseen that he would be upstaged so often and with such disastrous results.

Michael Wilson was born in Toronto in 1937. His father was president of National Trust, and Michael was groomed for leadership from the very beginning. He went to private schools and studied commerce and economics at the University of Toronto. When he graduated in 1959 he was recruited to work at the venerable English banking firm of Baring Brothers in London. It was the start of a long career in banking and finance that was uninterrupted until Wilson decided to run for office in 1979. He took on former Liberal Cabinet minister Alastair Gillespie in the Toronto riding of Etobicoke Centre and won by more than 8000 votes. In the short-lived Clark government, Wilson served as Minister of State for International Trade, a junior portfolio. When Clark resigned, Wilson made a bid for the party's leadership. He came in a distant fourth on the first ballot and threw his support behind Mulroney. His reward was the post of Minister of Finance, the toughest position in any government.

Wilson was well prepared for his portfolio and he immediately impressed the senior bureaucracy with his knowledge of finance and his grasp of the important issues. He was a quick study, he knew what he wanted to accomplish, and his views were similar to those held by the bureaucrats in the upper levels of his department. Wilson's working relationships with his staff were excellent from the very start. There was, however, one major difference between Wilson and his Liberal predecessor, Marc Lalonde. Lalonde had had a close relationship with Trudeau and, for the most part, was given a free hand in running the department. Wilson has no such freedom of action because Mulroney and the Prime Minister's Office have played a far more active role in orchestrating economic policy than Trudeau ever did. This has, on several occasions, undermined Wilson's power to impose his views on the government. In effect, Mulroney has acted as a senior minister of finance.

Wilson's takeover was eased considerably by the presence of Mickey Cohen, his deputy minister. Although many observers of the Ottawa scene expected Cohen's head to be among the first to roll when the Tories took power, Mulroney announced at the beginning of October 1984 that he considered Cohen a competent public servant and that he had confidence in him as a deputy minister. Wilson, who had worked with Cohen in 1979, also had a high opinion of him. Cohen therefore stayed, despite the belief of Tory backbenchers that he had been an architect of the National Energy Program.

The Tories needed Cohen. He had joined the government as a tax specialist in 1970 and had worked his way up to deputy minister in the Department of Finance, one of the most important posts in the public service. He was highly respected by senior public servants for his abilities and his professionalism. In the months before the election he began to distance himself from Liberal economic policy by moving two mandarins closely associated with Trudeau economics (Sidney Rubinoff and Glenn Jenkins) out of the department and replacing them with two men who enjoyed good relations with the business community, David Weyman and F. W. (Fred) Gorbet. This undoubtedly helped win over those in the PMO who thought Cohen had been blamed unduly for the National Energy Program. As one senior Mulroney adviser put it: "If Mike Wilson were to walk in and say, 'Mickey, we want to nationalize the economy,' he'd say, 'Give me a few weeks and I'll show you how.' . . . He represents the best of the public service tradition, which is to take direction and indeed to anticipate it."

* * *

Cohen's help was invaluable in the months following the election. Only minutes after his swearing-in, Wilson announced that he hoped to issue a statement of policy by December. Ten days later,

Treasury Board President Robert de Cotret also got to work and
called in his Cabinet colleagues to ask them for a list of possible
spending cuts to be submitted to him within ten days. The plan
evolved quickly—Wilson would issue a policy statement while
introducing a mini-budget that would demonstrate, in however
token a fashion, the government's determination to come to grips
with the deficit.

The Wilson policy statement grew out of the overview of government economic policy prepared under Cohen's direction by
the Department of Finance before the election. Throughout October the department hurried to flesh out the details and prepare the
proposals for a public airing while, at the same time, consulting
other affected departments, especially Health and Welfare and the
Treasury Board. The all-important Chapter IV, which laid out the
government's strategy for economic renewal, was circulated to
members of the priorities and planning committee. The document
was supposed to be strategic, not ideological, and it was intended
to undo the damage that finance department experts believed had
been caused by excessive interventionism. In the words of one
senior policy maker, "It placed the burden of proof on the
interventionists."

Wilson had his first important moment in the House of Commons spotlight on November 8, 1984, three days after the Speech
from the Throne, when he delivered his mini-budget and tabled
the policy document, *A New Direction for Canada: An Agenda for
Economic Renewal*. The budget measures were rather limited.
There were to be cutbacks in spending for the next year amount-
ing to about $2.2 billion, but these would be partially offset by
small increases in job-creation spending and social assistance programs. Some of the cuts were mere window-dressing. For example, the announced reduction in Petroleum Incentives Program
grants of over $200 million really reflected a lower level of oil
exploration activity rather than any real saving. Nevertheless,
Wilson announced that he was lowering the projected deficit for
1985-86 from $37.1 billion to $34.9 billion as a result of these
reductions. He promised even greater reductions in the deficit
when he delivered his first full budget in May 1985.

Observers such as the *Financial Post* had forecast for weeks that the Wilson discussion paper would open up the question of universality, despite Mulroney's sacred trust pledge. The forecasts were accurate. In *A New Direction for Canada*, the government insisted that the time had come for "a frank and open discussion [on universality]" and that there was "considerable scope for improving and redesigning social programs based on the twin tests of social and fiscal responsibility." Social responsibility, according to the government, "dictates that wherever possible, and to a greater extent than is the case today, scarce resources should be diverted first to those in greatest need." A series of rhetorical questions such as: "Is it fair to provide benefits of more than $500 per child to families with an income of more than $45,000 per year?" was posed so that Canadians would have little doubt about the government's intentions. A number of possible options were presented, such as the elimination of indexing for family allowances, or "reducing or eliminating the indexation of OAS while compensating pensioners in need." The paper concluded with a promise to launch a consultation process that would involve government, business, and the people of Canada and would be "flexible yet thorough."

On November 9, the day after Wilson presented his discussion paper, Mulroney declared at a press conference that the aim of his government was to determine the best way to get benefits into the hands of those who needed them most. Although he maintained that he would never challenge or review the universality of medicare, other social programs (presumably all others) were open for study. After all, he asked, was it proper for a bank president who earned half a million dollars a year to get a baby bonus? Later, however, in the House of Commons, Mulroney declared that he and the government remained "committed to the view that universality is a fundamental key to our social development."

(The question of whether or not the government could save money by cutting the family allowance or Old Age Security payments to Mulroney's bank president was later answered in an article in the *Globe and Mail* (November 26, 1985) by Professor E. P. Fitzgerald of Carleton University. Fitzgerald pointed out that according to Statistics Canada there were, in 1981, only 5800 Canadian taxpayers with gross incomes over $250,000. Together they received a little over $6 million in family allowance and OAS payments. Cutting this off would save only .018 percent of the projected federal deficit. If the 55,147 Canadians earning $100,000 or more per year were cut off from family allowances or OAS benefits, the total savings would amount to $53 million or 0.15 percent of the deficit. In fact, Fitzgerald pointed out, only one Canadian family in five had an income greater than $45,000 in 1981. These figures showed that the government would have to take benefits from middle-class Canadians—not just bank presidents—to make any substantial cuts in programs for the elderly and families or to redirect appreciable amounts to the poor and the needy.)

Wilson obviously disagreed with Mulroney. At a lunch given after the budget speech, he said that revamping social programs could create savings that would be used to cut the deficit and in a CTV *Question Period* interview taped November 9, he told reporters that the government believed an opportunity existed to redirect social spending to the poor and to "leave some money on the table that can be used either for deficit reduction or application in other ways to make a stronger economy."

The government continued to put forward its ideas in the days following the release of the Wilson position paper. On November 15, Jake Epp declared: "The value of . . . benefits should surely be greatest for those in greatest need and least for those whose needs are less." Who could argue with that? In a *Toronto Star* interview published on November 17, Mulroney claimed that the key question facing Canadians was whether or not "a better [system could be devised] that is more equitable, more cost effective, and consistent with our honourable traditions." He introduced a new element into the discussion by denying that deficit cutting was the objective. When asked if any savings gained by a rationalization of social programs would be used to bring down the deficit, he replied: "No, absolutely not." That must have been news to Michael Wilson and the Department of Finance.

It should have been obvious by the third week in November that Mulroney and Wilson were on different paths. Then, on November 22, *La Presse* published an interview with Jake Epp that added to the confusion. Epp maintained that universal benefits for families and the elderly would continue but that higher-income recipients would have to pay more taxes on those benefits. Since the family allowance and the OAS are already taxable, and since those who earn more generally pay higher taxes anyway, Epp was hinting at a special tax aimed only at the family allowance and OAS. Such a course had not been decided upon, let alone discussed, in Cabinet. When asked to respond, Wilson claimed that Epp's comments did not pre-empt the consultative process called for in the November 8 policy statement.

No one can argue against consultation. But what Mulroney, Wilson, and Epp were doing was not consultation, it was confusion and it resulted from disagreement over policy. Wilson's November 8 position paper was clearly a Department of Finance document even though other departments had helped prepare it. It had been approved by the priorities and planning committee and, presumably, by Mulroney himself. It should, therefore, have provided grounds for a common social policy. Despite the preliminary nature of the document, it described social policy fairly clearly: Canada could no longer afford to spend as much on social programs as it once had; Canada could no longer afford to pay the same benefits to the wealthy as it did to the poor; Canada was going to have to re-examine its social spending priorities and come up with programs more in line with the economic realities of the 1980s while, at the same time, continuing to maintain a comprehensive social safety net. Within those restrictions, all options were open.

Unfortunately, only Wilson took this seriously, and Wilson by himself did not count. When Mulroney said, less than ten days after the paper was released, that the government would not apply any savings on social programs to reducing the deficit, he removed the entire process from the deficit-cutting exercise that had supposedly been at the centre of Tory policy. He was also pledging that the government would not touch the more than 40 percent of its budget that made up social spending. Since it could not touch the more than 20 percent that goes to pay interest on the public debt, it was defeating the purpose of the exercise from the very start. That was also a defeat for Wilson and the Department of Finance. When Epp jumped in to declare that universality would not be tampered with, the government's options were restricted even further. What had started out on November 8 looking like a significant national debate was beginning to look like a farce. Mulroney, Epp, and Wilson had not yet learned that cardinal rule of government: get it straight before going public.

* * *

This confusion over policy became painfully obvious in December. During the week of December 9, Michael Wilson mused out loud to a Canadian Press reporter: "What we're saying is that there are people who don't need [social assistance]. Upper- and middle-income social programs cannot be afforded today." When asked why this had not been spelled out by the Tories during the election, Wilson replied: "If we had said in the election campaign that we're going to cut back on the family allowances for upper-income people . . . you know what would be said in Newfoundland, or the downtown core of Toronto? They're going to cut back on the family allowance, period . . . .It's the politics of fear."

Wilson's remarks sparked off nine days of the most rancorous debate yet in the new Parliament. On December 13, Mulroney tried to sidestep opposition demands that he clarify Wilson's statements by trotting out his old friend, the mythical bank president. "The poor and the dispossessed in our society need more benefits than the bank president making $500,000 a year," he declared. Later that day he told reporters that Wilson's remarks had been misconstrued and claimed that his government had only decided to explore alternatives in social policies after coming to power and discovering the true extent of the mess the Liberals had created. This, of course, did not impress the opposition and the attacks continued the next day. When the NDP's Steven Langdon asked whether or not Mulroney agreed with Wilson that "We cannot afford social programs for middle-income Canadians," Mulroney claimed that "the finance minister never said that." Wilson, of course, had talked about upper- and middle-income Canadians; Mulroney's distinction was, at best, hairsplitting. Later that day, Epp tried to create a middle ground for both Wilson and Mulroney when he called reporters into his office and told them that the term universality was being used indiscriminately and that current social programs were both universal and non-universal.

The following weekend provided a short respite for the government, but the furor in the Commons picked up again on Monday when NDP leader Ed Broadbent was thrown out of the House for accusing Mulroney of misleading MPs. Not to be outdone in the vehemence with which they defended universality, the Liberals competed with the NDP over the next few days by twice blockading Commons business using a trick invented by the Tories: they called for votes on adjournment and then failed to show up, leaving the division bells ringing. Liberal leader John Turner, at one point, even threatened to use his party's majority in the Senate to veto Tory social legislation. The pressure on the government grew. In the PMO and the departments of Health and Welfare and Finance, ministerial advisers scrambled to find common ground among their bosses. Epp played the role of peacemaker, not because he agreed or disagreed with universality from any ideological perspective, but in order to maintain party unity. It was no easy task, since Mulroney and Wilson appeared to disagree fundamentally over the government's objectives.

With the opposition attacking and the Cabinet split from within, this was no time to forge a policy on universality, let alone to do so publicly. Yet that is exactly what the government did. On Monday, December 17, Mulroney claimed the government would preserve universality by taxing benefits given to the rich. Wilson appeared to agree with him. On Tuesday, Epp announced that the government would use the general tax system to take back benefits from the rich because this would be easier than levying special taxes. He insisted there would be no reduction in benefits paid and that universality would remain. On Wednesday, Mulroney appeared to agree with this. On Thursday, however, he shifted ground slightly and said that a special tax could not be ruled out. Mulroney tried to fend off the opposition's attacks by urging them to wait for the government to publish position papers and for the national debate that would follow. He told the Commons: ''What we are trying to do and shall do is maintain the integrity of the universal system of delivery of social benefits to Canadians, to the elderly, to the dispossessed, to those who need help, while attempting to find a formula we hope will allow us to do more for those members of our society who genuinely need help.'' That locked the government in; it also shut Wilson out.

Epp completed the policy-making process on Friday, December 21, during a formal House debate on universality that the government had agreed to in order to end opposition attacks. He pledged that reductions in payments to the rich would be passed on to the poor and not used to reduce the deficit. The only object of the exercise was to see if money could not be better spent. Epp claimed that the government would not apply any special taxes to the OAS although such taxes might be applied to family allowances paid to upper-income Canadians. Under no circumstances, however, would there be a means test for family allowances or old age pensions. He charged that "the real fear of the opposition parties" was not that the Tories would dismantle social programs, but that they would "make them more rational and more equitable."

What had happened was evident: the government had fallen flat on its backside when the prime minister's ill-thought-out and ill-advised statements cut the legs out from under one of his senior ministers. What was not clear was how and why this had happened. According to one senior official, the root of the problem was that the prime minister and the Cabinet had not truly understood the implications of Michael Wilson's November financial statement. "The prime minister is not basically a policy man," the bureaucrat said. "I don't think he read carefully and thought through the implications of the November statement. That paper was small-c conservative, well-prepared, and well-thought-out. It was endorsed by the prime minister and Cabinet, but I'm not sure the prime minister recognized the implications." If so, that is as critical a comment as anyone has made about the prime minister. Moreover, the official continued, other "ministers are very sensitive to the position of the prime minister in these matters. They wait until he settles into a position, but he does have a tendency to flop around." The economic statement had been agreed to by all, but the agreement was more on how to handle the public relations, not on the content. That too says something serious about the government's priorities and competence.

All that left Wilson and Epp, and eventually Mulroney and his Tory government, in extraordinary difficulties. Once the prime minister had jumped in and made universality a sacred trust, he knocked Wilson's economic statement for a half-gainer. "We were back at square one," an official in Epp's department said. Wilson was a little slow to realize his weakened position, and he continued to defend the statement. After all, the prime minister had agreed to every word in it. Although he tended to concur with the finance minister on the economics of the question, Epp nonetheless thought that Wilson's comments on universality had been politically inept, and his role throughout was to find some ground on which the government could hold together and stand. It wasn't that Epp won a struggle with Wilson. Rather, his December 21 remarks in the House were simply stating the most defensible political position for the government.

* * *

The December Disaster, as it was called in some Ottawa circles, froze the government into a public posture on universality that it might not have taken and that was the result neither of a national consultation nor of an internal policy-making process. Even so, Wilson did not give up easily. In private he continued to push for a more fundamental realignment of social policy than Mulroney seemed willing to accept and he pressed the case for using funds saved by that realignment to reduce the deficit. This time Epp opposed him. He wanted to maintain universality. He was against using social program funds for deficit reduction and he wanted to use taxes, special or otherwise, to get at benefits paid to the rich. He strongly objected to any change in Old Age Security because, he argued, those persons already retired or soon to retire had made their plans in the belief that the OAS would be preserved and that the government had a social contract with them. Epp was worried about the political price the government would pay if it altered universality or used social program savings to decrease the public debt.

Epp had Mulroney and most of the Cabinet on his side. There was almost no pressure in Cabinet to cut spending fundamentally while Mulroney insisted that the public stance he had taken in December was now policy. Wilson simply did not have enough clout to sway his colleagues or the prime minister. That became apparent in the third week of January when the Cabinet met at Meech Lake, near Ottawa, to plan strategy for the next session of Parliament.

Mulroney was so upset over the failure of Wilson and Epp to

agree on a joint approach that he threatened to cancel a scheduled Health and Welfare policy paper on benefits for families and the elderly due out at the end of January. Epp's advisers, together with some advisers in the PMO, got the prime minister to change his mind only at the last moment and Epp was able to call a hasty news conference in Ottawa on January 18 to describe the government position. The conference was designed to defuse opposition attacks against the government's social program review when Parliament reconvened. Epp told the press that the government had no intention of changing universality and ruled out any special surtaxes for the rich on family allowances or OAS payments. He also said that the government would not use savings from social programs to reduce the public debt.

The Health and Welfare paper, issued on January 28, was a major defeat for Wilson. It was based on three principles that were clearly spelled out on the first two pages: first, that universality is "a keystone of our social safety net"; second, that there would be no means tests; third, that savings would "not be applied to a reduction of the deficit." If anyone still feared that the Tories were going to re-examine benefits for families and the elderly, the paper was supposed to calm their fears: "It should be stated at the outset that the government regards the present system as a good one, which is working well. The object of the present review is not to make radical changes in it, but to determine whether modifications or refinements can be identified which would make it work even better." A laudable objective—but certainly not the one the Department of Finance had in mind when the review of government spending policies had been initiated in the spring of 1984.

In line with Epp's approach (and, apparently, that of Mulroney), two modest examples of possible changes in benefits were proposed. One would reduce family allowances from the current monthly maximum payment of $31.27 per child to $20 combined with taxation changes that would bring more benefits to low-income families, less to those with higher incomes. The other left the family allowance payment the same but changed the tax system to produce a similar result. Under both plans, benefit reductions would begin at the $23,000-a-year income level, thereby hitting a large part of the middle class. Both Ottawa and the provinces would save money but Epp pledged to put those savings into other social spending areas. The paper had little to say about old age pensions: "After careful consideration, the government has decided not to put forward a consultation option for the reform of elderly benefits . . . .In the government's view no change is required in the Old Age Security/Guaranteed Income Supplements payments system." After all the public discussion that had occurred following Wilson's November 8 policy statement, the elephant had laboured and brought forth a mouse. The *Globe and Mail* labelled the process "the universality waltz."

* * *

The work of formulating the budget began after the Health and Welfare position paper had been released. Much was made of the consultation process. In February, Mulroney and Wilson met in Regina with the provincial premiers and finance ministers in a federal-provincial conference on the economy. With Conservatives controlling seven out of ten provincial governments, it was designed more to show the public how smooth federal-provincial relations were in the post-Trudeau era than to find any real answers to the economic problems facing the country.

In March, Mulroney hosted the National Economic Conference in Ottawa. The gathering, arranged by Montreal lawyer Stanley Hartt, brought together 136 representatives from most economic interest groups in the country. They came to Ottawa with their grievances, hopes, and suggestions for change, along with tens of thousands of pages' worth of position papers and policy statements. For two days the prime minister showed his adeptness at handling public discussions under the hot television lights. Few concrete suggestions emerged from the hours of speeches and debate, however, and the conference was useful only in demonstrating how far apart Canadians were on issues such as social policy or labour relations.

Throughout the late winter and early spring almost every interest group in Canada, from businessmen to artists, took Wilson up on his invitation to consult. He spent almost 150 hours in meetings with their representatives. The messages were as diverse as the delegations but one predominated: Canadians were ready to tackle the deficit as long as the burden of doing so was equally shared by all classes and occupational groups. This was the same message uncovered by Decima Research of Toronto when it polled Canadians on their attitudes toward the forthcoming budget.

The work of putting the budget together fell mostly on the shoulders of a small number of bureaucrats in the Department of Finance who worked with Wilson, Mulroney, and a number of Mulroney's advisers in the PMO. Epp and the other ministers most affected by individual budget provisions were consulted, of course, but Wilson and Mulroney exerted the strongest political influence on the final document. The manoeuvring room available to the budget makers in their attack on the deficit was severely limited by the events of December and January—more than 70 percent of federal spending was now politically untouchable. A decision was therefore made in the Department of Finance—and endorsed by Wilson, Mulroney, and the Cabinet—to launch an attack on indexation—the practice of automatically increasing federal payments and income tax exemptions by the amount of the increase in the annual cost of living. (Indexation, based on the notion that Canadians who were on fixed incomes or who were greatly dependent on governmental payments should be protected against cost of living increases, had been initiated in the 1970s when inflation became significant).

"De-indexation" was thought of as a broad, simple theme that was tough but fair. It would be sold to the Canadian people in the way that the Liberals had once sold "6 and 5" as a way of fighting inflation. If successful, de-indexation would save the federal government more than $6 billion by 1991. Starting in January 1986, both family allowances and Old Age Security payments would increase only by the amount of inflation less 3 per cent. (In other words, if the annual rate of inflation from one year to the next was 4 percent, the OAS would only be increased by 1 percent. If the inflation rate was 3 percent, there would be no increase at all.)

The bureaucrats in the Department of Finance also recommended that the impact of this partial de-indexation on the elderly poor be offset by "super-indexing" the Guaranteed Income Supplement—adding to the GIS not only the amount by which the cost of living increased, but also the 3 percent lost on the OAS. That would have saved the government from much of the criticism it subsequently received over the budget and was consistent with the claims made earlier by Epp and Mulroney that the government really aimed to redistribute its welfare payouts. Unfortunately, the advice was rejected by Wilson and Mulroney because super-indexing would restore about $860 million a year of the $1.6 billion saved by de-indexation.

Epp played only a small part in putting the budget together—it was basically a Wilson-and-Mulroney document—but he was consulted about the partial de-indexing of family allowances and old age pensions. He agreed to the former but opposed the latter because he believed that the elderly in Canadian society felt very insecure and that there would be serious political repercussions if the government ignored those feelings. His opposition, therefore, was political, not philosophical, as some commentators later claimed. His advice was not taken because the Cabinet believed that de-indexing was necessary to get the country back on track economically. Epp was persuaded to go along by assurances that the budget would spread the burden of fighting inflation across Canadian society. It didn't, and none of its provisions contributed as much to the general perception that the Tories intended to fight the deficit on the backs of the poor as did the $500,000 capital gains tax exemption.

A capital gain is the profit earned by selling an investment for a higher price than that at which it was purchased. For many years, Canada had no tax on capital gains because the government wanted to make Canada as attractive as possible for investors. A tax on capital gains was first introduced in the 1960s. The idea to include a lifetime $500,000 exemption on capital gains in the 1985 budget came from within the Department of Finance; it was intended to spur small businesses, encourage investment, and protect farmers. It was also intended as a visible and dramatic sign to Canadians and to the world that the Conservative government would do everything possible to stimulate growth in the private sector. All this would cost Ottawa as much as $1 billion a year.

Preparation of the final draft of the budget was completed in early May after consultations between Wilson and those of his Cabinet colleagues who were directly affected by the budget's provisions. When Wilson announced the budget date in the House of Commons on May 6, he told reporters: "I think the budget will be regarded as a tough budget, but I think [people will] regard it as a fair budget." His prediction could not have been farther from the truth.

* * *

Wilson's budget, introduced on May 23, was supposed to raise about $200 million in additional revenues through a variety of tax increases while cutting expenditures by about $1.8 billion. Full de-indexing of personal income taxes, the OAS, and family allowances would be discontinued and in future, inflation under 3 per cent would not be adjusted for. The future loss of family allowance income for poor families was supposed to be partially compensated for by an increase in the child tax credit, while wealthier families would keep less of their family allowance income (and other income) because of a reduction in the child tax exemption. No provision was made for the loss of OAS income to the elderly poor, even though Epp's position paper, issued on January 28, had pledged that the OAS would not be altered. Middle-income Canadians— those with incomes over $30,000 per year—were hit with a temporary surtax on their income tax. This, combined with the changes in child tax exemptions, would take an additional $250 out of the pocket of a Canadian earning more than $40,000 a year.

There were the usual tax increases on liquor and gasoline, provisions aimed at job creation, a promise of a cut in the civil service and in federal spending, and the elimination of a tax shelter known as the Registered Home Ownership Savings Plan. There were also tax breaks for corporations, a lifetime capital gains exemption of $500,000 (the biggest surprise of the day), increases and extensions of the federal sales tax, and a temporary surtax for large corporations. The result, according to Wilson, would be a decrease in the 1985-86 deficit from the $34.9 billion projected in his November 8 speech to $33.8 billion. He claimed that the deficit would be reduced a further $20 billion by 1990 and that the public debt would be cut by $75 billion in the same period. The budget, Wilson told Canadians, was realistic and fair.

Initial reaction to the budget was predictable. The Liberals and the New Democrats condemned it, business was guarded but positive, right-wing Tories complained that Wilson had not cut expenditures enough, and Dennis McDermott, head of the Canadian Labour Congress, called the budget "tough and very unfair."

The storm broke after the weekend. On Monday, May 27, Montreal Liberal MP Raymond Garneau made available figures from a finance department document that showed that the impact of Wilson's proposed changes to benefits for families and the elderly was going to be much greater than the finance minister had admitted in the documents tabled with the budget. Wilson's figures had indicated savings of only $650 million over the following two years but, according to the Department of Finance, the government would save more than $6.4 billion by the end of the decade and would earn an additional $2.2 billion from added revenues over the same period. The department's figures also showed that the much-vaunted change in the child tax credit, which was supposed to help compensate poorer families for the partial de-indexing of the family allowance, would have little real effect. At the other end of the scale, however, the $500,000 capital gains tax exemption would cost Ottawa about $1.2 billion by 1990-91. Southam columnist John Ferguson was quick to sound the alarm: "The figures suggest that this budget hardly spreads the burden fairly among all segments of society as claimed. The ordinary Canadian is bearing the brunt. The middle class pays a lot more in taxes and loses benefits. But the neediest are not getting the same amount in extra benefits that their prime minister promised them."

The Garneau revelations were followed by calculations released by the National Anti-Poverty Organization which showed that the de-indexing of the OAS would reduce it, in real dollar terms, by about $100 per year. Since half the recipients of the OAS were poor enough to qualify for the Guaranteed Income Supplement, the sum was significant. Chaviva Hosek, head of the National Action Committee on the Status of Women, pointed out that more than two-thirds of elderly women lived below the poverty line: "For them, $100 a year is heat in the winter or protein." At the same time, figures released by the Canadian Press indicated that de-indexing would cost hundreds of thousands of pensioners close to $1500 each by the end of the decade. "It gets worse and worse over the years," said Ken Battle, executive director of the National

Council of Welfare. "It is the medium- and long-term impact that is really severe."

As the attacks on the government increased, Wilson committed two gaffes that exacerbated the government's difficulties. On Thursday, May 30, Wilson spoke to 200 economists at a meeting in Montreal and told them, "It would be just delightful if we could solve our fiscal problems by asking only rich people to carry the burden of restoring fiscal responsibility. But that brings us face to face with another one of those sobering realities . . . No matter how we define the term, Canada has an acute shortage of rich people." The remark made perfect sense in context—there are not enough wealthy Canadians to carry the burden of fighting the deficit alone. But the headline writers had a field day: "Wilson laments 'shortage of rich people,' " trumpeted the *Calgary Herald*.

Several days later he got into trouble again by suggesting that the government issue bonds that were fully indexed to the rate of inflation. NDP leader Ed Broadbent jumped on the proposal and asked Wilson whether it was "his concept of justice . . . to bring in a budget that reduces indexation for pensioners and then . . . introduce indexation to protect the income of all those rich Canadians." Broadbent knew that indexing bonds would protect the government; Ottawa would no longer have to guess the future rate of inflation and then try to attract investors by paying interest rates higher than it thought inflation might be. Southam News columnist Don McGillivray noted that Wilson seemed "to have spent six years in the House of Commons and attained high office without losing a degree of naiveté that would doom a municipal councillor."

The government badly underestimated the public reaction to the partial de-indexing of the OAS and the family allowances. The issue became the focal point for all the grievances and complaints about the budget itself and seemed to offer the greatest proof to the government's detractors that the Tories were the party of the rich and the privileged. Even Epp felt betrayed. He had been led to believe that the sacrifices demanded of the public would be evenly spread across Canadian society. He had not known about the $500,000 capital gains exemption until almost the last moment.

On May 31, Ed Broadbent stood in the House of Commons to

wave a copy of a telegram from Charles McDonald, president of the 400,000-member National Pensioners and Senior Citizens Federation, protesting against the end to full indexation for the OAS. Broadbent and the NDP became the lightning rod for much of the protest. The NDP leader went to Vancouver and, on June 4, declared the start of a cross-country crusade. He described the budget as the most unfair he had seen since entering politics in 1968 and he promised that his crusade would produce such an outcry that the government would be forced to abandon its plans.

The outcry did grow, whether induced by Broadbent or not, and even traditional Tory allies deserted the government. On June 11, representatives of the Canadian Chamber of Commerce, the Business Council on National Issues, and the Canadian Organization of Small Business declared that pensions for the elderly should be fully indexed and that the government could find the money to reduce its deficit elsewhere. Mulroney was furious. But the desertion by the business lobby was only the latest episode in what was beginning to appear as a national upswelling of anti-government anger. All across the country, seniors—traditionally Conservative supporters—organized to collect signatures, send telegrams, confront Tory backbench MPs at constituency meetings, and mount demonstrations. As Charlotte Montgomery of the *Globe and Mail* observed, ''When angry war veterans and grandparents gather on the lawns of Parliament, some to charge publicly that their prime minister has lied to them, it is a scene from a politician's nightmare.''

For two weeks the government refused to relent. Seniors would have to accept the budget, Mulroney and Wilson declared, there would be no changes. But as the pressure mounted, the back-pedalling began. On June 12, Mulroney told the House of Commons that the plan to cut back on indexation of Old Age Security payments was actually only ''a proposal.'' Wilson repeated this preposterous statement two days later in a speech to the Toronto Society of Financial Analysts. But the signals emanating from the government were mixed; on the day of the Wilson speech, members of the Tory caucus urged Mulroney not to give in. One MP told the press: ''The only place this is an issue is with the Liberals and the NDP in the Commons.''

The conflicting signals resulted from confusion inside the government. Wilson and the Department of Finance were determined not to relent, Epp was convinced that a political disaster of major proportions was in the making, and Mulroney was increasingly uneasy about the no-win position he was finding himself in. His confrontation with Solange Denis on June 19 was apparently the last straw. The story was front-page news in every newspaper in Canada and the lead item on every telecast. So what if Denis was mistaken about the exact nature of the prime minister's pledge? So what if she did not grasp the larger economic issues? The television screens showed an angry old woman arguing with a wealthy, smooth-faced prime minister to keep her husband's $277-a-month pension intact. Denis could not lose.

The end came in the week of June 24; Mulroney decided on a full retreat on the de-indexation of the OAS. According to Rod McQueen, writing in *Saturday Night*, Wilson felt that he had been "hung out to dry" and insisted that Mulroney take some of the public blame for the entire episode. Mulroney agreed and on Thursday, June 27, Wilson rose in the House of Commons to announce that "Old Age Security payments [would] remain fully indexed to the Consumer Price Index." To make up the difference in the budget ($260 million by 1987), two new measures were announced: the temporary surtax on corporations that Wilson had announced in the budget was extended from twelve to eighteen months to yield an additional $200 million, and excise taxes on gasoline and other fuels were to be increased by one cent a litre starting on January 1, 1987. The business community had been repaid for its disloyalty.

The government's retreat from the partial de-indexation of OAS buoyed opposition groups beginning to mount a national lobby campaign against the de-indexation of family allowances. "De-indexation of family allowance is the next in line and we are going to fight it," declared Louise Dulude, vice-president of the National Action Committee on the Status of Women, in early July. Her sentiments were echoed by spokesmen for the Liberals and NDP in late August as preparations were made for the re-opening of Parliament. Liberal MP and caucus chairman Doug Frith declared: "Both opposition parties will be going into the House with a good frame of mind to carry on the demolition work."

The government introduced the bill to alter the full indexation of family allowances on September 14 and the opposition fulfilled its promise to fight the measure every step of the way. It was aided by the National Action Committee on the Status of Women and a variety of coalition groups that tried to mount the sort of nationwide campaign that had helped kill the partial de-indexation of OAS. Solange Denis even attended one anti-government rally on Parliament Hill. But the issue never generated the sort of wideranging emotional outpouring that had occurred in June and that had given the opposition in the House of Commons its real leverage. On January 20, 1986, the bill was passed for the third and final time.

* * *

The May 1985 budget was a watershed in Canadian history. When Wilson next rose in the Commons on February 26, 1986, to present his second full budget to the Canadian people, there were no cutbacks in social spending, no de-indexation plans, no attacks on universality. There was, instead, an increase in taxes despite all the evidence that tax increases threaten economic recovery. Wilson made much of the savings the government was realizing from the economies in its own operations recommended by the Nielsen Task Force and he pointed to the first actual reduction in the cost of government in many years. But those savings are a tiny part of the total cost of government. Wilson took great credit for getting the deficit under $30 billion for 1987, but much of this achievement should be chalked up to the general improvement in the Canadian economy that began even before the Liberal defeat of September 1984. That improvement might be choked off, however, if the government persists in raising taxes, because every dollar paid to the government is a dollar less for cars, houses, new factories, and new employees.

Any further examination of major social programs will be carried out with great circumspection. For one thing, the Department of Finance is not the place it once was. In the midst of the antibudget uproar of early June 1985, Mulroney announced that Mickey Cohen would be leaving the government to accept a position with the Olympia and York empire of the Reichmann family of Toronto. (There was some speculation that Cohen was being nudged out because of the budget's unpopularity but, in fact, he had indicated his desire to get out long before.) His replacement was Montreal lawyer Stanley Hartt, a close friend of Mulroney, who had helped organize the National Economic Conference in March. Hartt's appointment signalled to the Department of Finance that Mulroney intended to be much closer to the decision making than before.

If the Hartt appointment was intended to serve notice on Department of Finance mandarins that Mulroney did not trust their judgement, as some have alleged, Mulroney was looking for scapegoats in the wrong place. He should have started his search by looking in the mirror. Since he made the final decision to go with an across-the-board de-indexation, he must bear the greatest responsibility for the debacle.

Wilson too deserves considerable blame. He was told by officials in his department that the budget was unfair and yet he decided to go ahead with it. He gave the prime minister bad advice and the government suffered because of it. He weakened the government's ability to fight the deficit and his already-depleted authority in the Cabinet and the country. Wilson may be in reality just what he appears to be on the surface—a political greenhorn. Such people do not make good ministers of finance, whatever their economic or financial acumen.

The de-indexation of OAS payments had been bungled from the start. It was patently unfair because it placed an additional burden on one of the weakest groups in Canadian society, the elderly poor. If de-indexation was a worthy goal, necessary to battle inflation and to save the government money, then the elderly poor should have been protected by a super-indexation of the Guaranteed Income Supplement. The government would have saved less, but it would have succeeded in getting its policies through. In the long run, it would have saved far more than it will now.

Wherever Canadians stand on the question of social programs, most will admit that it is time at least to re-examine some of the basic assumptions that have been held since the end of World War II about universality, indexation, and other important questions. The election of the Mulroney government opened up the possibility that this re-examination would be undertaken, but the mistakes of that government have prevented it from proceeding beyond the questions raised by Michael Wilson on November 8, 1984. An important opportunity was lost. That, and not the alleged violation of a "sacred trust," is surely one of the greatest blunders the Conservative government has committed.

Chapter Seven
The Perils of Privatization

Few of the world's stories of business success can match that of Air Canada. The airline was created by an act of Parliament in 1937 as a subsidiary of Canadian National Railways—the government-owned railway company established by Prime Minister Sir Robert Borden's Tories in 1917. When it began operations in 1938 under the name Trans-Canada Airlines, its fleet consisted of one biplane and two small twin-engined aircraft called Lockheed Lodestars. There were box lunches and oxygen masks for the passengers; stewardesses were picked for their courage and knowledge of first aid; pilots waved to each other as eastbound planes passed those heading west. It wasn't much, and calling it a national airline reflected more hope than reality. But the federal government, urged on by Minister of Trade and Commerce C. D. Howe, wanted to stake out the field of commercial aviation before it became dominated by private companies. Whatever else might happen, they reasoned, there would at least be a government-owned and protected airline that would serve the national interest as Ottawa saw fit.

Dissolve to 1985: Trans-Canada Airlines has become Air Canada, one of the largest and best airlines in the world. It no longer needs government protection to ensure its growth, let alone its survival. The virtual monopoly on transcontinental flights that it once enjoyed has disappeared. Canadians and foreigners now fly by Air Canada because they want to, not because they have to; and yet it remains a government-owned airline. More and more Canadians, in and out of the aviation field, are beginning to wonder why.

One of the first and most prominent people to question the need for the continuation of government ownership of Air Canada was its president, Claude Taylor. In 1979 he pointed out that the airline, although government-owned, was managed like a private corporation: "You have to operate under the rules of the private sector," he said, "so why not be part of the private sector?"

In early 1984 a group of Air Canada employees approached Liberal Transport Minister Lloyd Axworthy with a scheme to buy up to 40 percent of the shares of the corporation. In December 1984, Air Canada's current president, Pierre Jeanniot, pointed out that government sale of the airline would free it from the need to raise capital through the government: "Once you can diversify your source of equity, you can grow on your own merit. You don't have to simply wait to become a priority of the government."

There are, today, compelling reasons why Air Canada should become a private corporation. Airlines in the United States are now vying with each other in the fiercely competitive world of deregulation and in Canada both Liberal and Conservative governments have been moving in the same direction. Competition in both the domestic and international markets has never been tougher. Airline managements need all the flexibility they can get to compete effectively on new routes with new equipment and with innovative services. In this world of modern air travel, Air Canada is still held back by government ownership and government financing. The Tories, everyone thought, would change all of this. The Tories, everyone thought, believed in "privatization." After nearly eighteen months of Conservative government, there are good reasons to doubt that assumption.

The Conservative Minister of Transport, Don Mazankowski, was supposed to be responsible for the privatization of Air Canada. There were many questions that had to be answered before the process could begin. Should the purchase of Air Canada shares be limited to Canadians? Should the company be sold off a bit at a time? What was Air Canada worth? Within a month of the election, Mazankowski had asked Michael Cochrane, a former Air Canada vice-president of finance and now chairman of Sydney Steel, to examine some of these issues. Cochrane was expected to recommend the establishment of a special task force to study the sale of the airline.

In mid-January 1985, Mulroney got into the act. He emerged

from a meeting with Louis Laberge, president of the Quebec Federation of Labour, to announce that Air Canada and the Canadian Broadcasting Corporation were not for sale: "Some people want to buy the CBC. The CBC is not for sale. Air Canada is not for sale. There may be some persuasive arguments in the case of Air Canada that some people can make in regard to the disposition of equity. I'll take a look at it. But Canada needs a national airline." And that was that. As the *Globe and Mail* noted, an opportunity had been lost. "What was the election for?" its editorial asked. What indeed?

* * *

Direct government involvement in the market economy is as Canadian as the maple leaf. When Canada's first railways were built in the 1840s and 1850s, they were built by private entrepreneurs who relied heavily on government support in the form of guarantees, subsidies, and outright grants. One mid-nineteenth century Canadian political leader summed up the prevailing attitude of the period when he proclaimed: "Railways are my politics." Despite the cynicism, there was a rationale of a kind behind it all. If British North America was to survive, it needed a strong transportation network, thriving commercial businesses, and, eventually, a growing manufacturing sector. To achieve this, tremendous obstacles had to be overcome. The British colonies were sparsely populated, they were spread out, and they existed alongside one of the world's most dynamic and increasingly powerful economies. British North American entrepreneurs were prepared to take risks in order to earn returns, but they were not completely foolhardy. Almost from the beginning they sought, and received, government support in their pursuit of profits.

Since it was accepted that government aid to business was both useful and legitimate it was not long before it was accepted that government ownership could also be necessary, and for many of the same reasons. One of the most important conditions for the joining of the Maritime colonies to Confederation was the construction of a railway to connect Canada with those colonies. The railway that resulted—the Intercolonial—was government-built, government-owned, and government-operated and became one of the greatest sources of patronage in Canadian history. In 1917 the

Conservative government of Prime Minister Robert Borden nationalized the bankrupt Canadian Northern Railway and set in motion the further nationalization of two other railways, the Grand Trunk and the Grand Trunk Pacific. The Liberal government that followed Borden completed the job and consolidated all government-owned railways under one crown corporation—Canadian National Railways. The theory behind the crown corporation held that even though government ownership might be necessary, government operation was highly undesirable because of the temptations it held for patronage and political interference. Crown corporations were structured in such a way that, in theory at least, they were to be independent of interference. As well, they were to be run along the same lines as private corporations. In other words, they were to be profitable.

Up to the present, government ownership in Canada has been supported and carried out by both Liberal and Conservative parties at the federal and provincial levels. In the last seventy years the Conservatives have established Canadian National Railways, the Canadian Broadcasting Corporation, and the Bank of Canada, while the Liberals have set up Air Canada, Petro-Canada, and a host of other corporations. Not a single instance exists of a major crown corporation established by one party being privatized by another after a change of government.

There was, until the late 1970s, a clear agreement among the major political parties and the majority of Canadians that government ownership was sometimes necessary to serve the national interest and was not, by itself, a bad thing. In the boom era of the late 1970s, that attitude appeared to change. The new generation of Canadians that arose to political maturity had not known the privations and sacrifices of the Depression and World War II. Unlike their parents, they did not look upon government as the giver of all blessings and they seemed to demand smaller, less intrusive government. When the Canadian economy experienced a severe recession in late 1981, the Tories, with their talk of less government, of privatization, and of closer cooperation with the business community, appeared to present a clear alternative. The Liberals themselves thought that the political winds were changing and tried to change with them. In the final year of the Trudeau government, Transport Minister Lloyd Axworthy began to move toward deregulation of the airline industry, while John Turner called for a government sell-off of a number of crown corporations. When the Mulroney Conservatives swept into office in September 1984, they had, it appeared, a clear mandate for change.

But had they? Although the talk among the pundits, the experts, the high-level bureaucrats, and the Tory policy makers was of the need to move to the right, it is by no means clear that the majority of Canadians experienced any real change in attitude toward government or toward government ownership. The polls, in fact, indicated that most Canadians still believed that government had an important role to play in certain areas of the economy. Were the "experts" all wrong? Yes and no. Canadians, unlike Americans, do not harbour an innate mistrust of government. They traditionally think of government as friend and partner and have relied on the collective power of the people to do through government what they could not, as individuals, do for themselves. Canadians have never been dogmatic about matters such as this. But at the same time they tend to be deeply conservative about money and are generally unwilling to take risks. Deficits, therefore, run counter to the Canadian way of thinking even if government ownership does not. For the most part, Canadians appear to want governments to run their financial affairs the way the individual is supposed to run a household — with the chequebook balanced. It was in the linking of deficit cutting with privatization, therefore, that the experts tripped up.

It is not clear whether the Tories really thought all this through. After all, they were in favour of privatization in principle, they declared, and even though they never promised to get the government out of all the businesses it was in, they clearly implied that everything was going to be under review. Mulroney's announcement, in mid-January 1985, about Air Canada shows that certain things were not. In fact, the Conservative government's policy on privatization has been marked by hesitation, confusion, and delay. On the matter of privatization, leadership has come from the polls, not the policy makers.

* * *

In 1983 the Tories began to work out a privatization strategy by setting up an eight-person study group under Senator William Kelly to examine the government's crown corporation holdings and to suggest a plan for getting rid of them. Kelly gave Mulroney his report in May 1984, and Mulroney told a caucus meeting that it would become the blueprint for future Tory action. The report, never made public, listed those corporations that should be sold off and outlined the policy issues that had to be resolved before each was put on the block. Kelly also recommended that the Treasury Board be responsible for privatization and that the Tories wait at least ninety days after coming to power before taking any action.

After the Tories were elected in September 1984, the Kelly report was kept secret but Kelly himself told a business group toward the end of October that too-hasty privatization would create more problems than it would solve and would be unpopular with the electorate. He pointed to public opinion surveys which showed that only about one-third of the Canadian people thought there was too much government ownership in the Canadian economy. The Mulroney government would have to recognize that there was still substantial support in Canada for what Kelly called the "public enterprise culture." Kelly claimed that privatization would not help the new government reduce the deficit and might even cost the government money. The new government should manage its crown corporations better and proceed cautiously with its sell-off program.

In the first weeks after the election, Sinclair Stevens, Minister of Regional Industrial Expansion, moved quickly to take control of privatization policy. Stevens was a man more feared than understood in Ottawa. As head of the department that combined the former Department of Industry with the Department of Regional Expansion, he was largely responsible for protecting Canadian industry. When he was President of the Treasury Board in the Clark government in 1979, he earned the nickname of "Slasher" for threatening to cut 60,000 jobs from the civil service. In his long years on the opposition front benches, he had strongly attacked what he claimed was Liberal extravagance in bailing out some industries and subsidizing others. He was, it was thought by the uninitiated, a true free-enterprise man. (He was forced to resign in the spring of 1986, because of conflict of interest allegations— his wife had negotiated an interest-free loan from a company that was receiving grants from Stevens's department).

Whatever Stevens's political philosophy, he was a hard-headed realist on matters such as subsidies and bailouts. He knew that companies such as Canadair and de Havilland needed government support in some form, whether they were owned by the government or not. He also knew that ending government support to industries such as textiles, which provide what few jobs there are in some depressed areas of the country, would be political suicide: "You have to accept the world the way it is," he told Deborah McGregor of the *Financial Times* in June 1985. "If you say that you feel an industry should be completely free to withstand whatever competition you throw at it . . . you are then saying . . . there will be no textile industry in the country; there will be no footwear [industry] in the country. I think that is the type of rash, almost theoretical approach that is so devastating." It became clear very early in Stevens's tenure, therefore, that, as Jeffrey Simpson of the *Globe and Mail* put it, the Conservatives were not ideologically committed to freer markets at all. The Tories were not about to sell off crown corporations simply because it was the ideologically pure thing to do.

Stevens made this clear in the second week of October when he reassured the public that the government would probably not close down money-losing crown corporations in a period of high unemployment. From this and other statements the message began to emerge that Stevens and his Cabinet colleagues were well aware that an unemployment rate of more than 10 percent was going to make it almost impossible to approach the question of government ownership from an ideological perspective. Stevens, the one-time champion of free enterprise and free markets, rapidly became a defender of tariffs, quotas, and, in some cases, bailouts. It was, as Giles Gherson of the *Financial Post* put it, a "sobering reintroduction to power."

Stevens was not the only one having second thoughts about notions once held dear by "free-enterprise" Tories. On a visit to Britain in November (made partly to study privatization), Treasury Board president Robert de Cotret told reporters that the government recognized the differences between crown corporations that existed as a result of "policy mandates" and that were, therefore, "unsuitable for privatization" (presumably the CBC was one of these) and those that were of "a more obviously commercial nature.'' Inside high government circles the realization had taken hold that if the first few privatization deals were disastrous, the entire effort would be in jeopardy. There would be no quick decisions, no hasty moves to take advantage of so-called windows of opportunity, no fears generated among Canadians that, in the words of one high-level political adviser, "They had elected Attila the Hun as prime minister.''

* * *

Sinclair Stevens was the minister responsible for the Canada Development Investment Corporation, a crown-owned holding company. At the time of the 1984 election, CDIC held de Havilland and Canadair (aircraft manufacturing companies which had once been privately owned), Teleglobe Canada (a profitable company holding a monopoly on overseas telephone communications), and a mixed bag of companies and investments—Canada Development Corporation, Eldorado Nuclear, and five million preferred shares of Massey-Ferguson. In late October, Stevens fired CDIC president Joel Bell and replaced him with Paul Marshall of Calgary, the president of Westmin Resources, a company in the Brascan empire. Stevens told a press conference on October 30 that the move was meant to signal the new government's attitude toward involvement in the private sector and to set "the right atmosphere for business," meaning that Bell was a Liberal and no longer welcome in so important a post. He made it very clear that Marshall, brought in for a salary of $1 per year plus a $5000 director's fee, would be responsible for selling off the CDIC's assets: Teleglobe, Eldorado, Canadair, de Havilland, and the Canada Development Corporation. Stevens intended to convey the message that the Tories were serious about privatization even though the government had not established a policy on selling off crown corporations at that point.

Stevens's headlong rush to impress the business community left important issues unresolved. For example, Teleglobe owed much of its profitability to its monopoly control. Would the government take steps to make sure that a privately owned Teleglobe would enjoy the same status? No one knew. These were the types of problems that the Kelly task force had foreseen and that needed to be resolved before there could be any real move to sell off a company. Paul Marshall had once worked in government (in the early 1950s he served for two years as executive assistant to Brooke Claxton, Minister of National Defence) and he knew that decisions there usually had as much or more to do with politics as with efficiency or profitability. A company like de Havilland could not simply be sold to the highest bidder; there were other considerations to be kept in view, such as jobs, the future of the Canadian aerospace industry, and so on. Stevens, therefore, had created the expectation that there would be quick movement even though quick movement was impossible.

On November 8, 1984, Finance Minister Michael Wilson called for a new privatization policy in his quasi-budget speech setting out the Tory "agenda for economic renewal." Wilson gave the clear impression that the new government wanted to open up all such questions for discussion and that hard decisions would be made in the months ahead about the role of the government in the economy and the need for government ownership: "Although each [crown] corporation was established to serve what, at the time, might have been an important public policy purpose, we must ask ourselves whether that remains the case. If it does not, it is surely important to consider whether the corporation should be retained . . . .There are several crown companies which are predominantly, or in some cases entirely, commercial in character, and it is appropriate to consider whether continued public ownership is in the best interests of either the company or the country."

Wilson's statement put privatization near the top of the government's agenda. With both Stevens and Mazankowski beginning to formulate privatization policy, it was obvious that the Cabinet had to impose order. The senior ministers in whose bailiwicks the crown corporations could be found finally got a chance to study the Kelly report and took a decision to split the privatization task among themselves: Mazankowski would be in charge of Air Canada, Carney would handle Petro-Canada, Stevens would look after the CDIC, and the entire program would be run by the Treasury Board and supervised by a Cabinet privatization committee consisting of Treasury Board president Robert de Cotret; the Minister of State for Finance, Barbara McDougall; and the Minister of Energy, Mines and Resources, Pat Carney. The plan might have worked if de Cotret had been a more vigorous and active minister and if the Treasury Board had been strengthened. He was not, it was not, and the plan fell into abeyance almost from the start.

By the summer of 1985, the new government was acting very much like the old, even though it was making different noises. The Trudeau government, for example, had taken over de Havilland and Canadair to keep them going, not as a matter of principle. The Liberals claimed that they never intended to make the two aviation companies permanent wards of the state, and that they would sell them once they were viable and the government could get a fair price for them. Most of the crown corporations that the Tories wound up were small, inconsequential, or defunct. Three small Liberal creations were quickly terminated—Loto Canada Inc., Canadian Sports Pool, and Canagrex. Next came a handful of companies that really existed more on paper than in reality. (Canadian National (West Indies) Steamships Ltd. was typical of these. It had sold all its ships to a Cuban bank in 1958 but was kept alive solely because the last payment due it, $470,400, had been trapped in a United States bank ever since the United States froze all Cuban assets in 1963.) The government sold two small but active and profitable corporations, Northern Transportation and Canadian Arsenals Limited, and also disposed of the bulk of its shares in the Canada Development Corporation (a majority of shares in this corporation were already privately owned). But it made no move to sell Air Canada, Canadian National, or Petro-Canada and although there had been a great deal of talk about selling Teleglobe Canada, there was no action. The sell-off talk concentrated, instead, on de Havilland and Canadair, the former a money loser, the latter alive only because the previous government had assumed most of its debt.

* * *

Although the free-enterprise philosophy that the Tories were thought to have adhered to since 1979 made much of the need for selling off "unnecessary" crown corporations, the Tories also claimed that much of the vast network of government support for private business was also wasteful and unnecessary. Here they were touching upon a theme that was dear to the hearts of many voters who resented tax breaks, subsidies, grants, and other forms of government largesse for apparently profitable companies.

In the 1972 federal election, the New Democratic Party, led by David Lewis, campaigned on that very theme. Lewis attacked the "corporate welfare bums"—private businesses, many of them huge and profitable, that received handouts from Ottawa. If Canadians really wanted to know who was ripping off the system, Lewis charged, they should look to private industry, and not to those on unemployment insurance or welfare. Lewis's campaign struck a responsive cord and the NDP won 31 seats in the House.

Lewis's campaign theme was largely bombast, but it was based on a very real phenomenon. There is a corporate welfare system in this country every bit as pervasive as the public welfare system that Canadians take for granted. The government continually bails out the losers, be they banks, trust company depositors, or major corporations. But it is not only the losers who can count on government largesse. In the corporate welfare system, even the winners rely heavily on government for help. There is, for the most part, little real free enterprise in Canada. Business people who mouth pious odes to free competition and attack government interference can often be found standing in line waiting for the public handout that will take as much risk as possible out of their enterprises. Canadian business has operated in this way ever since colonial days and nothing has changed. In this society of The Great Handout, business too wants its share.

There is, as usual, a rationale for all this. Under certain conditions, government assistance helps businesses earn profits and profitable businesses create jobs, pay taxes, and help improve the balance of payments. All Canadian governments have maintained the corporate welfare system—there is little to choose between them in this regard. In the late 1970s, however, many Canadians began to question whether or not businesses that were supported by government in one fashion or another were efficient enough to compete in international markets. They also began to wonder whether it was fair that small businesses were allowed to fail when the government always seemed to spread out a safety net for large corporations. The Tories appeared to offer these Canadians an alternative. The system was neither fair nor efficient, the Tories said, the government should not be a source of handouts for private enterprise. If Canadian business were to become tougher and leaner, the Tories claimed, private industry had to be weaned from the public welfare it had depended upon for so long. The Tories, therefore, vigorously denounced federal subsidies and bailouts to private businesses, especially those in Quebec. In November 1982, for example, Michael Wilson, then finance critic, attacked Liberal support for private corporations in this way: "The government should consider . . . less giveaways and less bailouts than has been its custom . . . encouraged as it has been by socialists on our left." Once in charge, however, the Tories kept the federal subsidy and bailout trough almost as full as the Liberals had. Nowhere was this more apparent than in the case of Domtar.

Domtar is a large Quebec-based pulp and paper company that is 45 percent owned by the government of Quebec through two provincially owned investment companies. In 1984 it made a profit of almost $90 million. Early in 1985 Domtar approached the Quebec and federal governments with a request for approximately $200 million in grants to help finance a $1.2 billion modernization program for its fine-paper manufacturing plant at Windsor, Quebec. The plant employs 700 of the town's 5500 people and the expansion promised to create an additional 250 jobs in the surrounding area. The Quebec government was willing to give Domtar $83 million if Ottawa would kick in the additional $117 million. Stevens and senior advisers and bureaucrats at the Department of Regional Industrial Expansion were reluctant to give government funds to a company that had turned a handsome profit the year before. They questioned the need for the additional manufacturing capacity which the company would create. They were also deeply worried about American reactions to an outright grant, because United States pulp and paper companies were already complaining about what they claimed was unfair Canadian competition. This last point was brought home to Stevens in interviews with the Canadian ambassador to the United States, Allan Gotlieb, American trade officials, and some members of Congress during a short visit to Washington just after the Domtar request came through. Although Domtar chief James Smith met privately with Mulroney in mid-February, Stevens rejected the Domtar request.

Domtar went public and mounted a campaign to pressure Ottawa to change its mind. Construction work at the Windsor mill was halted immediately after Stevens's announcement on February 22 and a local "survival committee" sprang up. As Domtar pressed its claims for the money on the front pages, Quebec Tory backbenchers were quick to respond. The pressure mounted on the government and within days Mulroney started to backpedal. He emerged from a caucus meeting to tell the press that although his government would not give Domtar a $100 million blank cheque, other forms of aid might be possible, and he revealed that he would be discussing the matter with Quebec Premier René Lévesque. For the next several weeks Ottawa, Quebec, and Domtar examined alternatives. On April 5, a deal was announced: the Quebec government's Société de développement industrielle would lend Domtar $150 million, to be repaid over ten years, and Ottawa and Quebec would pay the interest on the loan on a fifty/fifty basis. Quebec would also give Domtar a $21 million grant. The deal would cost Ottawa about $38 million.

Although the Conservative government has been less generous with bailouts and subsidies than its Liberal predecessor (it actually allowed White Farm Equipment, an Ontario-based company, to fail) it is also under greater budgetary constraint. This may be the only difference between the two, because the Domtar episode shows that the basic approach remains the same. If large numbers of jobs are seen to be at stake or if the area of the country affected has significant political clout, Ottawa can be depended upon to bestow its favours. How else can a $38-million-dollar gift to a profitable company be explained? In the 1984 election campaign, Mulroney declared that his government's support for the maintenance of the welfare state was a "sacred trust." As far as the corporate welfare system is concerned, he has kept his promise.

* * *

If the Tories had one dominant target for privatization, it was Petro-Canada—the company that right-wing Tories love to hate. When Mulroney was elected in September 1984, Petro-Canada was already the fifteenth largest company in the country with annual sales of about $3.4 billion. It had been founded by the Trudeau government in the summer of 1975 with a mandate to expedite petroleum exploration and development, especially in the high-risk frontier regions. The company was a nationalist's dream because it ensured that at least one of Canada's major oil companies would answer as much to the dictates of national interest as it would to the necessities of the balance sheet. When the company began to acquire retail outlets through the purchase of existing, mostly foreign-owned oil companies, the red and white maple leaf design began to dot the roads and highways of Canada. Petro-Canada was "ours," company advertising stressed, and most of the people of Canada took Petro-Canada to their hearts. Despite highly questionable moves (such as the 1981 purchase of PetroFina at a price many observers considered much too high, a purchase financed by consumers through a federal tax imposed at the gas pump), Petro-Canada quickly became a sacred cow.

When Joe Clark was elected to office in the spring of 1979 he brought with him Tory enmity toward this Grit creation and Tory promises that Petro-Canada would be sold off. The company was "a turkey," Clark proclaimed, and a task force was formed to study the best way to privatize it. Nationalists rallied behind Petro-Canada and the heat on the Clark government was turned up. Caught between his right wing, which demanded privatization, and the political reality that the company was popular in Ontario, Clark failed to act. When he was defeated and Trudeau returned in the 1980 election, the future of Petro-Canada seemed assured.

During the 1984 election campaign the Tories made no specific promises about Petro-Canada, remembering how voter mistrust of Clark's intentions toward the company had led to his downfall. On the other hand, Conservatives had been making noises about privatization at almost every opportunity and it was known that many party members were less than thrilled about the expansion of Petro-Canada since its founding in 1975. Alberta MPs in particular appeared to assume that the election results were a mandate for action against the crown-owned oil company.

Energy Minister Pat Carney did move quickly on Petro-Canada after the election, but not nearly far enough to satisfy the party's right wing. The chief executive officer, Wilbert (Bill) Hopper, was called in and told not to expect any more federal money to help finance the company, even though Petro-Canada was slated to receive $275 million in 1985. This marked the start of the one consistent message that the Tories have put out on Petro-Canada; no more taxpayer dollars would be pumped into the company. If Petro-Canada needed money it would have to raise it internally or borrow it from nongovernmental sources. Hopper was expected to run the company like a private corporation and run it in the black. Not long after this Hopper told the *Financial Post* that his company could, if asked by the government, sell shares to raise money and dilute the government's ownership interest. The day following the appearance of this story, nine members of Petro-Canada's fifteen-member board were asked to resign—they were too Liberal for the Tory government's taste. But Hopper, Mulroney made clear on December 14, would stay.

* * *

Shortly after Hopper was confirmed as chief executive officer of Petro-Canada, the Reichmann family of Toronto, owners of the multibillion dollar Olympia and York real estate empire, approached, or were approached by, the government (the real story has yet to emerge) to begin the process by which they and Petro-Canada eventually acquired most of the assets of Gulf Canada. Gulf Canada's American parent company had been purchased by Chevron in March 1984. That purchase also transferred ownership of Gulf Canada to Chevron and this transfer had to be approved by the Foreign Investment Review Agency which was, at the time, still functioning. FIRA okayed the deal with one major proviso: Chevron had to sell off its interests in Gulf Canada to a Canadian buyer by April 30, 1985, if one could be found.

One was found. The Reichmann family wanted Gulf Canada's exploration and production assets but, primarily for tax reasons, they did not want its refineries and retail outlets. Petro-Canada provided the solution. If it could buy the Gulf Canada refineries and service stations from the Reichmanns, it would expedite their purchase of Gulf Canada and would make Petro-Canada the largest retail supplier of petroleum products in the country. Petro-

Canada would probably have preferred to buy Gulf's piece of Hibernia but the Reichmanns would not stand for that.

The crown-owned oil company needed Cabinet approval to borrow $1.8 billion for the purchase of Gulf Canada's five refineries and 2500 service stations, and Carney pushed hard for the deal. But as the negotiations between the Reichmanns and Chevron reached a climax in early July (FIRA's deadline had been extended), resistance in the Cabinet grew, particularly from Wilson, Stevens, and de Cotret. Why? No one knows for sure, but some good guesses can be ventured: a large loan to Petro-Canada might push interest rates up; the Tories did not intend to make Petro-Canada the nation's largest oil company; the government was nervous about taking more political flak just after it had taken a beating on the de-indexing of the old age pensions. It is clear that there was growing opposition in the oil industry to a deal, especially among retailers. Tory backbenchers from Quebec and Alberta were strongly opposed.

On Friday, July 12, the Cabinet approved Petro-Canada's role in the deal despite its growing misgivings and issued an order-in-council authorizing Petro-Canada to borrow the money. The deadline for the Reichmann/Chevron deal was Monday, July 15, at 8 p.m. Newspaper reports over the weekend of July 13 and 14 presented the clear impression that the government was solidly behind the Reichmanns. Just before the deadline, however, the Reichmanns asked Chevron for a forty-eight hour extension. They received it. But on Wednesday evening, just before the deadline expired, they pulled out, thereby forfeiting their $25 million deposit.

Much confusion surrounds the details of what happened. Most press stories and reports from those close to the Reichmanns suggest that Mulroney himself turned against the agreement on Wednesday afternoon and ordered Hopper to back out. That forced the Reichmanns to withdraw because they could not renegotiate a new deal in time. Those close to the government tell a different story: they blame the Reichmanns for the collapse of the deal by trying to get a better price out of Chevron at the last moment.

The Reichmanns were still interested in buying Gulf Canada, however, and quickly reopened negotiations with Chevron. This time the government was not involved and things went much more smoothly. By August 2, the arrangement for the Reichmann buyout of 60 percent of Gulf Canada stock had been completed and the deal announced. Ten days later, Petro-Canada agreed to buy four Gulf Canada refineries and 1800 service stations for $886 million, making it Canada's largest oil company.

Although a number of Alberta Tory backbenchers were upset (Calgary North MP Paul Gagnon called the agreement "asinine"; Calgary South MP Bobbie Sparrow termed it "a dumb move"), Carney, Mulroney, and others were quick to take credit for the deal and to point out that Canadian ownership of the energy sector— "Canadianization"—had been significantly advanced by it. Carney told the press on August 21 in Vancouver (where a Cabinet meeting was being held) that the arrangement had been inspired as much by governmental policy considerations as by commercial ones, while Mulroney claimed that it was "Conservative policy to Canadianize the oil industry" and that the transaction had "enhanced Canadianization by almost five percentage points." That was true enough; it had also been true on July 17 when the original agreement had fallen through. Mulroney did not add, and no one seemed to notice, that all this had been made possible by FIRA, the Tories' favourite whipping boy, which by August had been killed off.

And what happened to privatization along the way? On August 16, four days after the Petro-Canada/Gulf Canada deal, a story was leaked to the press by a Petro-Canada director that a task force had been appointed by the board of directors several months earlier to examine privatization. Carney told reporters on the CTV news program *Question Period* on August 23 that Petro-Canada might raise money by "the sale of shares" but this would not mean selling off Petro-Canada completely. If the company went to the public for money, she insisted, it would not be for philosophical reasons but "as a sound corporate way" of raising capital. Hopper had said this the previous fall.

What is the likely future direction of the government's policy on the privatization of Petro-Canada? It will probably follow these lines: Petro-Canada will remain a crown corporation but it will, at some point, begin to raise its capital requirements through public offerings of shares or debentures. This will dilute the government's interest in Petro-Canada, but the government will continue to retain a significant and perhaps a controlling interest in the company. The company will not be totally privatized. The public offering of Petro-Canada securities will be made only when the government is certain that the tiniest detail has been ironed out and that the company will get full value for the equity it sells. That is not likely to happen any time soon because low oil prices have depressed energy shares. Before anything is done, however, hard decisions will have to be made about what role the government should play in the affairs of a partially privatized Petro-Canada. So far, there is no evidence to show that those decisions have been made.

* * *

The government did carry out one important privatization deal in its first year and a half in office—the sale to the Boeing Aircraft Company of de Havilland Canada. That sale was one of the few instances in which the government showed determination to use its parliamentary majority to accomplish an objective with which the opposition and some of the press strongly disagreed.

De Havilland Canada, located at Downsview, Ontario, was established in 1928 as a wholly owned subsidiary of the British aircraft manufacturing firm of the same name. In 1946 it began to build Canadian-designed aircraft and from then until the early 1970s it specialized in the production of small transport aircraft for military and bush flying purposes. The company had become a pioneer in short take-off and landing (STOL) technology by developing two twin-engined aircraft, the Twin Otter and the Buffalo. In the late 1960s, de Havilland Canada began to consider entrance into the STOL passenger market and started design and development work on the four-engine Dash 7, based roughly on the Buffalo. The Dash 7 first flew in March 1975 after de Havilland had spent about $120 million in initial development costs, 80 percent of which was paid for by Ottawa. Sales of the Dash 7 were disappointingly slow and although over 100 of the aircraft have been sold around the world, the development costs have not yet been recovered. Despite the lag in Dash 7 sales, work on the twin-engined Dash 8 began in the fall of 1980.

When start-up costs on the Dash 7 began to escalate in the early 1970s, de Havilland's British parent became anxious to unload the company. In 1974 the Trudeau government bought it and placed it in the CDIC portfolio. From the very start of de Havilland's status as a crown corporation, the Liberal government made it clear that it was ultimately looking for a buyer, either in whole or in part. In fact, the Liberals were in the process of negotiating a partial sale of de Havilland to Boeing on the eve of the September 1984 election.

De Havilland was a foreign-owned company from its establishment in 1928 until the government bought it in 1974. In fact, almost every important aviation company in Canadian history has been foreign-owned and most of the significant technological developments in Canadian aviation have been accomplished by these foreign-owned firms. Avro, now defunct, was British-owned when it carried out its pioneering work on the C102 jetliner and the CF100 interceptor in the late 1940s and early 1950s, and when initial design and production work began on the CF105 supersonic interceptor in 1953. Canadair was American-owned when it produced the Mark VI Sabre, one of the most successful jet fighters of the 1950s, and when it began the initial stages of development of the Challenger business jet. And, of course, de Havilland was British-owned when it began to develop STOL technology with the Twin Otter and the Buffalo. Research and development in the aviation field has always been extremely expensive and no privately owned Canadian company has yet successfully combined the cash requirements for advanced R&D with the needed expertise and marketing networks that would ensure the financial success of a new product. There are, in fact, very few countries in the world with successful indigenous aviation industries and most of those either have populations and industrial bases much larger than Canada, or nurture their industries with heavy government subsidies, or both. Cost has dictated that aviation development become an international business.

Recent de Havilland history bears out this story; the company has been a money loser for much of the last decade. From May 1976 to May 1982, it accumulated a total net profit of $19.2 million. But business turned sour and from then until December 1984, it piled up a total net loss of $542 million. Ottawa has pumped $760 million into the company since 1982—$240 million of this was in 1984. Despite these large cash transfusions, de

Havilland still had a long-term debt of $54 million in December 1984. Ottawa was forced to keep de Havilland afloat because it employs about 4400 people at Downsview, does business with 1100 suppliers and subcontractors across Canada, and generates seventy jobs elsewhere for every 100 persons employed at the main plant.

* * *

According to the government, the privatization of de Havilland began with the appointment of Paul Marshall to head the CDIC shortly after the election. He assembled an advisory team which included representatives of major Canadian and foreign investment banks and which sought the advice of a number of accounting, legal, and financial companies on everything from insurance to real estate values. The government claims that over 130 prospective buyers were contacted but that only three serious candidates emerged. These were: Rimgate Holdings, a Canadian/Dutch consortium which included Fokker, the Dutch airplane manufacturer; Dornier, of West Germany, which was also interested in Canadair; and Boeing.

Ian McDougall, president of Rimgate, later claimed that the government stacked the rules of the sale against it because of its insistence that Rimgate have its financing committed and in place before allowing it to do an in-depth analysis of de Havilland's books. This, according to McDougall, loaded the dice in favour of Boeing, which did not need to arrange financing. Marshall denied the charge and hinted that Ottawa believed Rimgate's interest was really a cover for a Fokker attempt to eliminate de Havilland, a rival in the field of small passenger-carrying aircraft. Neither Rimgate nor Dornier ever made a bid on de Havilland. Boeing did, and its offer was recommended to the Cabinet's privatization committee by the CDIC's board of directors.

On Monday, December 2, Ottawa announced that an agreement had been reached to sell de Havilland to Boeing. Boeing was to pay $150 million for de Havilland, with $90 million to be paid in cash up front and the remaining $65 million in installments over 15 years. For every $5 million in Boeing orders placed in Canada, however, Ottawa agreed to forgive $1 million of the $65 million, thus providing a powerful incentive to Boeing to place contracts in Canada. Ottawa agreed to assume all liabilities for de Havilland aircraft produced up to that point at an estimated cost of $30 million. Boeing was also to be eligible, as a result of planned reinvestments in plant and equipment, for some $60 million in federal grants and loans.

Boeing is clearly interested in running de Havilland, not closing it down. It agreed to give the company a world product mandate for the design, development, production, and marketing of its products and accepted a government veto over foreign production of de Havilland products. Research and development on STOL-type aircraft will continue at Downsview with maximum use being made of the facilities and personnel located there.

Despite these assurances, it appeared to some observers that the Tories had given de Havilland away. The uproar began even before the formal announcement of the agreement. On Thursday, November 28, Liberal MP Robert Kaplan told the House of Commons that he thought de Havilland should not be sold at all and if it were, it should be sold only to a Canadian company. As soon as the announcement was made, former Transport Minister Lloyd Axworthy claimed that although de Havilland was on the verge of profitability, the government was ''giving it away, virtually . . . the fix [in favour of Boeing] was in from the start.''

The NDP announced a motion of nonconfidence in the government because of the agreement and claimed that the sale would mean the loss of Canadian jobs. They predicted that Boeing would transfer the manufacture of the Dash 7 and Dash 8 to the United States and close de Havilland down. This, in fact, made little sense: Boeing would have had to build a totally new, much more expensive plant somewhere in the United States just to accomplish what it can do much more cheaply at Downsview. Its plants in the state of Washington produce 747, 757, and 767 aircraft, which are about as different from the Dash 7 and Dash 8 as a Greyhound bus is from a Volkswagen Rabbit. But even if Boeing throws all good business sense to the wind and tries to close Downsview down, Ottawa would be sure to step in and take control. To do otherwise would be to court political disaster.

The Liberals also opposed the sale and made charges as preposterous as those levelled by the NDP. On December 3, Turner raised the ghost of the Avro Arrow in the House of Commons. (The Arrow was a jet interceptor developed for the Royal Canadian Air Force that was cancelled by Diefenbaker in 1959 because of excessive cost.) Turner claimed that the de Havilland deal was "a similar type of transaction," and that "Canadian expertise in aeronautics, in space, in short takeoff and landing aircraft [would] no longer belong to [Canada]." This technology transfer through foreign ownership could, of course, happen, but it has not happened in the past. None of the important and uniquely Canadian aeronautical developments which were carried out by foreign-owned firms were ever transferred abroad and thus lost to Canada. Why de Havilland should do, under American ownership, what it had not done under British ownership is something Turner could not be bothered to explain. (Besides, the analogy to the Avro Arrow was inaccurate. When the Diefenbaker government cancelled the Arrow contract in 1959, the result was the complete shutdown of Canadian Avro and the loss of some 14,000 jobs. The agreement with Boeing had been designed to ensure its continuance, not its closure.)

Some press commentators echoed the Liberals and were clearly angry about the sale. Columnist John Ferguson wrote immediately after the announcement, "It looks like we just gave away an aircraft company," while Christopher Young, who published at least five columns on the subject over the next few weeks, wrote on December 5: "Canada, the government is saying, is not only open for business—large chunks of it are for sale, and some of it you can have free."

Other press reports were more objective. Christopher Waddell's article in the *Globe and Mail* on December 7 pointed out that the Tories had pushed too hard for the sale, allowing Boeing to take advantage of their eagerness, and that they had apparently given little thought to anything except a straight deal for the whole company. But Waddell still thought the sale to Boeing was "the obvious answer for the government." He pointed out that Ottawa could not afford to continue to pump in development money and that such money would be needed in the future to ensure the viability of de Havilland in the decades to come. He noted that Boeing had a long-term strategic interest in keeping de Havilland alive—it wanted to continue to sell jets to Air Canada—and had the resources to do so. He also attacked the Liberal argument that the sale was premature because de Havilland was on the verge of profitability, with the development costs of the Dash 8 mostly paid. If the Liberal claim of imminent profitability was true, Waddell pointed out, it was actually a point in favour of the sale because a potentially profitable de Havilland was a more attractive product than one with a totally gloomy future. Despite Waddell's effort to introduce some sanity into the debate, the storm of stridently nationalist rhetoric continued: "The issue is not selling crown corporations," Christopher Young thundered, "it's selling them to foreign interests, or, in this case, giving one of them to a foreign corporation, something that Turner never proposed."

In the House of Commons, the Liberals and the NDP demanded that the government place the agreement before a parliamentary committee and at first the government, led by de Cotret, stonewalled. On Thursday, December 19, however, it reversed its position when Sinclair Stevens, who had been in hospital, returned to the Commons. In a "good guy, bad guy" routine that could have come from a Hollywood script, Stevens presented a pleasant contrast to de Cotret. He promised to release all relevant information on the sale except "that which may have some commercial sensitivity to it," and he announced that the conclusion of the deal would be postponed until the end of January to give a Commons committee time to hold hearings on the agreement: "I certainly have no objection, and neither do my colleagues, including the President of the Treasury Board, to the matter being considered at an appropriate time by a committee of this House." De Cotret had flatly refused this the day before.

Stevens could afford to be pleasant because, in fact, he had given nothing away despite the opposition's cheers of victory. The government did release additional information about the sale showing that de Havilland's projected losses were placed at $83 million for 1985 and $50 million for 1986. (The original estimates given to prospective buyers were $60 million for 1985 and $14 million for 1986, followed by three years of rising profits.) But the government never had any intention of seeking the approval of the committee for the sale and, in fact, there was no legal requirement for it to do so. The Commons hearings were little more than pro forma, especially when the government made plain that the sale was going to go through regardless of what the committee found or determined.

On January 29, Stevens announced that the sale would be completed without further delay. A turnabout at that point would probably have doomed a sale of de Havilland (or, for that matter, Canadair) for some time to come. No company would have been willing to follow Boeing's example if the government had cancelled or even substantially delayed the agreement. A decision had been reached and this time the government would show that rare resolve that had been lacking on other, more important occasions. The closing documents were signed that day and the deal went through on January 31, 1986.

Throughout the fuss that followed the announcement of the Boeing/CDIC agreement, the opposition made a valid point—that the government had been too eager to sell de Havilland and may not have received the best possible price. The opposition, however, failed to put its case clearly to the public. The NDP did not launch a national debate on the question of whether or not the Canadian aviation industry should, in principle and in perpetuity, be government-owned even though that position was at the heart of NDP criticism of the transaction. The Liberals did not launch a national debate on whether or not the Canadian aviation industry should be Canadian-owned. To do so would have been to ask other key questions. For example, should de Havilland and Canadair be kept by the crown until an appropriate Canadian-owned company could emerge? Is any Canadian company suitable? How long should the government wait? How much should the government be prepared to pay to make a Canadian-owned operation viable and for how long? Because these questions were never asked, they were never answered.

De Havilland has been sold. Canadair, Teleglobe Canada, Petro-Canada, Air Canada, and all the others remain. Was the sale of de Havilland evidence of the government's determination to reduce its own role in the economy and to take itself out of manufacturing and service sectors wherever possible? No. De Havilland was and is a money loser kept alive by government funds because of the 4400 Canadians it employs directly and the thousands of others who work for companies that do substantial business with it. The sale of a drain on the public treasury is no measure of the government's commitment to privatization; it is only a measure of the government's determination to cut its losses. So far there is no evidence that the Conservatives are substantially more committed to privatization than was the previous government. In fact, a Turner Liberal government might well have done more in the way of privatizing Air Canada or Petro-Canada than the Tories have done. In politics, it seems, it is only the guardians of the sacred cows who are allowed by the voters to wield the slaughtering knife.

Clearly the Tories have sacrificed privatization to the realities of politics. There is nothing wrong with this approach if the sole purpose of achieving power is to hold it and if the voters are cynical enough to accept this way of governing. But there are still a substantial number of Canadians who clearly expect that the governments they elect will lead and will present clear policy choices. Pat Carney's drive to deregulate the petroleum industry was a model of this kind of behaviour in one field. She moulded government policy and government action to achieve a political and philosophical objective. In doing so, she gave Canadians a choice even though they have not yet decided which policy they prefer in this era of low oil prices. But she and the rest of the government promised the very same kind of action on privatization and, to date, they have not delivered. If they truly believe that less government ownership will mean a stronger Canadian economy, their duty is to try to lead the public to that conclusion, whatever the polls say. If they do not believe it, why didn't they say so in the first place?

Chapter Eight
The Carney Show

Pat Carney was determined to kill the National Energy Program long before she became Minister of Energy, Mines and Resources in September 1984. A business writer and energy consultant prior to entering politics in the June 1979 election (she was defeated by less than 100 votes in Vancouver Centre but was elected on her second try in February 1980), Carney had worked and travelled extensively in the North in the early 1970s. She had prepared an economic impact report on the Mackenzie Valley Pipeline for the Canadian Arctic Gas Consortium and had concluded that the proposed megaproject would bring great economic and developmental benefits to the North. From this and other work, Carney became convinced that a prosperous Canadian energy industry could stimulate the rest of the Canadian economy. In order for that to happen, she believed, the NEP would have to go.

The NEP had its genesis in the defeat of the short-lived Clark government in 1980. That government had tried to force Canadians to accept the high energy prices that had followed the Arab oil boycott of 1973 and the series of dramatic price increases imposed upon the energy-consuming world by the Organization of Petroleum Exporting Countries. The previous Trudeau government responded to the sharply higher prices by creating a two-price system—one frozen price for Canadian crude, which the government could control, and another rising price for foreign oil, which it could not. But frozen Canadian crude prices discouraged exploration and development in Canada, and thus the two-price system was modified in the late 1970s with one low price reserved for so-called "old" sources and a new, higher price, for oil from "new" and unconventional sources, such as the Alberta oil sands. The Clark Conservatives planned to do away with this patchwork system by raising all Canadian oil prices to world levels. They believed that this would spur exploration and development and encourage conservation. Clark and his finance minister, John Crosbie, were also determined to take a larger share of the massive oil and gas revenues that were going primarily to the producing provinces (especially Alberta) and the industry. In 1979, for example, federal revenues from oil and gas amounted to less than $1 billion, whereas the provinces, especially Alberta, and the oil industry earned about $4 billion each. Federal officials feared that if this situation continued, the provinces and the oil industry would earn as much as $23 billion between 1979 and 1985, and Ottawa's share would be a paltry $3 billion.

The government tried to accomplish these objectives through a revenue-sharing agreement with the producing provinces, but the effort was a failure and Clark was forced to take unilateral action. In November 1979, Crosbie introduced a budget into the Commons that included an 18-cent-a-gallon excise tax on gasoline that consumers would pay every time they pulled up to the pumps. The public howled and the opposition Liberals attacked the government for raising gasoline prices so quickly. They charged that Ontario consumers were going to be bled white because the government had been unable to force Alberta into a fairer distribution of energy revenues. The Clark government had bumbled from crisis to crisis from the time of the June election; the Liberals smelled power once again. They defeated the government on a motion of nonconfidence in the House in early December 1979 and tossed the Conservatives out of office in the February 1980 election.

The Trudeau Liberals, with Marc Lalonde holding the energy portfolio, made a perfunctory effort to arrive at a revenue-sharing agreement with the producing provinces. There was too much at stake for Alberta and Ottawa in terms of both ego and money, however, and the effort ended in bitter recrimination. In October 1980, therefore, the government announced the National Energy Program, a comprehensive new scheme for the achievement of Liberal political objectives. It had been generated entirely within the federal government—neither the provinces nor the industry were consulted about the new system. It was, in typical Trudeau style, simply imposed.

Based on the assumption that oil and gas prices would never drop and that energy revenues would continue to grow as a result, the NEP was a grandiose scheme designed to meet several objectives at the same time. It would increase Canadian ownership of the oil industry; it would achieve Canadian energy self-sufficiency by the end of the century by increasing Canadian production and by reducing the demand for imported oil; it would continue to shield Canadians from high world prices and it would dramatically increase Ottawa's share of oil and gas revenues. There were to be new taxes, new incentives, and greater federal intervention in the energy industry than at any time since World War II.

The NEP contained a number of dramatic new measures. The most important of these was the Petroleum and Gas Revenue Tax (PGRT)—a tax of 16 percent on gross revenue earned by the oil and gas companies. The PGRT broke all precedents because it was not deductible for income tax purposes. An oil company could not deduct the PGRT from its gross income in calculating either provincial or federal corporate income taxes. The effect was double taxation. In addition, a system of grants called the Petroleum Incentives Program (PIP), which favoured Canadian-owned companies, was introduced to encourage exploration in frontier areas. At the same time, the government reserved for itself the right to step in and unilaterally take up to 25 percent of the production of companies drilling on federal lands—areas, such as the Arctic, which are directly under Ottawa's jurisdiction. This was known as the "back-in" provision. The two-price system for oil was kept in place, as was an oil import compensation system designed to even out the differences between lower-priced Canadian oil and higher-priced foreign crude.

The NEP sparked a two-year war between Ottawa and the producing provinces, led by Alberta. Although the price structure of the NEP was modified slightly in 1982 after negotiations between Ottawa and Edmonton, the policy itself, with its PIP grants, the back-in, the PGRT, and other taxes, remained. The basic political objectives of the NEP were too important to Trudeau and Lalonde to allow for any real modifications. Dollars might be shifted here or there, tax points might be redistributed, but the NEP as such would remain.

The introduction of the NEP coincided with the onset of a world-wide recession that dramatically reduced the demand for oil and gas and brought an end to escalating prices. The Canadian energy industry reeled under the two hammerblows of the NEP and the sharp reduction of demand. In Calgary, a boom city through much of the 1970s, unemployment rose to over 12 percent, the rate of bankruptcies soared, and buildings under construction were boarded up. Easterners headed back down the Trans-Canada highway by the thousands, their dreams shattered.

Although the industry, the producing provinces, and the federal Conservative party naturally enough blamed the NEP for all their woes, the industry's total revenue actually rose from about $6.9 billion in 1980 to $12.4 billion in 1984. The Alberta recession was real enough, but other oil-producing countries such as Mexico and Nigeria experienced similar difficulties and they did not have an NEP. What was it about the NEP that really bothered producing provinces and the energy industry? First was the realization that Ottawa had stepped into the energy field and had used the resources of the Western provinces and the earnings of the industry to bolster Liberal support in central Canada. Second was the belief that profits and net revenues would have been higher without the NEP.

The grass is always greener on the other side of the fence: in the first two years of the NEP, the oil rigs heading for the United States jammed border crossing points in Saskatchewan and Alberta. Given Pat Carney's long-held belief that the energy industry is the mainspring of Canada's sustained economic growth, the NEP became an obvious target for the Mulroney-led Conservatives.

Carney became energy critic in 1983 and quickly got to work studying the NEP. Although most Canadians supported the policy, she, like other Tories, felt strongly that it was politically divisive and economically unwise. She set up industry study groups, solicited advice from the oil companies, and held discussions with the leaders of the producing provinces to get a firm grasp on what they thought was wrong with the NEP, and specifically, how the nation's economy and the needs of the industry could be better served by some other program. By early 1984 it was clear that she intended to dismantle the policy and substitute a market-oriented, non-interventionist approach to the energy industry.

Carney was convinced that the industry, freed from the shackles of the NEP, would eventually generate as many as 300,000 new jobs across the country. In June 1984 she told the Petroleum Society of the Canadian Institute of Mining and Metallurgy in Calgary that her prime objective was "to make the oil and gas industry an engine of growth for the whole economy." She made it clear that Canada had to move to world prices and hinted strongly that under Tory rule, provisions of the NEP most hated by the industry, such as the PGRT, would be removed. Despite such speeches, Carney remained vague about the specifics of how the NEP would be approached by a Conservative government. The vagueness was, of course, deliberate. The fuzzier the approach, the greater would be the freedom to manoeuvre when negotiations with the producing provinces took place. Although the provinces, the industry, and Carney agreed on general principles, a deal was by no means guaranteed, and Carney had no intention of tipping her hand prematurely.

Carney's campaign was aided by falling world prices and by a growing disenchantment with much of the NEP, not only within the Department of Energy, Mines and Resources, but even among friends of the Liberal government. The NEP was based on a false premise—that oil prices would remain high for generations—and its very foundations were already being eroded when the Tories took over. Suddenly, the acute energy shortages that had marked much of the 1970s disappeared; by 1984, there was a world oil glut. That made Carney's job easier but it was no guarantee of success.

Carney's appointment to the energy portfolio in September 1984 was welcomed by the industry. The president of the Canadian Association of Oilwell Drilling Contractors, Jack Williams, told the press a few days after she took over the portfolio that his group was "very pleased" because Carney, in meetings with the association, had proved herself "able, responsive, and receptive." Despite this goodwill, Carney had a hard task ahead. The NEP was still popular among Canadians, it was deeply ingrained in legislation, and it had been a cornerstone of Liberal policy. More important, the federal government had come to depend on NEP revenues and the disappearance of those revenues would make tackling the deficit even harder. In putting a new policy in place that would meet the Conservative political agenda, therefore, Carney had to satisfy the competing needs of the producing provinces, the consuming provinces, the industry, and the federal Department of Finance.

* * *

Carney brought two men into her office who shared her view of Canadian energy policy. Harry Near, Carney's chief of staff (at a salary later reported as approximately $10,000 a month), had served as a policy adviser to Energy Minister Ray Hnatyshyn in the short-lived Clark government and had returned to private industry as an energy consultant after the Clark defeat. He stayed in touch with politics through his involvement with the Clark leadership forces in 1983 and worked for a time with Carney after she was made energy critic by Mulroney in 1983. Near was not eager to return to Energy, Mines and Resources full time, and he made it clear that he would stay only until agreements had been reached with the provinces and Carney had the department running the way she wanted it. He left at the end of May 1985.

The other political appointee was Steve Probyn, who was named senior policy adviser. Probyn had had extensive experience in the energy field before joining Carney's staff. Although Canadian-born, he had worked on energy policy for the British Conservative Party after his graduation from the London School of Economics. He had also worked on the Venture natural gas project while employed by the Nova Scotia premier's office under Conservative John Buchanan. In 1982 he attended Harvard University to study United States energy policy and natural gas law.

Near and Probyn got along well with deputy minister Paul Tellier, even though Tellier had a reputation as a Trudeaucrat and was seen as a possible obstacle to the achievement of Conservative political objectives. Carney soon found out that he was, in reality, a good administrator and manager with little interest in developing policy. He and other high-level bureaucrats in the department had realized for some time (possibly from the day that

Trudeau announced his retirement at the end of February 1984), that the NEP was due for a radical transformation. From the start of the Liberal leadership race it seemed likely that John Turner would become the new leader, and Turner had hinted strongly on several occasions that he intended to review the NEP. Besides, the NEP was becoming not only a difficult policy to administer as world oil prices fell but also a very expensive one because of the PIP grant program. Under Tellier's direction, therefore, a variety of policy options were developed within the department in anticipation of changes that might be made either by a revamped Liberal government under Turner or by the Tories. At their very first meeting, Tellier handed Carney a memo outlining the ways in which the Conservatives could achieve their policy objectives. The atmosphere in the room, chilly until then, is said to have warmed considerably.

The relationship between the minister's office and the bureaucracy was helped by a clear demarcation of responsibilities. Near and Probyn helped Carney establish the specific political objectives that would allow her to achieve her overall aim of dismantling the NEP, and Tellier told them how to accomplish what they wanted. Tellier took part in all the formal negotiations with the provinces and acquitted himself so well that Carney was deeply disappointed when, in July 1985, Mulroney named him Secretary to the Cabinet and Clerk of the Privy Council, the highest public service post in the land. Despite the good relationship between the minister's office and the upper level of the bureaucracy, however, Carney took only Near with her when she made her first ministerial trip to the West at the beginning of October 1984; Tellier stayed in Ottawa in an obvious break with tradition. This was a clear message to the provinces; even though most of the faces in the department would remain the same, there were new political masters.

* * *

Carney's specific objectives in the negotiations with the producing provinces were to deregulate Canadian oil prices and allow them to move to world levels while at the same time eliminating much, if not all, of the special tax structures the Liberals had put into place as part of the NEP. But this had to be done in such a way as to allow industry a larger share of the revenues to plow back into job creation. Ottawa would not forgo revenue just to increase the size of Alberta's Heritage Fund. Nor would it let those revenues flow south of the border in increased dividend payments. Carney also knew that the government had to tackle a $35 billion deficit and that the PGRT brought more than $2 billion a year into federal coffers. If the PGRT had to go, was there an alternative that would allow Ottawa to keep some of the tax revenues, perhaps under another name? How could Ottawa guarantee that the revenues it was giving up would be used by the private sector for job creation? Would the provinces or the industry accept a "use-it-or-lose-it" tax that would ensure re-investment by industry? These were the major considerations, but there were others. Ottawa wanted to end the PIP grant program, which tended to reward drilling more than production, but had to replace it with some other incentive program to offset the high cost of exploration in the uncertain frontier areas. The complex gas-pricing structure also had to be tackled if Canada was to have a truly unregulated energy system. One issue not on the table was the NEP "back-in," which was applicable wholly to exploration on Canada lands and therefore not a matter for federal-provincial negotiations.

Carney's five-day swing through Ontario and the West began on October 1 with a visit to the office of the Ontario energy minister, Philip Andrewes. More a courtesy call than anything else, Carney had no intention of including Ontario in the negotiations. Her most important meeting was with the Alberta energy minister, John Zaozirny, in Edmonton.

Zaozirny had already notified Carney publicly that he and Alberta Premier Peter Lougheed expected Mulroney and Carney to stick to their pre-election promises. But Lougheed had been helpful when he had announced several weeks earlier that he would not object to a modest extension of the federal-provincial oil and gas revenue-sharing agreements that were due to expire on December 31. Almost everyone recognized that there was little chance of a comprehensive agreement by then. Carney reciprocated by raising Canadian oil prices to bring them more into line with world prices, an important (albeit token) gesture.

Carney and Zaozirny emerged all smiles from their meeting.

Both ministers agreed that it was necessary to get the negotiating machinery in place and that the discussions should not be rushed or held to rigid deadlines. The mood was more conciliatory than at any other recent meeting between a federal energy minister and an Alberta counterpart.

In Ottawa, matters were not so smooth. When Finance Minister Michael Wilson took over his portfolio, he discovered that the federal financial picture was worse than he had imagined. Wilson's deputy minister, Mickey Cohen (who had earlier served in the Department of Energy, Mines and Resources), pointed out that dropping the PGRT would deprive the federal treasury of some $2.2 billion per year over the next few years. He urged Wilson to keep the tax in some form and Wilson agreed to try.

The Wilson/Carney discussions pitted economic realities against political necessity. Wilson needed the revenue. This was a direct challenge to Carney's view that the energy sector would stimulate economic growth if it could be freed from overregulation and overtaxation. Jobs could not be created overnight, no matter how quickly the NEP might be dismantled, and this meant that any increased revenues from economic growth would be years in coming. Despite his reservations, Wilson's major policy statement, *A New Direction for Canada*, presented to the House of Commons on November 8, 1984, seemed to reflect Carney's view. But Wilson (and Cohen) did not give up easily, and in the months that followed, Carney found herself caught between the finance department, which wanted to keep the PGRT in some form, and the producing provinces, with their demands that the PGRT be dropped.

* * *

It was obvious even by late fall that Carney would have no easy time of the negotiations with the Western producing provinces or indeed, with the federal Department of Finance. What was needed was an easy triumph, something that could demonstrate Carney's important place in the Cabinet and that would show suspicious Western producers that the confrontations of the Trudeau era were a thing of the past. The Atlantic Accord gave Carney just what she needed.

Exploration for oil and gas in the waters off the coast of New-foundland had started in 1964, but it was not until 1979 that the first major discovery was made at the Hibernia field, a little over 300 kilometres east-southeast of St. John's, on the Grand Banks. The Hibernia discovery well flowed at the rate of 20,000 barrels of high-quality crude oil a day, indicating that a major new oil field lay under the sea. Oil companies were soon scrambling to drill discovery wells on the Grand Banks.

Three important questions had to be answered before full-scale development of the off-shore fields could begin. Which government actually owned the resource? Which government would manage it? Which government would benefit the most from it? In Alberta or Saskatchewan the oil and gas came from wells drilled on dry land and provincial ownership was not in doubt. Hibernia and the other wells were far out at sea, and although Ottawa claimed jurisdiction and appeared to have a strong case, the New-foundland government led by Conservative Premier Brian Peckford claimed that Newfoundland had not given control of its resources to Ottawa when it joined Confederation in 1949.

Ownership was actually the least important of the three questions, unless the government that owned the resource took its ownership as giving it the right to manage the resource and be the chief beneficiary of it. That seemed to be the view of the Trudeau Liberals in dealing with Newfoundland. They were determined to settle the ownership question and were confident that they would win. This would allow them to dictate terms when it came to settling the much tougher political issues involved.

The federal government went to court with Newfoundland in the spring of 1982. By 1984 it had secured decisions from the Newfoundland Supreme Court and the Supreme Court of Canada that it did indeed own the off-shore resources. This answered one of the key questions, but others remained unresolved and could be answered only by the politicians, not the courts. The Liberals, therefore, also entered into negotiations with the Peckford government to try to find a political solution to the questions of management and benefits. Their negotiating team, led by Energy Minister Jean Chrétien, proposed a joint-management scheme similar to the one between Nova Scotia and Ottawa but in which Ottawa would have the final say in case of disagreement. It was a good proposal, but it could not be turned into an agreement because of Peckford's mistrust of Trudeau.

The Supreme Court of Canada's decision that Ottawa was the sole owner of the off-shore resource was handed down in March 1984; three months later, with a federal election in the offing, Peckford and Mulroney, then opposition leader, signed a letter of intent on the off-shore resources that had actually been negotiated by Carney and the Newfoundland energy minister, William Marshall. The Carney/Marshall agreement was based on the earlier Liberal proposals but with a crucial difference—Ottawa would have no built-in advantage in the management or control of the resources.

The agreement was contained in a letter sent to Peckford by Mulroney on June 14, 1984. In it Mulroney pledged that a Conservative government would "recognize the right of Newfoundland and Labrador to be the principal beneficiary of the wealth of the oil and gas off its shore consistent with a strong and united Canada." To this end there was to be a joint management agency, with equal representation for both parties and independent arbitration in the settlement of disputes. Ottawa would have a preponderant decision-making power over the mode of exploration and the pace of production only until "national self-sufficiency" and security of supply were reached or if, having been reached, were in danger of being lost. The existence of such danger was to be decided by an independent evaluation. Normally, Newfoundland was to make the ultimate decisions in matters affecting the mode of development. This could be overridden by the federal government only if Newfoundland, in the opinion of an independent evaluator, was delaying "the attainment of self-sufficiency and the security of supply." In addition, Newfoundland was to be entitled to the same share of the revenues it would have received if the oil had been found on lands under its jurisdiction. The question of actual ownership was secondary, Mulroney declared, and his government would even be willing to have the agreement entrenched in the constitution by the normal constitutional amendment procedure.

The Mulroney/Peckford agreement was a good start toward an Atlantic Accord, but it was only a start, and after the Conservatives took office in September 1984, Carney placed the achievement of such an accord at the top of her priority list. Not only would it remove a long-standing irritant in Ottawa-Newfoundland relations, it would also be a sign to the other provinces, and especially to the Western producing provinces, that the Mulroney government was ready to make a deal.

Carney went to Newfoundland at the end of November to begin the negotiations. Paul Tellier headed the federal team as he had under the Liberals, but this time Steve Probyn and Harry Near also took part. Carney, Near, and Probyn were very conscious that the establishment and maintenance of trust would be the key to reaching an agreement.

The Mulroney/Peckford understanding had covered considerable ground, but many crucial details remained to be settled, including the size of a promised federal development fund. Negotiations began on November 22, when Carney met Marshall and Peckford in St. John's. There were few problems. Carney told the press on December 13 that agreement had been reached on "all substantive issues" and that the only matters remaining were technical questions that would be ironed out presently. She admitted that she had been in touch with Ontario Premier William Davis to keep him informed about the progress of negotiations and that he had given his approval.

The Atlantic Accord was signed in Ottawa at a meeting between Carney and Marshall on February 7, 1985. Carney had offered Marshall $225 million to underwrite a fund for the upgrading of Newfoundland's oil-related operations and equipment, but Marshall had tried to hold out for more. In Ottawa, Carney was able to convince Marshall that this was the most she could get out of the Cabinet. He accepted and the agreement, based substantially on the Mulroney/Peckford understanding reached the previous July, was complete. It was given Cabinet approval in both capitals the next day and Mulroney and Carney went to St. John's on February 11 to sign it. Peckford told the press that "no other document, including the terms of union . . . come[s] as close to achieving economic and social equality for the people of Newfoundland and Labrador as this." This was as good an example of political hyperbole as Canadians had heard for a long time.

Back in Ottawa there was a standing ovation for Carney in Cabinet and a celebratory dinner for the federal negotiating team.

Jean Chrétien claimed that the agreement was little different from the one he had offered Peckford and that Newfoundland would have been better off financially if it had dealt with him. Perhaps so, but Newfoundland did not deal with him, primarily because of the poisoned atmosphere that had infected federal-provincial relations under Trudeau and that had made the simplest agreements difficult to achieve. In this case it was personality, not ideology, that had made the difference. Carney had given Mulroney his first triumph only five months into his term of office. It was to be his last easy victory.

*   *   *

The negotiations that produced the Atlantic Accord were carried on at the same time as the discussions with the Western producing provinces. They began on October 29 in Vancouver when Carney met the provincial ministers from Saskatchewan, Alberta, and British Columbia: Paul Schoenhals, John Zaozirny, and Stephen Rogers. Through the meeting and those that followed, the most important discussions took place between Carney and Zaozirny. Schoenhals's interventions were limited almost exclusively to heavy oil, Saskatchewan's major concern, while Rogers was interested primarily in natural gas.

Zaozirny and Carney got along well at the start and there was almost immediate agreement on the need to deregulate the Canadian oil price structure and allow prices to move to world levels. But agreement ended there. Although Zaozirny was just as committed as Carney to strengthening the private sector and dismantling the NEP, conflicting interests emerged that dogged the talks for the next several months. Alberta, supported by the other provinces, kept reminding Ottawa of its promises to do away with the PGRT and insisted that there could be no deal if the PGRT were retained in any form. When the October 29 meeting ended, a formal agreement was signed extending current oil prices until the end of January 1985 (thus formalizing the proposals first mooted by Lougheed in early October), and the ministers returned to their respective capitals. In the meantime, the bureaucrats were asked to keep negotiations going.

Carney met with her western counterparts three more times before the end of January—on December 17 in Vancouver, on

January 19 in Ottawa, and on January 27 in Vancouver again—
and she continued to consult quietly with both the Canadian Petroleum Association and the Independent Petroleum Association of
Canada. Carney remained optimistic in public and claimed that
the talks were going well and that it was "better to be slow than
sorry." But there was little real movement on fundamental issues.
Alberta insisted that the PGRT had to go, and federal negotiators
kept coming up with alternatives that would have preserved aspects
of it. One such attempt was called the "mezzanine tax"—a tax
halfway between the PGRT and nothing.

While federal negotiators fended off provincial complaints in
the conference rooms in Ottawa and Vancouver, Carney, Wilson,
and Mulroney tried to come up with a compromise of their own
that would have preserved PGRT revenues, even temporarily, while
meeting the provinces' major objections. When Carney met
Zaozirny and the others in Vancouver on January 27, it was clear
there would be no deal before the deadline ran out. March 31 was
set as a new deadline. Although the ministers were not even close
to agreement on the omnibus issues, they decided to scrap price
controls on oil exports to the United States and to cancel a scheduled increase in natural gas export prices. Both moves were designed
to preserve the Canadian position in the United States where a gas
surplus had started to force prices down.

Although there were no ministerial meetings in February, Ottawa
and the provinces kept the discussions going from a distance while
Zaozirny increased the pressure on the federal Conservatives with
a quick trip to Ottawa to meet the twenty-one Alberta MPs. He laid
out the provincial government's position in detail and the MPs
began to pressure their Cabinet colleagues to make concessions so
as to avoid an Alberta-Ottawa showdown. When Supply and Services Minister Harvie Andre, MP for Calgary Centre, attended a
closed policy workshop on the Alberta economy in Edmonton on
the first weekend in March, he was forced to admit to the press
that Alberta Tories were growing increasingly worried that the
delays in the negotiations were due to Ottawa's failure to dump
the PGRT. As the new deadline neared, Lougheed and Zaozirny
refused to discuss negotiating positions or to speculate about the
outcome of the talks. But by mid-March both business and government sources were telling the press that prospects for an energy
agreement were deteriorating by the hour.

As the deadline loomed in the last two weeks of March, the pace of the discussions quickened. By then it was clear to almost everyone that the PGRT remained the major stumbling block. On March 21, Mulroney moved to break the logjam by agreeing to allow Carney to trade away the PGRT. Since it was obvious that the success of the talks was on the line, Mulroney, Wilson, and Carney decided to phase out the PGRT over several years, but with only a slight reduction in the first two years.

On Monday, March 25, the four energy ministers sat down in the Okanagan room of Vancouver's Four Seasons Hotel to make one last effort to reach an agreement before the deadline ran out. Carney had already met several times with industry representatives in the weeks before this, but neither she nor anyone else could predict the course of the discussions. Three bargaining sessions were held that day and two more the next. The ministers emerged to announce that a Western Accord had been reached. Ottawa's decision to give up the PGRT had been the key to success.

The Western Accord went most of the way to dismantling the NEP. The federal government agreed to phase out the PGRT over a four-year period beginning in 1986, when the 12 percent tax was to drop to 10 percent. It would disappear totally by January 1, 1989. The elimination was scaled in such a way that half the tax would be gone by 1988 and the rest by 1989, thus preserving most of the PGRT for the first three years of the phase-out. Other taxes connected with the NEP were also to be dropped. These included the Petroleum Compensation Charge, the Natural Gas and Gas Liquids Tax, the Incremental Oil Revenue Tax, and the Canadian Ownership Special Charge. The PIP grant program was to be eliminated completely by December 31, 1987. Government price-setting of oil was to end and with it the two-price system for old and new oil first introduced in the 1970s. This, of course, meant world prices for Canadian oil.

At several junctures during the negotiations, Ottawa had insisted that guarantees be put in place to ensure that industry re-invested the revenues Ottawa was forgoing. This was the "use-it-or-lose-it" tax. But no such provision was included in the agreement. Carney told the press that it was in the best economic interests of the industry to re-invest the revenues, even though the Petroleum Monitoring Agency would monitor the degree of re-investment.

Carney believed that world oil prices would remain relatively stable even though they were likely to fall somewhat in the late 1980s before they recovered in the early 1990s. No one seems to have calculated how many jobs were supposed to be created, and in what time period, if prices held firm. Nor did anyone try to determine how far prices would have to fall before it would be virtually impossible for companies to earn profits from even conventional crude production. At that point, economic interest might lead the industry to use its revenues for other things—such as buying out rivals—instead of for job creation.

Although the federal Cabinet, the Alberta government, and most of the oil business hailed the new agreement, the rejoicing was far from universal. Ontario Premier Frank Miller, then in the midst of an election campaign, expressed concern over the possible impact of higher energy prices on Ontario consumers, while Ontario Liberal leader David Peterson claimed that the agreement could cost as many as 50,000 Ontario jobs. Federal NDP energy critic Ian Waddell called the deal a "windfall to the oil companies" and the *Toronto Star* published an editorial bemoaning "Mulroney's great giveaway."

The signing of the Western Accord eliminated most of the NEP and only the back-in and the Petroleum Incentives Program remained. The back-in was unilaterally cancelled by the federal government at the end of October 1985. At the same time Ottawa announced that the Petroleum Incentives Program was to be phased out by the end of March 1986 and replaced by a new Exploration Tax Credit. The move was not greeted with enthusiasm in the oil industry because Canadian companies benefit little from the new system. Calgary oilman and Tory MP Paul Gagnon, for example, fought to keep the PIP grants while the Independent Petroleum Association of Canada, representing most Canadian oil companies, claimed that its members would no longer have "the financial capacity" to continue exploration in the frontier regions once the PIP grants were phased out.

* * *

Natural gas is at least as important as oil in the overall Canadian economic picture and, like oil, had been a controlled commodity for some time when the Tories took power in the fall of 1984. Carney was determined to free gas from government regulation as she had freed oil, but the issue was so complicated that the energy-producing provinces and the federal government had not devoted much time to it during the negotiations leading to the Western Accord. They had, instead, agreed that "a more flexible and market-oriented pricing mechanism" was required and had then called for further studies and negotiations leading to an agreement by November 1, 1985.

The maze of provincial and federal regulations, and contracts between producers, consumers, and suppliers that made up the Canadian gas-pricing system began to develop soon after the completion of TransCanada Pipelines in October 1958. The pipeline was a result of the shared vision of C. D. Howe, Minister of Trade and Commerce in the early 1950s, and a number of pipeline entrepreneurs, for a great west-to-east pipeline to carry natural gas to markets in central Canada. It was at the time of its completion and it remains today the sole means of shipping Alberta gas to Ontario and Quebec—a monopoly.

From the beginning of its operations, TransCanada saw itself as more than just a pipeline. It involved itself in exploration and development and, more important, it became a major purchaser of Alberta gas. Instead of simply shipping gas, for a price, from the Alberta border to central Canadian consumers, it purchased outright most of the gas it shipped and then sold it to the consumers of Ontario and Quebec. This benefited Alberta producers because they sold gas to TransCanada even if there was no immediate market for it in the east.

When Peter Lougheed led his Alberta Conservatives to power in 1971, he was well aware of consistent complaints from some Alberta producers that TransCanada was taking advantage of its monopoly position to keep the price of Alberta gas low. The provincial Energy Resources Conservation Board investigated and concluded that gas was grossly underpriced in Alberta. The Lougheed government responded by passing the Arbitration Act, which gave the provincial government the power to intervene in gas contract negotiations in order to drive up prices. At the same time, the board was ordered to withhold all permits for new contracts with TransCanada until prices were negotiated upwards.

The actual transportation charge levied by TransCanada on the gas it carried (most of which it owned) was regulated by the federal government, first through the Board of Transport Commissioners and later by the National Energy Board.

This already complicated situation was made more so when Canadians awoke to the energy crisis following the 1973 Arab-Israeli war. In 1975, the Trudeau government passed the Petroleum Administration Act which gave Ottawa the power to negotiate "city-gate prices" with the producing provinces. (The city-gate price is the price that TransCanada charges for gas at the point of delivery in Ontario and Quebec, that is, the point at which the gas is turned over to the local gas distribution utility.) From 1975 on, city-gate prices resulted from Alberta/Ottawa negotiations and were tied to crude oil prices.

This was also true of export prices. To export natural gas had always been a principal aim of TransCanada's backers, including the federal and Alberta governments, and there had been much optimism in the late 1950s and early 1960s that Canadian gas fields would soon become suppliers to the United States market. When the federal government began to regulate domestic oil and gas prices in 1975, it also began to set gas export prices tied to Canadian prices. Although Canadian gas was priced about 25 percent higher than American gas in the United States, it sold well during the energy shortages of the late 1970s and the demand for it grew. In 1983 Canada sold almost $4 billion worth of gas in the United States. But when the United States deregulated its own gas industry in the early 1980s, this, combined with a growing over-supply caused by greater conservation, the introduction of Mexican gas, and the development of electric and nuclear alternatives, threatened the Canadian position in the United States market.

The gas price structure was also regulated in other ways. The National Energy Board enforced rules designed to protect Trans-Canada's monopoly position. One such rule was the "displacement provision" which stipulated that TransCanada had to carry gas for other companies only when their carrying contracts ran for at least fifteen years and when their gas represented a net increase in shipments through the pipe and did not simply replace gas that TransCanada would carry. Such protection was necessary because TransCanada was and is a very expensive utility that performs a vital national service. When such provisions were added to the regulations imposed on local gas-carrying utilities by the consuming provinces, the result was an intricate network of paper that was far more difficult to untangle than the entire NEP had been.

* * *

Carney's desire to deregulate the gas-pricing structure had been anticipated by the former Liberal government, which was not blind to falling American gas prices. In mid-July 1984, Liberal Energy Minister Gerald Regan announced a partial deregulation of export prices by allowing Canadian exporters to negotiate prices directly with United States buyers, provided they did not fall below the Toronto city-gate price. The contracts still had to be approved by Ottawa and in November, six Canadian export companies became the first beneficiaries of the new policy when contracts they had negotiated with American buyers were approved by the Mulroney Cabinet.

The partial deregulation helped preserve Canada's normal 5 percent share of the United States market but it did not satisfy the new Conservative government in Ottawa. There had been no time to deregulate the gas industry prior to the completion of the Western Accord, but the energy ministers set a deadline of November 1, 1985, the date by which export contracts had to be negotiated with American buyers. The job was given to the Summit Group, a body formed in 1984, representing the Canadian Petroleum Association, the Independent Petroleum Association of Canada, Trans-Canada Pipelines, and the Ontario utility companies belonging to the Canadian Gas Association and the Ontario Natural Gas Association. The Summit Group began its negotiations shortly after the Western Accord was signed.

If there were any illusions that this industry-based team would be able to avoid the pitfalls of political consideration, they were quickly dispelled. It soon became clear that deregulation meant one thing—lower prices—to Ontario-based consumer companies and another—maintenance of current domestic price levels and greater access to United States markets—to Alberta-based producer companies. These difficulties were compounded by the results of the Ontario election held in May 1985. (Premier Frank Miller's Tories were returned as a minority government by the electors. Within a few weeks, more than forty years of Conservative rule ended when the Liberals and the NDP agreed to throw them out.) Miller was replaced in June by Liberal David Peterson, who appointed Vincent Kerrio to the energy portfolio. Kerrio soon tried to influence the Summit Group negotiations by telling anyone who would listen that Ontario consumers, victimized by the Western Accord, were entitled to buy Alberta gas for less than the price it commanded in the United States.

As early as mid-June, Carney began to worry over the lack of progress. She told a meeting of the Canadian Gas Association in Jasper that the industry would have to set up a new gas pricing system or face continued government regulation. But as the summer dragged on, there was little progress. One reporter noted in July that the silence from the Summit Group spoke volumes "about the degree of uncertainty" surrounding the future of the Canadian gas-pricing system.

At the beginning of September, Carney sent Steve Probyn to Calgary to size up the situation. He found that there had been little progress and concluded that the governments had to get back into the negotiations or there might not be an agreement by November 1. He also discovered that the Western provinces, headed by Alberta, were not at all anxious to reach a deregulation agreement and were apparently acting on the assumption that gas exports were so important to Ottawa that Carney would allow lower export prices whether or not there was an agreement. This, Carney insisted, would not happen. Her only real hold over Alberta and the other producers was her control of gas exports through the National Energy Board. If she allowed the board to chop prices without an agreement, she would lose her hold over Alberta. The gas negotiations thus became a battle of wills between Carney and Zaozirny, with each hoping the other would give way first.

Probyn recommended to Carney that Ottawa concentrate on negotiating with Alberta alone, effectively benching the other players, and on October 11 the intergovernmental talks resumed in Edmonton. Things got worse by the hour. A 3 percent increase in TransCanada's rate for shipping gas was due on November 1.

This had previously been approved by the National Energy Board. If something were not done about it, deregulation would start with increased natural gas prices at a time when the new Liberal government in Ontario was demanding price reductions.

Then there was the growing problem of TransCanada's "take-or-pay" contracts. These were long-term contracts, entered into by TransCanada with producers in the West, under which the pipeline company bought and paid for its gas whether or not there were immediate markets for it. When central Canadian demand for gas dropped during the recession in 1982, TransCanada paid for a lot of gas it could not sell. It had incurred heavy debts and had worked out a repayment scheme with the support of the major banks known as "Top Gas." If, after deregulation, producers and consumers were able to negotiate contracts directly, they could undermine TransCanada's ability to repay its debts by selling off its surplus gas under the Top Gas program.

Other complications abounded. There was the National Energy Board requirement that gas not be exported unless there was a twenty-five year surplus for Canadian needs. Carney was also under increasing pressure from Ontario to deliver lower gas prices. She, in turn, was pressuring Alberta to lower its prices—the Alberta Border Price. Kerrio and his deputy minister Duncan Allan demanded deregulation, lower prices, the renegotiation of existing contracts, and guarantees that Ontario consumers would be able to buy Western Canadian gas for less than United States consumers. Allan, at one point, threatened to buy cheaper United States gas. Zaozirny said he wasn't worried; in public Carney played down the possibility but in private she was furious and told Allan to keep his mouth shut.

There was no agreement in Edmonton. Following the break-up of the meeting, Carney put tremendous pressure on Zaozirny to lower the Alberta border price by 8 percent. Zaozirny, isolated at that point because the Alberta Tories were engaged in a leadership race, resisted, although he agreed to work with the producing companies to absorb the forthcoming TransCanada toll increase. This would stabilize gas prices for Ontario consumers, but it would not lower them. There was, at that time, no compelling economic reason why gas prices in Canada should have been lowered, even though they were dropping in the United States.

Carney's pressure was designed to appease Ontario and resulted from charges made by the new Liberal government that the Western Accord had been a sellout of central Canadian consumers. When the energy ministers met again, this time in Vancouver on October 20, Zaozirny dug in his heels and Carney was forced to give up her efforts to get cheaper gas for Ontario. Even so, the Vancouver talks ended without an agreement after five hours of intense negotiations. The impasse remained: Carney would not allow freer access to the United States market without a domestic agreement; Alberta would not lower its prices; and the other issues remained unresolved.

When the talks resumed in Ottawa on October 30, the deadline loomed and many observers forecast failure. But this time, success was at hand. The answer as to how the rate increase was to be funded was provided by Doug Stoneman of the Canadian Petroleum Association, who suggested that the money come from the Market Development Incentive Program, a federal program meant to encourage the conversion of eastern homes to natural gas that was funded by the gas industry. This program would pay the toll rate increase.

With the funding of the toll increase settled, agreement came quickly on the remaining items. Alberta gave up its power to intervene in gas contract negotiations so as to keep prices up and Ottawa gave up its insistence that the export price of gas be tied to the Toronto city-gate price. Ottawa and the producing provinces agreed that by November 1, 1986, a free market in gas would come into existence. TransCanada's monopoly right to buy the gas that it was shipping east was to lapse. But TransCanada had to be protected: the National Energy Board was charged with solving the Top Gas problem, and it was made clear that the Top Gas burden would have to be shared by purchasers even after November 1, 1986.

Albertans claimed a victory; the government of Ontario saw matters differently. Vincent Kerrio told the *Toronto Star* that the Ontario government was "very, very disappointed the federal energy minister didn't take into account the need of provinces outside the West." But Carney had been forced to choose by Zaozirny's toughness and she had had little choice but to side with Alberta. She had had to find a way to get Alberta to agree to deregulation and to give up its right to intervene in the setting of gas purchase agreements inside the province, or there would have been no deregulation. Short of forcing the situation, there was little she could do. Natural gas is Canada's second largest export commodity. Neither Ottawa nor Alberta could afford to jeopardize Canadian access to American markets. By threatening not to allow the export price on gas to be lowered without a comprehensive agreement, she had pushed Zaozirny as far as she could, and she knew it. Thus the Agreement on Natural Gas Prices and Markets was signed on October 31, signalling the end of a decade of regulation of the Canadian energy industry. Carney had killed the NEP.

* * *

Will OPEC kill Carney's deregulation of oil and gas? The virtual collapse of world oil prices at the beginning of 1986 is having a drastic impact on the Canadian energy industry and on the federal treasury. With oil prices hovering between $11 and $14 U.S. a barrel (the price at the beginning of April 1986), virtually all frontier oil, from the east coast or the Arctic, is too expensive to develop, as is the oil from so-called alternative sources, such as the Alberta oil sands and the heavy oil deposits in Alberta and Saskatchewan. This will delay exploitation of these sources of supply and will increase Canadian reliance on cheaper Middle East oil.

What is worse for Ottawa, however, is that exploration and development in the Canadian energy industry is grinding to a halt. Of approximately 450 rigs in Alberta in mid-April, fewer than thirty were in operation. The entire industry, from supply contractors to petroleum engineering firms, is cutting back. At the same time, the price of natural gas is also falling much faster than most experts predicted. Gas, as one expert put it, will soon be treated like any other commodity.

Carney's "engine of growth" was apparently working until the fall in oil prices. In January 1986, the Canadian Energy Research Institute conducted a survey of 400 oil and gas companies and concluded that capital expenditures in the industry would rise by $1 billion in 1986 and a further $1 billion in 1987. That will not happen; much of the industry will be hard pressed just to hang on and the sector cannot be depended upon to fulfil the great expectations that Carney had for it. The engine of growth is seizing up.

By late April, various bailout and aid schemes were under discussion in Ottawa and the provincial capitals. Saskatchewan Premier Grant Devine suggested establishing a floor price, even though such a move would mean the reintroduction of federal regulation. This, Carney made plain, would not happen. Edmonton offered help to the industry in the form of royalty reductions and, in cooperation with Ottawa and Saskatchewan, promised aid for a heavy oil upgrader plant at Fort Saskatchewan. Ottawa and the producing provinces tried to put together an aid package rumoured to be worth about $1 billion. Included in the discussions were proposals to eliminate the PGRT immediately and drastically reduce provincial royalties. These steps would be far more significant than anything yet done, but they are not without their complications. Both Alberta and Saskatchewan rely heavily on oil royalties and the PGRT still earns Ottawa more than $600 million in revenues, even with the depressed energy market.

It is obvious, at this stage, that events are not turning out as Carney predicted. Of course, the fall in oil prices has in no way been caused by the ending of the NEP, and those who assert that the federal government would have been in a better position to cope with the emergency if the NEP were still in place have not really thought the matter through. True, the NEP allowed Ottawa to control prices and would have enabled the federal government to keep Canadian oil and gas prices artificially high to subsidize the industry. But imagine the hue and cry among the voters if prices at United States gas pumps dropped while those in Canada remained at the same level as before the price collapse! Such an uproar did, in fact, take place in early 1986 when Canadian gasoline prices did not drop as fast as some consumer advocates believed they could.

Carney's dismantling of the NEP may not now be an economic success, but it is one of the few political triumphs the Conservative government has had. This was supposed to be a government that believed in less governmental interference, more competition, and more freedom for private capital to plan, invest, produce, and either fail or prosper as the market dictated. So far, Carney is the only minister who has practised what the Conservatives preached before the September 1984 election. But more than that, the deregulation of the energy industry has been the single most important piece of evidence yet that the Mulroney government has made a clean break with the Trudeau government which preceded it in its conduct of federal-provincial relations. Ottawa is now more or less at peace with Newfoundland and the Western producing provinces and it has demonstrated to all the other provinces through the example of the energy negotiations that it will not impose its will the way that Trudeau once did.

Mulroney's greatest weakness as a prime minister has been his dislike of confrontations. That has led to policy disasters in areas as diverse as Canadian relations with the Americans (the *Polar Sea* voyage) and social policy (the Old Age Security de-indexation debacle). But it has been his greatest strength in the area of federal-provincial relations. He played little direct part in the negotiations leading to deregulation because he was content to give Carney as much leeway as necessary as long as she kept delivering. There were no threats. There were no ultimatums. There were no frosty declarations of the federal government's right to intervene in the energy industry to protect the national interest. The provinces were not treated like naughty or delinquent children. There was a greater measure of trust and civility than there had been for years and this laid the basis for success. Whatever else may be said about the Mulroney government, it has brought respite from the federal-provincial wars that have constantly plagued Canada, and Carney's dismantling of the NEP was an important part of the peace-making process.

Carney's energy policy also remains a workable replacement for the previous regime of regulation, despite the fall in oil and gas prices. The energy industry will finally begin to function in a free market and it will learn what other businesses already know—how to prosper in fat years and how to survive in lean ones. Ottawa will be far less responsible for the industry's successes or failures than it was before and it will also take far fewer rewards. That should lead to greater efficiency and, in the long run, more profits and more jobs. The companies that survive the oil glut of the 1980s will be in fighting trim when the inevitable shortages reappear later in this decade or early in the next.

Pat Carney entered her portfolio determined to shift a decade-old policy and take the federal government out of the business of regulating the distribution and pricing of Canadian energy. She had an agenda and she accomplished her objectives. Although her task was made easier by a growing world surplus and falling world energy prices, none of what she accomplished would have happened by itself. As Jeffrey Simpson of the *Globe and Mail* observed: "If other ministers had moved with the assurance of Miss Carney, no one would even contemplate a one-term Tory government."

Chapter Nine
Who Killed Cock Robin?
The Government
and the Bank Failures

When the doors of Edmonton's Canadian Commercial Bank opened on Monday morning, March 25, 1985, it might have seemed to employees and depositors that it was business as usual. But the bank had been able to open only after a series of hectic meetings involving the chief executive officers of Canada's largest banks, the Cabinet ministers and civil servants responsible for Canada's financial system, and the Governor of the Bank of Canada. When those meetings had started some ninety-six hours before, the Canadian Commercial Bank was on the brink of total collapse—something that had not happened to a Canadian bank since the bankruptcy of the Home Bank of Canada in 1923. The CCB was saved, or so it appeared, only by the hasty negotiation of a bailout package that involved the governments of Canada and Alberta and the six largest banks in the country.

*   *   *

For most of the twentieth century the Canadian banking system has been remarkably stable, perhaps more so than Canadians really deserved. The stability came from a strong conservativism in Canadian banking, the domination of the system by a few large institutions, and close government regulation and supervision of the banking industry, usually with the complete cooperation of the bankers. This situation was a marked contrast to the nineteenth century when many Canadian banks were all too eager to lend money, especially to anyone connected with a railway. (Mentioning a Canadian railway to a London banker in the nineteenth century, however, was a good way to get a door slammed in your face.) Between Confederation in 1867 and the outbreak of World War I, 36 percent of Canadian banks collapsed and, in a large number of those cases, criminal charges were laid. However, during this period, larger, better managed, and more conservative banks, such as the Bank of Montreal and the Bank of Nova Scotia, grew. Their managers favoured the British system of large, stable institutions that lent conservatively, rather than the loose network of local and regional banks that existed in the United States.

Although the overall success rate for American banks was higher than that for Canadian banks, this was due to the strength of the major banks in the great financial centres such as New York, Philadelphia, Boston, or Chicago. In fact, many American banks were far less stable, with narrower capital bases, than the major Canadian banks. Banks in the United States, however, were more responsive to local and regional needs than were the banks in Canada. By 1900 Canadian banking was concentrated in Montreal and Toronto and depositor dollars were flowing from the Maritimes and the West to Ontario and Quebec. Toronto and Montreal bankers were unwilling to lend money to small businesses in the Canadian hinterlands but only too glad to foreclose on Western farmers and Maritime fishermen. This was a constant source of regional grievance for most of the twentieth century.

The growth of the major Canadian banks was greatly enhanced by the foundation of the Canadian Bankers' Association in 1900. A powerful lobby group, the CBA had a strong voice in the decennial process of revising Canadian banking law and in choosing the Minister of Finance. The Association's birth coincided with an increase in the mergers and consolidations that lowered the number but increased the size of Canadian banks and that prompted social reformers to charge that a ''money trust'' was being created. These charges led to demands for government inspection of banks.

It took a major bank failure for the government to move. When the Bank Act was due for revision in 1923, Finance Minister W. S. Fielding claimed that government inspection would entail the creation of a large and costly bureaucratic apparatus that would provide no better guarantee against fraud and mismanagement than the independent auditing system that already existed. Several months later, the Toronto-based Home Bank of Canada failed.

The government investigation into the affairs of the Home Bank revealed a shocking tale of fraud and mismanagement. (Most of the bank's officers escaped punishment although the auditors were eventually hauled off to prison.) Demands for government inspection reached a crescendo, and in 1924 the government responded by creating the Office of the Inspector General of Banks (OIGB) within the Department of Finance. The era of instability had ended, or so it seemed, and although more than 5000 banks failed in the United States during the Great Depression, not a single one failed in Canada.

It was a good record on the face of it, but it was misleading and it lulled Canadians into complacency. Several banks that nearly collapsed in that sixty-year period were saved through merger. The Bank of Weyburn in Saskatchewan, for example, almost went under in the early years of the depressed 1930s. Banks also suffer hard times in periods of prolonged inflation. There were no such periods for almost fifty years after the early 1920s, but when inflation returned, so too did serious problems for Canadian banks.

* * *

The modern era in Canadian banking began with the creation of the Royal Commission on Banking and Currency by the Conservative government of R. B. Bennett in 1933. It recommended the creation of a government-controlled central bank to regulate both credit and the money supply. This was in part a response to reformers who claimed that the Canadian banking system was far too insensitive to the needs of farmers, workers, and small businesses. It was also a way of giving the government greater control over the flow of money in the banking system, something that both the British and American governments had enjoyed for years. The government responded by setting up the Bank of Canada in 1935 as a government-controlled but privately owned institution. Later, in 1938, the Liberal government of William Lyon Mackenzie King nationalized it.

By 1964, mergers and consolidations had lowered the number of federally chartered banks to eight. Only five of these—the Royal Bank, the Bank of Montreal, the Toronto-Dominion Bank, the Bank of Nova Scotia, and the Canadian Imperial Bank of Commerce—were truly national. These banks had also expanded overseas, to the Caribbean, and into the United States and ranked among the largest in the world. Despite this, or perhaps because of it, they remained conservative in their lending policies, giving rise to demands for more flexibility, more competition, or both. This was especially true in the West where a new class of entrepreneurs wanted Western-based banks that would respond to the needs of Western business. They appeared to find an ally in 1964 when the Royal Commission on Banking and Finance recommended "a more open and competitive banking system."

Although the government introduced few of the reforms recommended by the Royal Commission, fresh winds were clearly beginning to blow. The number of Canadian-owned banks expanded from eight to fourteen over the next fifteen years as a result of political pressures, and most of these new banks, like the Canadian Commercial and the Northland, were based in the West. In 1980 the Bank Act was changed to permit the existence of two types of banks; Canadian-owned (Schedule A) and foreign-owned (Schedule B). The latter were forced to live with numerous restrictions. By 1985 there were close to sixty Schedule B banks.

The new banks were primarily commercial banks. They were created to serve businesses, not small depositors. Not only were they small compared to the major chartered banks, but their capital bases were regional and thus narrower. Banks such as the Canadian Commercial loaned their money primarily to the burgeoning (in the late 1970s) real estate and energy industries. Few of their customers were to be found in the more stable service sector or in secondary manufacturing because these industries were under-represented in the West. They were much closer to American-style regionally based institutions than were the older chartered banks. This was something the depositors did not seem to realize. To most Canadians, a bank is a bank is a bank and all banks are equally stable, an attitude reinforced by the introduction of deposit insurance in 1967.

The Canadian banking system was changed dramatically by the rapid expansion of banks (and trust companies) in the 1970s and 1980s and by the movement of deposit-taking institutions into new areas such as the credit card field. But government regulation and inspection did not match this growth and depositors failed to exercise the discretion that all investors should practise whether the investment is a small savings account or a multimillion dollar deposit. They failed to see that banks can collapse and that many of the newer Canadian banks were particularly vulnerable to severe economic downturns. They ignored the warning signs such as the near collapse of the Unity Bank in the late 1970s (it was only saved by a merger with the Provincial Bank). Banks fail all the time in the United States. As Canada moved closer to the American type of system, governments, regulators, and depositors should have realized that Canadians were beginning to run the same risks.

*   *   *

The Canadian Commercial Bank opened for business in June 1976, in two rented rooms in the Edmonton Westin Hotel. As chairman and chief executive officer, Howard Eaton directed it to rapid early success. The late 1970s was the era of the high rollers in Western Canada as world demand pushed energy prices higher and higher. Deals worth hundreds of millions of dollars were made over lunch at the Calgary Petroleum Club. Land flips that doubled the values of properties almost overnight became commonplace. The banks—every one of them—were eager to lend to almost anybody who was drilling a well, building a rig, or buying commercial property. The CCB was no different. It was soon heavily committed in the three booming sectors of the overheated Western economy—energy, real estate, and construction. By the end of 1981, more than 40 percent of the CCB's loan portfolio was in these sectors, more than 43 percent committed in Alberta and British Columbia. That, by any measure, was a narrow capital base, especially because the three were interrelated—a crash in energy would cause a crash in real estate and construction. This began to happen by the end of 1981. The depression in world energy markets hit Alberta hard. Almost overnight the telephones stopped ringing in the offices of the developers, the land flippers, and the mortgage brokers. Bankruptcies rose sharply. Calgary became a ghost town.

The CCB's management may have been worried by the downturn but they, like many other Albertans, thought the boom would soon return. There was a world shortage of oil, wasn't there? Calgary was now a world oil town, wasn't it? So the bank refused to write down many bad loans, capitalized the interest on others (took back interest on loans to customers out of their principal— the equivalent of burning a candle from both ends), and failed to pursue delinquent borrowers. In this regard, the CCB was little different from most banks, large or small, during those times. The larger chartered banks, however, had broad enough capital bases to absorb the losses. The CCB did not. Nonetheless, it continued to look to the future and even expanded into the United States by buying a 39 percent share of the Westlands Bank of Santa Ana, California. The storms of economic depression raged outside but all seemed well within the offices of the CCB, even though by July 1982, the bank had more than $64 million in bad loans on its books.

Where were the inspectors during this period? For the most part, they were busy elsewhere. For years William A. Kennett, the Inspector General of Banks, had been fighting an uphill battle for funds to expand his office (in December 1985, there were only forty-three staff members in his office, supervising about seventy banks). Kennett had spent almost all of his life in government service. He served on the Royal Commission on Banking and Finance and rose through the ranks to be appointed Inspector General in 1977. The position is akin to that of deputy minister in other government departments and is not, as some Canadians assume, an autonomous post such as that of the Auditor General. Kennett, as a deputy minister, reports to his minister who is, in the Mulroney government, the Minister of State for Finance, Barbara McDougall.

As early as May 1982, Kennett told the House of Commons finance committee that he needed more staff. In this decade of budget paring, however, it was asking for too much. Kennett's office thus relied more and more heavily on the audits done by the accounting firms hired by the banks to prepare their annual financial reports. The information he had at hand, therefore, was not gained through independent evaluation, and government decisions based on that information rested on questionable knowledge.

Concerns about the CCB surfaced in Ottawa in late 1982. In January 1983, Howard Eaton had left the bank under something of a cloud because of his association with Leonard Rosenberg, a principal in an enormous Ontario trust company scandal; this, combined with the virtual collapse of the Alberta economy from the twin blows of the recession and the National Energy Program, had stirred rumours of trouble. The Bank of Canada was also warned about the overconcentration of CCB loans in the energy and real estate sectors and informed Kennett. He raised the matter with Finance Minister Marc Lalonde and with the CCB's auditors in January 1983. A few days later, however, Bank of Canada Governor Gerald Bouey gave the CCB a vote of confidence. Bouey's views were backed by an official of the Clarkson Gordon accounting firm, who told Donald Macpherson, the Assistant Inspector General of Banks for the OIGB, that he did not think the bank was in serious trouble over its real estate lending, even though it was hard to judge land values in the West at that point (there was virtually no market for real estate in Alberta). Despite this opinion, an OIGB report on the bank prepared in June 1983, expressed concern over the high rate of capitalization and the failure of the CCB to make adequate provision for loan losses in its financial statements.

The CCB also began to run into difficulties with its American operations. In October 1983, the United States Federal Reserve Board in California audited the Westlands Bank and found it to be in bad shape. The board ordered the bank to cease operations and to come up with at least $15 million U.S. by April 1984, or be closed down. This would have been a tremendous blow to the CCB, and CCB management decided to purchase the rest of the bank in order to keep it going. The total cost of this transaction eventually amounted to close to $100 million.

The CCB's problems mounted in 1984. By the end of that year, its total exposure to loans in the energy and real estate sectors amounted to almost $1.5 billion. An OIGB inspection in May revealed the bank's precarious position and the inspectors expressed concern about "the large amount of non-earning loans [on the CCB's books] and the bank's ability to properly monitor them." This was undoubtedly the reason why the bank added tax credits (owed by the government) to the income side of its ledger in preparing the figures for the audit of the 1984 annual report. The tax credits allowed the bank to claim a total profit for that year of a little over $800,000 even though the bank was, in fact, losing money heavily. Clarkson Gordon and Peat Marwick did the 1984 audit which, although technically correct by accounting methods, did not give a true picture of the bank's health.

The 1984 audit was later severely criticized from several quarters. Instead of giving a current estimate of the value of outstanding loans, the bank used what is called a "baseline value"—a combination of the current estimated value of the loan and the estimated future value of the loan in a more normal market. Although other banks did not use this method to estimate the value of their outstanding loans, they do use it for some accounting purposes. The auditors accepted the practice. The two firms also did not prepare their reports independently (there was no legal requirement for them to do so) and thus one could not be used to check the accuracy of the other. The audit, therefore, showed only what the CCB wanted it to show, yet almost everyone involved in the bailout was to depend heavily on it.

By the end of 1984, falling oil prices were ravaging the American oil industry and banks such as Westlands, heavily involved in energy sector loans, were having difficulty keeping afloat. The Federal Reserve Board audited the Westlands Bank again in September 1984, and found it in bad shape with a high percentage of non-performing loans. They informed the OIGB in Ottawa in February 1985 and added that they believed that about half of the assets of Westlands were bad. This meant that the CCB had to pour even more money into its United States subsidiary or watch it collapse. The situation was clearly critical. Neville Grant of the OIGB warned his superiors on March 6 that the CCB would be "hard pressed to survive in its present form." A meeting to discuss the United States situation was scheduled between Donald Macpherson and the CCB president for March 14, 1985.

* * *

For much of its short history, the Northland Bank story paralleled that of the CCB. It too was founded in 1976 to serve the needs of Westerners and although it was originally financed largely by prairie cooperatives and credit unions, its complexion had changed considerably by 1980. The Northland's first president, Hugh Wil-

son, concentrated on funnelling Northland's funds into foreign
loans, chiefly in Latin America. But this did not satisfy Northland's chairman, Robert Willson, who was anxious to turn the
Northland Bank from foreign to Western Canadian investments.
He engineered Wilson's dismissal in 1979 and the move of the
Northland into the Western energy and real estate sectors. In 1980
several Calgary businessmen bought into Northland, and Robert
Priscoe was lured away from the Mercantile Bank of Canada to
become president. Priscoe pushed aggressively into oil and gas
just before the big collapse of 1981. The bank's profit of $4.3
million in 1981 became a loss of $2 million in 1982 even though
Northland, like the CCB, used tax credits on its books to show a
$1.7 million profit for that year. In 1982, Priscoe was pushed out
and Bill Neapole moved in from Financial Trust of Calgary.

Neapole was determined to turn Northland around. He moved
quickly to reorganize and strengthen the capital base of the bank,
clear bad loans off the books at a reasonable cost, and initiate a
drive to attract retail deposits. He raised over $40 million in new
capital, added 10,000 new accounts and diversified the loan base
by putting new loans on the books, thus diluting bad loans. Neapole
introduced an innovation frowned upon by other bankers: his
bank moved out into the business world to help manage struggling
Northland borrowers in the hope of getting their businesses back
on track. Neapole seemed to have matters well in hand by early
1985. When Gerald McLaughlan of the CCB walked into Donald
Macpherson's Ottawa office on March 14, 1985, however, a train
of events was set in motion that wiped out all of Neapole's work
and brought his bank crashing down.

* * *

Barbara McDougall, the minister responsible for financial institutions, wanted to change the Canadian banking system. She knew
the system well, having spent years as a vice-president of A. E.
Ames, a Toronto-based brokerage house. She lost her job there
when A. E. Ames merged with Dominion Securities in 1981.

McDougall was born in Toronto in 1937 and graduated with an
economics degree from the University of Toronto. She went on to
make her mark as a financial analyst in the world of business,

working for companies such as the Canadian Imperial Bank of Commerce, the *Toronto Star*, and Northwest Trust in Edmonton. She developed a successful sideline as a business journalist in Edmonton and Vancouver in the mid-1970s. When she returned to Toronto to begin working for A. E. Ames, she began to get involved in politics, acting as policy and press adviser to Toronto mayor David Crombie in 1978 and as his campaign manager in the 1979 and 1980 federal elections. In 1984 she took on Liberal Cabinet minister John Roberts in Toronto's upper-middle-class St. Paul's riding, beating him by 4000 votes. As a new MP she hoped for an appointment as a parliamentary secretary, but she was called, instead, to become Minister of State for Finance. She was determined to leave her mark on the portfolio by introducing a series of radical changes to the Canadian financial system.

Canada's once-cozy financial world is supposed to rest on four pillars: the chartered banks, the trust companies, the insurance companies, and the investment brokerage houses. Each is supposed to have its own particular function. Although banks and trust companies both take deposits, the banks are primarily responsible for the vast majority of commercial loans that keep Canadian business in operation. The trust companies are something like United States savings and loan associations or Canadian savings banks and are generally limited to low-risk investments such as mortgages or government securities. The first Canadian trust company opened in 1872 and since the late 1960s there has been a tremendous increase in the size and number of trust companies. The distinction between trust companies and banks is clearly beginning to blur.

Canadian legislation was designed to keep the four pillars as separate as possible, to keep each set of institutions operating in its own independent world. In the highly conservative atmosphere that once shrouded the Canadian financial world, that worked well. But now the same competitive spirit that is beginning to prevail in so many other business sectors has hit the financial community: Canada's financial institutions want to compete with each other.

McDougall recognized these changes, welcomed them, and wanted to push them along. The former government had given her the means—an advisory committee composed of representatives of the finance industry who worked with Mickey Cohen, the deputy minister of finance, to draw up proposals for reform. William Dimma, chairman of Royal-LePage of Toronto, a real estate firm, chaired the group. Their conclusions formed the foundation for a green paper called *The Regulation of Canadian Financial Institutions: Proposals for Discussion*, released on April 15, 1985.

In a speech to the Association of Canadian Bank Analysts and the Toronto Society of Financial Analysts six weeks before the release of the green paper, McDougall outlined the "principles and purposes" she wanted served by the reform process: "The need to reduce conflict of interest and prohibit self-dealing; the need to enhance consumer protection and information; the need to expand competition and promote flexibility and efficiency; the need to keep Canada current with financial marketplace realities worldwide; and the need to foster the expansion of the financial community so as to create more sources of capital for small and medium-sized business—and the consumer."

The green paper proposed far-reaching changes to the Canadian financial system. Among other things, it recommended a new class of financial supermarkets offering one-stop financial services. This was to be done by allowing financial holding companies to own insurance companies, trust companies, stock brokerage houses (where allowed by provincial law), and even a new kind of bank, the Schedule C bank. Most of the regulations governing these new banks would be the same as those regulating the older chartered banks, but with one important difference: no one is allowed to own more than 10 percent of a Schedule A bank but this restriction would be waived for the new Schedule C banks. The measure would make them less responsive to shareholders and more capable of innovation, or so the green paper reasoned.

To police the system, the green paper proposed the establishment of a new financial conflict of interest office, modelled after the United States Securities and Exchange Commission, and the merger of the Department of Insurance (a unit of the Department of Finance responsible for policing the insurance industry) with the OIGB. At the same time, the range of investments open to insurance, trust, and mortgage companies was to be broadened.

McDougall hoped the green paper would be the blueprint for

change. She invited the financial community to give the government its views while the House of Commons standing committee on finance, trade and economic affairs, chaired by Tory MP Don Blenkarn, held hearings on the paper. She expected the Blenkarn committee to report back by September 30 and legislation to be introduced before the end of 1985. "The details of the paper are negotiable," she explained, "the principles are not."

There was some positive reaction to the green paper. William Somerville, president of National Victoria and Grey Trust, told the press that his industry had "fought hard for the latitude to put our deposits into more than just mortgages." Jean-Pierre Bernier, vice-president and general counsel for the Canadian Life and Health Insurance Association, claimed that the paper generally recognized "the reality of the market and the existence of financial conglomerates," referring to institutions such as the Trilon Financial Corporation, controlled by the Bronfman family. But these were the exceptions. Bankers and brokers generally condemned the green paper proposals. Andrew Kniewasser, president of the Investment Dealers' Association, claimed that the four pillars of the financial community would become two and that the two might eventually become one. Robert MacIntosh, president of the Canadian Bankers' Association, called the green paper "a strange document" and complained that it paid little attention to "the need for equal treatment of financial institutions." This need for a "level field" was to become the banks' major rallying cry against the green paper in the months to come.

The green paper was a clear signal that the banks were no longer the favoured institutions of government. McDougall denied that she was interested in "deregulating" finance in the way that Transport Minister Don Mazankowski was proposing to deregulate transportation. But it was clear that she intended to press ahead with the reforms, against the opposition of the banks if necessary. The political support of the new powers in the financial world was clearly seen by Ottawa as every bit as important as that of the older, more established world of high finance. But the bankers need not have worried. The green paper appeared less than three weeks after the CCB bailout and although few people drew any connection between the two events at the time, the destiny of the green paper was to be closely tied to that of the CCB.

The collapse of the Canadian Commercial Bank and the Northland Bank virtually killed the green paper.

* * *

The CCB crisis broke on Thursday, March 14, 1985, when 39-
year-old Gerald W. C. McLaughlan, one of the youngest bank
presidents in Canadian history, walked into the Ottawa office of
Donald Macpherson, Assistant Inspector General of Banks, to tell
him that the CCB was now carrying $255 million in bad loans on
its books—loans that would probably never be collected—which
amounted to almost 10 percent of its listed assets. The bank was in
danger of not being able to meet its obligations to its creditors or
depositors. It was, in other words, on the verge of collapse.

Macpherson knew the CCB was in trouble before McLaughlan
walked into his office but he did not know just how much trouble.
He thought McLaughlan had come to talk about the United States
situation but, instead, the CCB president revealed that his bank
was on the verge of bankruptcy. The two discussed a variety of
possible solutions before McLaughlan returned to Edmonton, but
nothing definite was decided. Macpherson then alerted his boss,
William A. Kennett, who was on vacation in the Caribbean and
Kennett made arrangements to return to Ottawa. After speaking to
Kennett, Macpherson told Bouey about the problem as well as
Elizabeth Roscoe, McDougall's chief of staff. He also wrote a
memo to McDougall telling her that a financial restructuring of
the CCB was the lowest cost option open to the government.

In an effort to save the CCB without government help, Macpherson phoned Allan Taylor of the Royal Bank and asked him if the
Royal would consider a merger with the CCB. Taylor responded
the next day by telling him that the Royal might be willing to
take the CCB over in order to liquidate it, but nothing more. The
following day, Saturday, March 16, Macpherson and Bouey agreed
to call upon the heads of the six largest Canadian banks for help.

On Monday, March 18, Macpherson dispatched Neville Grant
to Edmonton to examine the CCB's books. McLaughlan had told
Macpherson that the bank's problems stemmed from $255 million
of bad loans and Grant was charged with the responsibility of
finding out how accurate that figure was. He conducted a quick

examination at the CCB's head office and finished on Thursday afternoon, March 21. That night he phoned Ottawa to report that he had discovered a further $81 million in bad loans.

* * *

The Conservatives had been categorically opposed to bailouts before they came to power. They based their opposition on a simple argument—if the marketplace has condemned an inefficient company to bankruptcy either because of particular economic circumstances or because of the poor practices of the company's management, the government should not take taxpayers' money and use it to save the company. But now the Conservatives were in power and faced the first failure of a Canadian bank in more than sixty years.

Barbara McDougall was ambivalent about saving the CCB. She did not want to see a disruption of the Alberta economy if the CCB went down, but she was also reluctant to commit public money to its salvation. When Kennett arrived back from vacation on March 20, she told him that she was "inclined to liquidate the bank" and "wanted no investment of government money," even though she was concerned about the possibility of a "disruption of borrowers and business." But her view was overruled when she met with Cohen, Macpherson, Bouey, Kennett, and Finance Minister Michael Wilson at a breakfast meeting on the morning of March 21. At that meeting, Wilson insisted that the bank be saved and that Alberta be brought in on the salvage operation. Cohen roughed out a way of doing it and McDougall agreed with the arrangements.

Although Wilson wanted to save the bank, he could not have known if the bank could be saved, or at what cost, on the basis of any information he had at that point. The fact is that he and Mulroney, who was now being brought into the picture, were in favour of a bailout because of political considerations. Wilson and Mulroney were determined not to let a Western bank go down for fear of losing Western votes and Western strength in the Tory caucus.

At this point, and in the days to follow, Wilson, McDougall, and Bouey were relying on information about the state of the CCB from the Inspector General's office presented to them by Kennett. It later turned out that he was not passing everything along. For example, he never gave McDougall copies of the Federal Reserve Board reports on the CCB's California operations. Those reports would have shown that the CCB's American subsidiary was in deep trouble. There is confusion as to exactly what he told and to whom. The bankers involved in the bailout claim they were never told of the additional $81 million in bad loans identified by Grant on Thursday evening, nor about an additional $35 million in bad loans uncovered over the weekend and reported to Kennett by Grant the following Sunday night. In any case, much of what Kennett did pass on was gained not from his own people, but from the CCB's auditors and he never made this clear to his political masters. At one point a minister asked Kennett if a $240 million package would be enough to save the bank and he responded positively. But the bailout package was not nearly enough and a thorough examination of the CCB's books at that point would have told him so. However, the decision to bail out the CCB was a political one. It would not have mattered much what Kennett said unless he was prepared to resign and place the issue before the public.

There is further evidence of the political nature of the decision to save the bank. Although McDougall and Wilson were constantly briefed by Kennett and Macpherson during the crucial ten days, they never asked for, and were not given, a formal recommendation from the OIGB and this, after all, is one of a deputy minister's chief tasks when government decisions are pending. They relied heavily, instead, on advice garnered from their political staffs and from political advisers and friends outside the government. No one seemed to be interested in whether the bank could be saved at a reasonable cost and if the salvage operation was likely to be a success. Doubtless Bouey, Kennett, and Macpherson gave their opinions on this (as did Mickey Cohen) but most of these opinions were of necessity based on gut feelings, not facts. They did not have the facts. Nor did they have recommendations from the department to guide them.

On Friday morning, March 22, Gerald Bouey welcomed William Mulholland, chairman of the Bank of Montreal; Michel Belanger, chairman of the National Bank; Donald Fullerton, chairman of the Canadian Imperial Bank of Commerce, Cedric Ritchie, chairman of the Bank of Nova Scotia; Robin Korthals, president of the Toronto-Dominion Bank; and Allan Taylor, president of the Royal Bank to the new boardroom in the Bank of Canada Building. Alberta's deputy treasurer Alistair McPherson, Cohen, Kennett, and McLaughlan were also there. Bouey came to the point quickly: the CCB was on the verge of bankruptcy. A decision whether or not to bail the bank out would have to be made by Monday morning, before it was due to open for business. It was the start of a very long weekend.

McLaughlan left to fly back to Edmonton shortly after the meeting began; the other bankers met virtually non-stop with Bouey and the other government officials over the next seventy-two hours while Wilson and McDougall waited in their offices, several blocks away. The bankers were not entirely happy with the information that was provided to them and later claimed they were given only the CCB's first quarter balance sheet and a list of $255 million in bad loans. They were given an opportunity to verify the situation for themselves by sending representatives to meet with Grant in Edmonton on Saturday morning to go through the CCB's books but because of a mix-up, the representatives did not join Grant until Sunday morning. They worked at the CCB's offices most of the day and by evening had discovered an additional $35 million in bad loans. Grant reported this to Kennett by phone but the bankers in Ottawa claimed that they were never told about it. All weekend, therefore, they mulled over the bailout under the mistaken assumption that the CCB was holding slightly more than $250 million in bad loans, when the real figure, it later emerged, was closer to $1 billion.

On Saturday, March 23, Mulroney intervened directly in events at a meeting with Wilson, McDougall, Bouey, Cohen, and Kennett. He wanted the bank saved. He did not want his government anywhere near a bank collapse, especially not that of a Western bank. From this point on, therefore, it was full speed ahead. The bankers returned to Toronto on Saturday afternoon, met there on Sunday morning and flew back to Ottawa Sunday afternoon. They then went into a marathon session Sunday evening that involved negotiations with the CCB's debenture holders, who refused to help out. When the bailout group approached them (most of them trust companies) on Sunday evening to seek a postponement of the payments due to them, they ran into a stone wall: the debenture holders wanted their money. The problem was solved only after British Columbia, Alberta, and Ottawa agreed to buy $39 million worth of CCB debentures from the holders. With this, the last roadblock to a bailout had been passed; the deal was settled at about 6 a.m. on Monday morning.

* * *

Banks are built and sustained on public confidence. Once that confidence has been shaken, it is very difficult to restore. As of Monday, March 25, the public knew about the troubles of the Canadian Commercial Bank and depositors began to leave in droves. By late April the run on the CCB's wholesale deposits threatened the bank once again and the Bank of Canada made what was supposed to be a short-term cash advance to the CCB to cover the disappearing deposits. It also issued a news release to reassure Canadians that it would provide the CCB with whatever support the bank needed to survive. The news release was a signal to the six chartered banks that had participated in the bailout that Bouey was going to cover the CCB's lost deposits no matter what; they began to withdraw their deposits from the stricken bank. By the time the CCB collapsed in late August, they had pulled out $400 million. It was an obvious sign of lack of confidence in an institution they had just helped bail out. Had they learned so quickly the real state of affairs at the CCB and decided to cut their losses? Bouey called the bank heads about this in April but he received little satisfaction. For the next four and a half months, therefore, the Bank of Canada kept pouring more money into the CCB to replace the withdrawals; the total eventually reached $1.2 billion.

The CCB bailout helped kill the Northland. Many large wholesale depositors suddenly grew skittish about leaving their money in small Western banks and the Northland lost $100 million in a three-week period. It too lost deposits from the six chartered banks and was forced to rely on Bank of Canada deposits as replacements. In May and June Neapole struggled to rebuild the deposit base and for a while it appeared that he might succeed. But in June matters suddenly grew worse and the bank's dependence on the Bank of Canada increased. The Northland eventually absorbed about $600 million in Bank of Canada funds.

When the CCB tried to sell off many of its loans in May and June, potential customers offered only 30 to 35 cents on the dollar. On June 12, the House of Commons standing committee on finance, trade and economic affairs issued its report on the circumstances leading up to the CCB bailout. The committee had met in May and early June to investigate events up to March 7. They attacked the bank inspection system and the 1984 audit but reserved their harshest criticism for CCB management: ''In the final analysis, questionable accounting practices, inadequate disclosure, and lax supervision do not by themselves cause bank failures. Bad management and lax credit practices do. Management alone carries responsibility for all its decisions.'' CCB management responded by accusing the committee of ignorance and the selective use of facts. Two weeks later the bank discontinued its regular weekly and monthly internal liquidity tests, a sure sign that management knew the bank was losing the struggle to survive. Although the committee's report could not have inspired much public confidence in the ability of CCB management to save the bank, there was not much public confidence left in the CCB by mid-June.

By July the situation was clearly critical. Wilson began to sound out members of the banking community on what might happen if the CCB were allowed to collapse. Kennett dispatched George Hitchman, retired deputy chairman of the Bank of Nova Scotia, to Edmonton to look into the CCB's loan situation. Hitchman took two former bank executives with him and for thirty-nine days the three examined eighty-four of the bank's 2010 loans. It was a small sample to be sure, but the examination revealed that sixty-one of the eighty-four loans were weak. Hitchman concluded that the CCB would need between $800 million and $1 billion to cover future loan losses. The CCB's total loan portfolio at that time was $2.4 billion. Hitchman submitted his report to Kennett on August 12. In it he concluded, ''The fact that real estate prices went down or drilling rigs were not in demand might have been an added feature [contributing to the collapse], but these loans should not have been made.'' Kennett was ''surprised at the extent of [the] condemnation.''

The whole Hitchman exercise is illuminating. Hitchman and two former bankers had to spend over one month poring over the CCB's books before they were able to get anything like a true

picture of the state of the bank. In March one man—Neville
Grant—had been given three days to size up the bank's condition.
But even then his cursory examination had uncovered far more
damage than bank president McLaughlan had revealed to the
OIGB. This again points to the political nature of the bailout deci-
sion and the scraps of faulty information on which it was based.

While Hitchman was in Edmonton going through the CCB's
books, Bouey and McDougall turned their attention to the Northland. Two inspectors were sent to Edmonton to examine the bank's
loan portfolio while Neapole and Robert Willson were given a
limited time to reorganize or find a merger partner. Ottawa favoured
the National Bank but after National Bank representatives turned
up to examine the Northland's books in late August, they rejected
a merger. Besides, Neapole was against it and was determined to
fight on.

It was a losing battle. By late August the Hitchman report on the
CCB, and the OIGB report on the Northland had convinced Mulroney,
Wilson, and McDougall that nothing further could be done to save
the banks. The Bank of Canada had poured $1.8 billion into the
two banks to keep them afloat and that was enough. It was time to
close them down. On August 30, officials of the other chartered
banks were told of the impending closures and on Sunday, September 1, McDougall announced that the Canadian Commercial
Bank was to be closed immediately and the Northland was to be
placed under supervision in the hope that a merger or buyout of
some sort could be arranged. It was a vain hope. The Northland
was closed on September 30.

*   *   *

There was turmoil in the House of Commons when it resumed.
Opposition leader John Turner charged the government with making "a monumental billion-dollar goof." Calls for the resignation
of Wilson, McDougall, Bouey, and Kennett echoed through the
halls of Parliament. As the uproar mounted, McDougall agreed,
in a meeting with Wilson and Mulroney, to take the blame, even
though she had been the only one of the three to question the
wisdom of a bailout. Wilson had so many disasters to his credit by
this point that one more might have spelled his political doom.

Mulroney defended the bailout in the House of Commons by

citing the need to help ''two fledgling Western-based corporations in need of assistance.'' When the story of the bank withdrawals emerged, he threatened that if anyone had acted illegally, ''immediate prosecutions will be started against them.'' There was, of course, nothing at all illegal about the bank withdrawals. But Mulroney seemed to have a need to show just how stern he could be with the ''fat cats'' of Bay Street. ''It would be preposterous in the extreme, for [those who] contributed money on a Wednesday, to withdraw it on a Thursday . . . If it's the case, we will deal with the utmost severity with the banks of Canada.''

As pressure mounted for a full-scale parliamentary inquiry into the bailout and the collapse, McDougall announced on September 30 the appointment of federal Supreme Court Justice Willard Estey to conduct a judicial inquiry into the bank failures. The opposition and the press were outraged but Mulroney was unmoved: ''The irresponsible and dilatory conduct of the opposition'' had prevented any objective examination by a parliamentary inquiry, he charged. One columnist, John Ferguson, called it ''the old political sidestep'' and claimed that Estey's terms of reference would exclude the government's role in the bailout.

Estey began his hearings in Ottawa on October 2 and later went to Edmonton and Calgary to hear testimony. The charges made by the press and the opposition proved, once again, to be without foundation. Estey dug deeper and deeper and the government provided hundreds of classified documents, many of which were highly embarrassing to it. The inquiry concluded in May 1986 after hundreds of hours of testimony, most of which pointed to basic flaws in the procedures governing the regulation and inspection of Canadian banks and the poor business judgement of those responsible for the Canadian Commercial and Northland banks. Inspector General William Kennett did not wait for the Estey Commission findings before deciding his own future course of action. On Monday, March 10, 1986, he announced his early retirement at the age of fifty-three.

* * *

The bank collapses dragged down the green paper, at least for the time being. Cohen left the Department of Finance at the beginning of June 1985, to join the Reichmann financial empire in Toronto and when he left, much of the impetus for sweeping reform had disappeared. The failure of the CCB and Northland did in the rest. As trust company magnate Hal Jackman (chairman of E-L Financial Corporation) put it: ''The bank situation is so urgent it means all the really controversial aspects of the green paper will be left to one side for a while.'' McDougall was quick to see the writing on the wall and quickly retreated from the strong stand in favour of change she had taken in April. In late September she told the *Financial Post* that the green paper had only been ''a discussion document''; she made plans to implement the green paper recommendations to beef up the OIGB and the Superintendent of Insurance, but did not move on the more radical proposals regarding financial holding companies.

Don Blenkarn's standing committee on finance, trade and economic affairs conducted hearings on the green paper (increasingly referred to as the ''groan paper'') in October. Even before the committee issued its final report in early November, Blenkarn predicted that it would make the green paper ''look like a bunch of crap, which it frankly is.'' He was not far off the mark. The committee recommended scrapping most of the radical changes to the financial system suggested in the green paper, although it called for more competition among banks in Canada and more liberal rules for foreign banks. The committee could see no reason for Canadian banks ''to expect protection from foreign competition in domestic markets.''

Blenkarn was scathing about the inspection system: ''I don't think the people of this country would put up very much longer with an inspection system of banks of the class and kind we've had heretofore,'' he said, calling it a ''tea-and-cookies'' system. Not surprisingly, his committee recommended the creation of a national financial administration agency to police financial institutions. It would be a super-agency, replacing the OIGB, the Superintendent of Insurance, and the Canada Deposit Insurance Corporation (CDIC). It would operate as a crown corporation and its board would consist of representatives from the federal and provincial governments as well as the finance industry. It would have wide-ranging powers to inspect, regulate, and close down financial institutions, and to take action against individuals caught cheating the system. Although pressure began to mount on McDougall in early April 1986 to get on with the job of reforming Canada's financial institutions and the rules by which they do business, there is still, at present, no omnibus legislation on the horizon. It is sorely needed.

At the beginning of April 1986, Imasco Limited launched an attempt to take over the Genstar Corporation, which owns 99 percent of Canada Trustco. If successful, Imasco might have had direct access to Canada Trustco funds to finance Imasco operations. This would have left depositors unprotected and McDougall was forced to introduce ad hoc legislation to ensure that Imasco and Canada Trustco remained separate despite the takeover.

* * *

The government moved quickly to assure uninsured depositors of the Northland and Canadian Commercial Banks who were not covered by the CDIC (the limit of CDIC insurance is $60,000 per depositor) that they would be repaid in full. Affected depositors ranged from a publisher (Mel Hurtig in Edmonton) to small cities (Wetaskiwin, Alberta, and Kanata, Ontario). The largest uninsured depositors were banks, mostly foreign (about $200 million), provincial governments (about $165 million), and corporations ($142 million). Credit unions ($130 million), investment dealers ($110 million), and municipalities ($82 million) ranked next. Individuals— the so-called retail depositors—were owed about $27 million or 3 percent of the total. The bill was $935 million—approximately $525 million to CCB depositors and $411 to those at the Northland Bank. This was over and above the payout of the CDIC to those who were covered by the $60,000 limit; this payout amounted to about $593 million. There was little discussion in government circles over the decision to repay the uninsured depositors: in one way or another all depositors at recently failed deposit-taking institutions (Pioneer Trust and Capital Trust, for example) have been reimbursed. It is clear that whatever the CDIC limit, putting money into a deposit at a Canadian bank or trust company is a sure thing and the normal rules of risk and return do not apply.

McDougall justified the government's action this way: ''The

government of Canada encouraged these depositors and depended on the support of these depositors who continued to participate in the effort to preserve the viability of an important financial institution. We are honouring that implied commitment in the same spirit of responsibility in which it was created.''

The payout legislation was introduced into the House of Commons on October 3. The bailout group was not covered. The government claimed that the six banks involved in the bailout (and Alberta) would realize some return from the sale of CCB assets after the Bank of Canada took its bite; it was CCB's only secured creditor. The bankers were clearly unhappy about the failure of the government to compensate them for their losses. Fullerton of the Canadian Imperial Bank of Commerce claimed that they were protected in writing but Taylor of the Royal Bank and Belanger of the National disagreed, even though they argued that the government had a moral obligation to compensate them for the $60 million they had put in.

* * *

When the government made the original decision to bail out the CCB in March, one of the considerations had been the impact a bank failure would have on the entire Canadian banking system. It affected the small regionally based banks, but the system as a whole sustained the collapse without much damage. Shortly after the Northland collapse, a run on the Mercantile Bank began when the Canadian Bond Rating Service lowered the credit rating of the Mercantile Bank and the Continental Bank. This, combined with depositor nervousness about small banks in general, started a run on the Mercantile. In early October, it was propped up, at government request, by the six banks that had been in on the CCB bailout. At the end of October it was forced to merge with the National Bank of Canada.

As a result of the Mercantile's troubles, rumours began to circulate about the stability of the Continental Bank and the Bank of British Columbia. The OIGB decided it was time to take action to stop further bank runs from developing. The chartered banks lent Ottawa thirty-five auditors, who fanned out across the west to comb the books of the Western and Pacific Bank, the Morguard Bank of Canada, and the Bank of British Columbia, all in Vancouver, and the Bank of Alberta in Edmonton. The audit showed all four to be financially sound.

On October 31, Continental Bank president David Lewis announced that a support package of $1.4 billion had been arranged from the Bank of Canada. In addition, the six largest chartered banks had agreed to extend a $1.5 billion line of credit to the bank. Don Blenkarn, for one, noted the changed attitude of the banks. In the CCB bailout, the six chartered banks had acted like competitors, he charged, yet by the end of October they had started to "realize they are in the same business" and had helped to bail out the Continental. The difficulties faced by the Mercantile and the Continental had one other repercussion. In late November, Morguard was sold to Security Pacific Corporation of Los Angeles.

These events are a strong indication that regionally based banking is on its way out, at least in Western Canada. On February 24, 1986, the CBC broadcast a story that alleged that the Bank of British Columbia had unsuccessfully approached the federal government and the four Western provinces with a request for $800 million in financial assistance. Bank executives did not deny the report and called it "old news" but the next day, the Bank of British Columbia launched a libel action against the CBC and everyone else involved with the story. That did not stop the Canadian Bond Rating Service from alerting its clients on Wednesday that it was now closely watching the bank and could downgrade its bonds at any moment. Bank stock plummeted as rumours of a collapse circulated. In the first week of April 1986, the bank announced that it was closing nineteen of its prairie branches. There can be no doubt, therefore, that the CCB/Northland affair has made the financial community very wary about the viability of Western banks. The virtual collapse of oil prices will make matters even worse for these banks.

There had been fourteen Canadian-owned or Schedule A chartered banks at the beginning of 1985. By the end of the year there were only ten. Nevertheless, 1985 turned out to be a banner year for the six largest Canadian chartered banks. Lower inflation, lower interest rates, and the reawakening of Canadian eco-

nomic activity after the longest and deepest recession since the
Dirty Thirties brought a flood of profits into the major banks. The
CCB and the Northland were dead, but the system lived on.

* * *

Who was responsible for the collapse of the Canadian Commercial Bank and the Northland Bank? The managers of those banks,
who pushed them aggressively into oil and gas, real estate, and
construction in the early 1980s, and who lent money to every
warm body with a deal on a building lot in Calgary or a drilling rig
in Edmonton, were clearly to blame for the banks' shaky finances.
Most of these loans were bad loans from the beginning. Many of
them were capitalized on the basis of highly inflated statements of
net personal worth and were secured by personal guarantees that
were of dubious value. It is no mystery why the banks collapsed.
The mystery is: why did the government try to bail them out?
What information did the government have when it arranged the
March bailout package? What information did the bankers have
and why did they participate in the bailout? How much was lost by
extending the life of the CCB by five months? What does the
episode say about the ability of the government in the spring of
1985 to make tough decisions, quickly, during a time of crisis?

Wilson and Mulroney were determined to save the CCB because
it was a bank and because it was Western. Ideology and theory
went out the window in the face of the stark reality that no government had been touched by a bank failure in sixty-two years. This
young government, so dependent on Western support, was not
anxious to break precedent. The government clearly had very
little real information about the true state of the CCB at its disposal
when it made the decision, but then, the decision was a political
one anyway. Mickey Cohen, for one, later told the Estey inquiry
that the exact numbers did not really matter over that hectic weekend in March. It was the principle of the thing that counted.

Politicians cannot, of course, be blamed for acting like politicians. But the Conservative government had insisted that it would
not intervene in the marketplace as soon as the first crisis came
along. In the banks affair, Tories acted exactly as the Liberals had

done before them. McDougall was played up as a minor hero when it was discovered, as a result of documents tabled at the Estey inquiry, that she had originally opposed the bailout. But if she did so on principle, why did she choose to stay in the Cabinet when the policy she was forced to swallow turned out to be disastrous?

The decision to bail out the depositors was also political, and was the easiest course of action the government could choose. But it perpetuated the belief that "a bank is a bank is a bank" and that there are no risks in dealing, as depositors, with banks. No one told the investment dealer who handled the funds for the City of Kanata to put so much money into a single bank. No one told the city's leaders to approve such an action. That was an investment decision. But the government saved the city (and the dealer) from the consequences of their bad judgement.

No one can possibly determine how much more money, or how much less, would have been lost if the CCB had been allowed to collapse in March. The investors, those who held CCB securities, lost their money in the fall of 1985 as they would have six months before. The bill to the government and to the CDIC might even have been higher in March. Since the government probably would have bailed out the uninsured depositors in any case, it may, in fact, have saved money (even if inadvertently) by keeping the CCB alive until September 1. This is because the two banks had fewer depositors and fewer deposits when they were closed, owing to the loss of investor confidence in them in the preceding months.

As the CCB's only secured creditor, the Bank of Canada will likely recover a large chunk of the money it poured into the CCB from April on. Once the Bank of Canada gets its money back from the sale of the assets of the collapsed banks, the rest of the creditors—the chartered banks who helped with the bailout and the Government of Alberta—will have to stand in line. The banks lost a lot of money but then, in the long run, they may have gained more than they lost by contributing to the death of the green paper proposals to establish financial holding companies and Schedule C banks. The governments of Alberta, British Columbia, and Canada were not as fortunate. They purchased $39 million worth of CCB debentures on the night of Sunday, March 24, which turned out to be worthless. On top of that, the government of Alberta pumped $60 million into the bailout that it will probably never recover.

The collapse of the CCB and the Northland revealed that basic weaknesses had crept into parts of the Canadian banking system because of the rapid expansion which began in the late 1970s. It showed that the inspection and regulation system needed to be overhauled. It demonstrated the incredible naiveté of Canadians when they are dealing with deposit-taking institutions. But most of all, it strengthened the belief among many Canadians that the government did not know what it was doing and that it was afraid to take strong action. In the long run, that may have been the most important result of the banks affair.

Chapter Ten
Marcel Masse
and the Culture Vultures

As Marcel Masse, the Minister of Communications, settled into his new offices, he quickly learned that his transmogrification into the Canadian André Malraux would be more easily said than done. First of all, he took over responsibility for nurturing Canadian culture in a society in which the vast majority of the population placed a higher value on constructing highway overpasses than it did on cultural activities. Second, his mandate was shrinking; the budgets of the various cultural agencies under his aegis had suffered both cutbacks by his Liberal predecessors and the nibbles of inflation. In addition, his own party had come to office believing that big government was an octopus strangling the initiative of Canadians. His department and agencies were not exempt from the Tories' determination to slash spending.

Masse suffered an additional disadvantage. Most politicians can camouflage their actions with smoke and mirrors. But whenever he took to the podium in front of his natural constituency, the minister would be confronting the men and women of the literary and cultural establishment. His audience might, in the minister's view, be composed of decrepit Toronto culture vultures, aging separatists from Montreal's Carré St. Louis and the buy-your-own-theatre crowd from Calgary, but these individuals hold effective and articulate control not only of well-organized lobby groups and newspaper and magazine by-lines, but also of the scholarly establishment.

Masse's powerful position in the new Conservative government could not be denied. He was a member of the Cabinet's priorities and planning committee and was acknowledged from the start as a leading French-Canadian Cabinet member. Despite this, the new minister was virtually unknown to the arts community and to the cultural bureaucrats, who had expected either of the two Toronto MPs, David Crombie or John Bosley, to fill the communications position. Some of the signs were promising—originally a history teacher, Masse had helped found a summer music festival in Joliette. He had also been on the board of the Montreal Symphony (rumour had it that he represented his company, Lavalin, on the board, and although he attended the symphony's business meetings, he did not go to concerts). At the age of thirty, he had served in the Union Nationale government of Daniel Johnson in 1966. Originally on the extreme nationalist wing of his party, he left in 1971 after losing a leadership contest. By then, he had served variously as Minister of Natural Resources, of Education, and of Intergovernmental Affairs. After two unsuccessful tries in 1974 and 1979 to win election to the House of Commons as a Conservative, he carried the Eastern Townships riding of Frontenac in 1984.

Although Masse arrived in the Department of Communications as an unknown, before three months had passed, the press had given Canadians as much information about Marcel Masse as they could easily digest. At the same time, Masse seemed to delight in keeping the departmental printing facilities busy. His office put together hundreds of press releases that outlined the minister's ideas for what he called the "cultural industries." An ambitious man, Masse cast aside the cultural policies that had been developed by the Conservatives in opposition and floundered around to find replacements. In many ways, Masse showed a distinctly conservative bent. Initially he did not want to restrict Canadians' access to foreign culture but to ensure that facilities existed for them to learn about their own. This led him to promote culture not as art but as "big bucks." For the first few months, however, Masse spent his time trying to find ways of establishing political control over his various fiefdoms. It was rather odd that as a former history teacher he had not looked at the past.

* * *

Ever since the founding of the National Gallery on March 6, 1880, the Canadian government had taken upon itself the role of nurturing national cultural institutions. Axiomatically, such intervention lays politicians open to attack, but as long as the government confined itself to providing homes for national treasures, it was fairly safe.

The situation began to change during the 1930s, when the government expanded its functions to include broadcasting and film. Nationalism fueled this intervention and remained the real reason for the government's new role—that of regulation and participation through public corporations that directly delivered services to the Canadian public. The country ended up with private and public systems of broadcasting and film production. Regulation was firmly vested in the hands of the federal government. Until 1958, when the government formed the Board of Broadcast Governors (the forerunner of the Canadian Radio-television and Telecommunications Commission), the Canadian Broadcasting Corporation was both regulator and broadcaster. In 1939, the National Film Board was established to interpret Canada to Canadians through the cinema.

Modelled on a British prototype, the Canada Council set up shop in 1957 to grant money to encourage the arts, humanities, and social sciences. The council was intended to have the freedom to make its grants to performing artists, arts organizations, and academics without government interference. At first, the council maintained its self-sufficiency by using its endowment—the $50 million death duties on the estates of two wealthy Canadians—to make its grants. Under its act, the council was not a government department nor the servant of the minister through whom it reported to Parliament, but was an independent corporation reporting to Parliament directly. This arm's-length relationship was designed to protect the artists and scholars from political figures who might attempt to influence them. The council itself became part of the arts scene by appointing artists to its advisory panels and hiring them as staff members.

But as the Canada Council expanded, it needed more money. In the mid-1960s, it began to receive additional funds from the government to cover its yearly expenses. After 1967, funds for the council appeared annually as part of the government's regular expenditures. The council's financial dependence exposed it to pressures to conform to the government's policy.

Inevitably, the danger of political controversy involving the arts increased as the government took an increasingly active role. Private broadcasters and film makers complained about unfair competition, given the subsidization of the CBC and the National Film Board. There also remained the unresolved question of the degree of freedom that crown agencies should possess. No matter how sympathetic they might be to the arts, politicians resent picking up the arts tab without having complete control over spending.

* * *

Shortly after he took office, Masse was required to recommend spending cuts for inclusion in a financial statement that the Minister of Finance, Michael Wilson, would present to Parliament on November 8. This was undoubtedly difficult for Masse, who had not had time to familiarize himself with the operations under his control and might lay him open to charges of misjudgement based on poor information and prejudice. Naturally, he relied on the bureaucrats who were closest to him—Robert Rabinovitch and David Silcox. Masse was told that the agencies would benefit from some trimming of administrative fat and that this would not affect their programs. It was just what the minister wanted to hear. He had the excuse that he wanted to show the ''nest of Liberals'' who ran the agencies just who was boss.

In making his cuts, Masse did not take into account the legacy he had inherited. In its last months, the Liberal administration had threatened the independence of the Canada Council with Bill C-24, which was designed to tighten governmental control over all crown corporations. The philosophy of the bill was that the government was their sole shareholder and had the right to direct their policies. Prime Minister Trudeau found the idea of the arm's-length relationship of the arts agencies difficult to accept: if they took government money, they should be accountable in the same way as other agencies. This shift in control brought a gentle glow of pleasure to the higher bureaucrats in the Department of Communications, who had long yearned for more clout in the cultural areas.

Timothy Porteous, director of the Canada Council, felt that the bill presented a direct challenge. Since any grants to artists could be viewed as ''inefficient,'' the bill could expose every element of the council's operations to departmental scrutiny. In June 1984, when Bill C-24 came before the House of Commons committee on miscellaneous estimates, the Canada Council was the only federal cultural agency to request an appearance. Robert Rabinovitch, the deputy minister of communications, forbade the council's director or its new chairman, Maureen Forrester (appointed in December 1983), to appear. The council decided to defy the gag order and on June 7, the scheduled day for the committee meeting, Mavor Moore, the former chairman of the Canada Council, published an article in the *Globe and Mail* condemning Rabinovitch's interference as a sinister sign of things to come.

With this, the issue shifted from substance to scandal and the future of the bill was now in doubt. The Conservatives threatened to delay the legislation by proposing amendment after amendment unless the government respected the independence of the agencies. Furious at being outfoxed, the Liberal government caved in and agreed to exempt the agencies in order to get the bill through before the end of the session.

During the election campaign that summer, Brian Mulroney and David Crombie, the Tories' chief spokesman on the arts, remained fierce partisans of the cultural agencies and promised, if elected, to respect the arm's-length relationship and to maintain funding for the arts. But after the Conservative victory, the communications portfolio went to Marcel Masse, whose voice on cultural issues during the campaign had been—to say the least—subdued.

Although Masse did not appear to heed the Conservatives' election promises, the heads of the cultural agencies had them very much in mind in early November when Masse called them together to discuss the cuts. The original invitations were issued to the titular chairmen of some of the agencies, even though the chief administrative officers would have to redo the budgets. Substitutions were finally allowed.

Most of the heads of the cultural agencies seemed almost relieved that the chop was not more severe. Rumours had been rife that the CBC would lose up to $200 million, but the final figure was only $85 million. The Canada Council, however, which had been led to expect a loss of $1 million, was told to prune $3.5 million from its administrative budget of about $14 million (its total government appropriation was $72.4 million). Telefilm Canada was the only agency to escape. A senior departmental official then took the floor with a cautionary word that all those present should sing from the same hymn book.

It may have been the same book, but each member of the chorus sang a different tune. The various boards met in panic to assess the best manner of dealing with the situation. Some bureaucrats in the cultural agencies decided to deal directly with the minister because they felt that the departmental staff was not presenting their cases fairly. The relationship between the minister and Rabinovitch had fallen apart. Masse had obviously not been warned about the ensuing storm by his deputy, one of those most closely identified with the *ancien régime*. The deputy was replaced in January 1985 by deMontigny Marchand. David Silcox, the assistant deputy, lacked the minister's confidence. Patricia Findlay, a policy adviser on the minister's staff, became one of the chief conduits to her boss.

Fearing that a massive cut would change its very nature, the Canada Council decided to slice only $1 million from its administrative budget. In effect, it dared the Department of Communications to retaliate. On November 15, Porteous stated his concern that the Canada Council might have to lay off half its staff because Masse was "very misinformed."

Even those who put the government's plan into effect got caught in the cross-fire. François Macerola, the head of the National Film Board, dutifully carried out his instructions although in one sense he was presiding over the NFB's dismantling. Some of the heads of the other cultural organizations felt he had sold out. Under the Liberals, Macerola had set about making cooperative arrangements with the CBC and private film producers in line with Francis Fox's policy. This greatly displeased the film board's staff, who felt that the board would become little more than a training centre. The Conservative government's November cuts chopped the NFB budget by $1.5 million and eliminated $10 million for administration over the following five years. Although it had prided itself for years on interpreting Canada to Canadians, the board's co-production ventures seemed to swamp its identity. It lacked the influential constituency enjoyed by the CBC and the Canada Council; no one would lobby in its defence. Some serious students of the film industry even felt that the board was blocking the development of that industry in Canada. And the board could not even count on the loyal support of its own staff to keep its national headquarters intact. The heads of the regional film units looked upon the cuts at the Montreal office as a chance to expand their own power bases.

The CBC's response was, in the words of its president, "to adapt to new circumstances." This meant implementing pre-existing plans to reduce its staff and to trim some programs and expansion plans. Juneau then went on the air in a national closed-circuit news conference to announce that some 750 employees would be laid off and that another 300 might leave on early retirement. It was so long Friendly Giant. The CBC also froze its spending for the broadcast fund for film development that was administered by Telefilm Canada and effectively stopped the cameras rolling for independent film producers across the country. Masse appointed an outside committee of three to advise the corporation on how to implement the cuts. This group effectively, if temporarily, usurped the function of the CBC's board of governors, an ineffective body in any case. Masse ignored one fact: if the CBC were to be independent, it had to retain an autonomous board to decide on medium- and long-term policy.

Task forces tend to be hit-and-run—they have no responsibility for implementing the recommendations they make and they suffer from the temptation to propose sweeping changes without paying much attention to detail. Masse's task force left the minister open to charges of political meddling and interference in the CBC's internal affairs.

And yet without Masse's task force as a watchdog, there were doubts as to where the brunt of the CBC cutbacks would fall. On December 18, the press reported that the corporation was trying to cut programming and regional stations rather than the corporation's administration and personnel departments. Naturally, Pierre Juneau denied the allegation, not altogether successfully. Further evidence of tension appeared on the following day, when the minister strongly intimated that the press reports were correct.

In part, the dissension could be attributed to the publicity the cuts had received. The defenders of public broadcasting argued that the cuts would greatly alter the CBC no matter where they were applied. On December 12, the opposition let loose in the House of Commons with a concentrated attack. "The arm's-length relationship has been respected," responded the prime minister. The communications minister further clouded the issue by arguing that the range of French-language programming had to be expanded. Radio-Canada would not rob the CBC; the expansion "would not necessarily come at the expense of the public purse," but rather through marketing francophone productions.

Artists began mobilizing to attack the government. They saw the cuts as a threat to their financial stability. In the regions, many individuals or organizations could not get by without the portion of their income that came from either the CBC or Canada Council grants. They began organizing a series of meetings and rallies that were planned to culminate in late March with a march on Parliament Hill. Thousands of arts supporters attended rallies from Vancouver to Halifax to protest against what they called the threat to Canadian cultural life. The danger that the artists and the Canada Council perceived was that the government was shifting the power in funding cultural activities away from the cultural agencies and toward Masse's own department. They feared that the system of awarding grants after an assessment by peers would be replaced by cultural patronage. (Of course, many of them forgot that the arts establishment tended to favour those who reflected its own image.) The artists' case was strengthened because Masse had sponsored Bill C-20, amendments to broadcasting legislation, which gave the minister power to issue directives to the Canadian Radio-television and Telecommunications Commission.

During the next few months, the cuts, particularly those to the CBC, provoked much debate in the media. On the eve of St Valentine's Day 1985, 1300 people calling themselves the Friends of Public Broadcasting purchased a two-page spread in the *Globe and Mail* for an open letter to Brian Mulroney. It was a denunciation by the cultural and academic establishment of the government's stinginess toward public broadcasting. "We object strongly," they said, "to what we see happening. Budget cuts are being made blindly, with little or no knowledge or concern for the consequences. Canadian culture is too fragile, and the CBC too essential to its healthy development for policies to be formulated by default." The CBC's defenders cited fifty years of service during which the corporation linked Canada from coast to coast—and provided employment for artists. Satellite dishes and advancing technology had weakened remaining barriers to American cultural influences and the best means of defence was to spend money on providing good programs to entice the population to tune in to domestic radio and television. Criticism surfaced even among the government's supporters. Dalton Camp called CBC radio the "best national broadcasting system in the world," and argued that it "really does not need to be put upon at this time, even in so vital a cause as economy."

There were, however, some who approved. From Western Canada, the right-wing columnist, Ralph Hedlin, understandably denounced the protesters as a central Canadian lobby with a Toronto centre of self-interest and concluded that if the CBC were to serve the nation, it had to decentralize. A group of businessmen wanted the CBC's English-language television network sold to private enterprise. In mid-January, Brian Mulroney stopped any speculation about this possibility when he intoned, "The CBC is not for sale."

At the same time, Robert Fulford, the editor of *Saturday Night*, argued that CBC television had long needed the re-evaluation that the cuts might provoke: "I've come to see it as a nearly extinct dinosaur, wandering across the Canadian landscape, forlornly searching for something to do . . . even those dedicated to it can no longer clearly explain why it's needed." In the 1950s, it had had to be all things to all viewers; by the mid-1980s, CBC television programming duplicated that of other Canadian and American networks. The CBC was, said Fulford, "hopelessly confused about its mission." Canadian taxpayers therefore, were paying large sums of money for services that were available elsewhere at no direct cost. The CBC's administration had done nothing to correct the problem. Fulford argued that the corporation should concentrate on the things that it did best: news, documentaries, science and children's programs, and cultural events. A smaller CBC, he concluded, might have a more important place in Canadian life.

Immediately, the *Globe and Mail* weighed in with support. It argued that the Committee of Concerned Canadians and the culture vultures had forgotten the difference between the institutions and culture itself. The *Globe* compounded its heresy by suggesting that Pierre Berton, Farley Mowat, Doris Anderson, Mel Hurtig, and Peter Newman—members of the original postwar cultural establishment—were giving way to a new generation that was more self-reliant and less in need of institutional support.

The Mulroney government, faced at the same time with the ruckus over the threat to universal social programs, was learning costly—but valuable—lessons. The first was that almost every area in which the government spends money develops its own constituency, ready to take to the barricades to defend a threatened spending program. The second was that any government challenge to Canadian cultural institutions would generate a great deal of vociferous disapproval.

Marcel Masse appeared to digest both of these lessons very well. Throughout the fracas, he adopted a position of sweet reason. He would, he admitted, have been wiser to adopt a cultural policy before making cuts, but the party's commitment to reducing the country's deficit had taken precedence. Most unwillingly, he had had to bow to the wish of Cabinet. Of course, Canadian cultural activities needed more money; his series of policy papers on such issues as telecommunications, the performing arts, and the role of other government departments would provide him with a case for increased funding. He hoped to achieve better cooperation through discussion with all cultural groups. He prescribed the all-purpose Tory panacea: better management for the ills besetting deficit-ridden orchestras and theatre companies. "Don't ask us," he urged, "to solve all the situations after three months."

This was the line that Masse took in the winter of 1984-85, as he tried to build up support from his provincial counterparts. In December, he set up a joint committee with the Quebec minister, Jean-François Bertrand, to examine the problems facing French-language television and to recommend a course for the future. At the February 28 meeting of all federal and provincial ministers responsible for culture (the first since 1982), Masse argued that in a period of restraint, they had to collaborate to get the most out of every dollar spent on cultural activities.

This argument may have enabled the minister to talk turkey with his Cabinet, but he still had to reassure the Canadian arts community of the government's commitment to promoting cultural activities. On the National Day for the Arts in late March, 500 artists protested on Parliament Hill. Representatives of cultural organizations and the arts community met with members of the Cabinet and with the minister to express their concerns.

The fuss by the arts lobbyists strengthened the minister's hand when it came to prying concessions from his colleagues. In addition, although the Tories had recognized cultural endeavours as one of their "sacred trusts," it helped to have one of the most powerful Cabinet ministers in charge of the Department of Communications. Masse ended months of uncertainty about the review of Telefilm Canada by increasing from 33 to 49 percent the amount that it could put up for a completely Canadian film production. While the CBC would still have a central role, film makers from the private sector would have a larger part to play as long as they made commitments of air time and funds.

* * *

Just when these efforts at accommodation were getting Masse's relations with the arts community back on track, a public hue and cry about threats to the arm's-length relationship sent him back to square one.

Ever since he had taken office, Masse had been making discontented noises about the Liberal appointees under his authority. Press rumours, fuelled by interviews with the minister, had it that heads were going to roll. Pierre Juneau had served in Trudeau's Cabinet as Minister of Communications in 1980 before his appointment to the presidency of the Canadian Broadcasting Corporation. André Lamy, the head of Telefilm Canada, was Juneau's brother-in-law. Timothy Porteous had worked in Trudeau's leadership campaign and then in the Prime Minister's Office. Gérard Pelletier, the chairman of the board of the National Museums Corporation, had also served in the Trudeau Cabinet. Along with Donald MacSween, the director-general of the National Arts Centre, and Leo Dorais of the Museums, they all claimed that they had earned their spurs as non-partisan public servants. Understandably suspicious, Masse erred in lumping them all together without checking a little deeper.

André Lamy, the head of Telefilm Canada, was the first to go.

Although Masse asked for Lamy's resignation in April, the director-general, in fact, wanted to retire and took advantage of generous severance provisions without a fuss. Masse could not replace Pierre Juneau at the CBC because of the terms of his appointment, but that did not preclude a certain amount of guerilla warfare to try to entice Juneau to quit. Donald MacSween, the director-general of the National Arts Centre, was similarly protected and was a personal friend of Brian Mulroney's to boot. Rumours ran around Ottawa that Marcel Masse had sent indirect messages to Gérard Pelletier to ask him to consider resigning. But without a direct request, Pelletier flatly refused. François Macerola of the National Film Board was dutifully carrying out the government's plans and seemed to be safe. That left Leo Dorais, the secretary general of the National Museums Corporation, and Timothy Porteous of the Canada Council most exposed to enforced resignations. Because they served "at pleasure," the minister had the right to replace them. The persistent rumours of their departures undoubtedly compromised their effectiveness in their jobs.

The Conservatives' commitment to cleaning out Liberals in the cultural agencies also caused some discomfort as the government began to make appointments to the various arts boards. The Liberal-appointed heads of the cultural agencies were not consulted. Consequently, some of the professional arts administrators felt saddled with board members who knew little about the arts at all—let alone the operations of a particular institution. From Port Moody, British Columbia, the Conservatives appointed Alan Egerton Ball to the Canada Council, an optometrist and a Tory worker. Another British Columbian involved in the arts commented, "If you were making up a list of people in B.C. who know something about the arts, I don't think I'd be hard pressed to name 500 people who would be ahead of him." To be sure, the Liberals had indulged in patronage but, the argument ran, they had seldom appointed anyone with no artistic qualifications or interests as a patron of the arts.

Some Conservative appointees wanted to make decisions in the absence of professional staff advisers—a recipe for disaster. The problem seemed to be particularly acute at the Canada Council. Among the thirteen new Conservative appointees, vice-chairman Jacques Lefebvre was a friend of Marcel Masse. Lefebvre had some knowledge of arts organizations for he had served as the chairman of the board of Les Grands Ballets Canadiens in Montreal. But on the council he was seen as the mouthpiece for the minister rather than an independent board member. In newspaper interviews, he espoused the government's initial line that the council was badly run and argued that the artists' protests against the November 1984 cutbacks were misguided. But following the meeting of the Canada Council in June 1985, Lefebvre told several leaders of arts groups that he supported the arm's-length relationship and denied that he was a Tory apologist.

Fears for the arts organizations' independence grew apace with the speculation that MacSween, Porteous, and Dorais would lose their jobs. Finally, Mulroney called his friend MacSween to assure him that his job was safe—a gracious but irrelevant gesture. On June 14, the *Vancouver Sun*'s arts critic, Max Wyman, named July 2 as the day that the director of the Canada Council would be dismissed.

The firings and the patronage appointments were seen as preludes to stripping from the Canada Council the prerogative to make independent decisions about funding for arts groups. The Department of Communications, in fact, had already set a precedent by awarding money to some organizations that had been turned down by the Canada Council and to others for capital expenditures. Worse yet, the groups that enlisted a high-level Tory to plead their case with Masse tended to get preferential treatment. Meanwhile, the Department of Communications had not responded to the Canada Council's request for an additional $10 million to ease the debt burden of some arts bodies that no longer had the funds to sustain the debt. Some of the major arts groups, strapped for funds, were willing to sacrifice the arm's-length principle for cash on the barrelhead—no matter what the source. The council's fight seemed lost on them, even though they might become political eunuchs with regiments of Tories on their boards, afraid to take issue with government policy.

Amidst the rumours of Porteous's dismissal, Maureen Forrester, the chairman of the Canada Council, telexed Mulroney in mid-June and asked for a meeting. She got no reply and went to the press who lapped up her story. The prime minister seemed unwilling to antagonize an important Quebec minister.

Masse tried to nip the controversy in the bud. On June 26, he announced the creation of a task force to examine the financing of the arts in Canada, and to explore the possibility of private fundraising. The following day, his office denied any intention to restructure the Canada Council's arm's-length relationship in achieving his main objective of broadening public and Cabinet support for the cultural sector in Canada. The minister also agreed to see Maureen Forrester on June 28. He assured her that no decision had been made about Porteous's future.

That afternoon, Parliament began its summer vacation. As the MPs fled Ottawa, the deputy minister of communications, deMontigny Marchand, called the director of the Canada Council with an invitation to lunch on July 2. During the course of their telephone conversation, Marchand spilled the beans: the government wanted to replace Porteous and to announce his successor the following week. In return, the department would create a job for Porteous, selling Canadian films and television programs in Los Angeles. Porteous was to respond the following Tuesday.

The reply was not quite what Marchand expected. Determined to take advantage of the threatened dismissal, Porteous launched a broadside to preserve the independence of the cultural agencies at a press conference that afternoon. Word had spread and hundreds attended. He claimed that arts funds would be distributed according to political rather than artistic criteria. The Minister of Communications, he told the audience, had consulted Maureen Forrester neither about his dismissal nor about any possible replacement. Between November and the end of June, Masse had not even met with her. Porteous then slammed the Department of Communications for funding arts organizations directly rather than funnelling money through the council, a politically neutral body. The department had not allocated its money with any thought of the long-term effects. Capital or equipment grants from the department, he pointed out, would increase operating costs and in turn these costs would lead arts bodies to seek more money from the council.

The following day, July 3, the Department of Communications released a letter from Marchand to Masse denying that the conversation with Porteous was to have initiated a dismissal. The intent of the lunch was to be the discussion of "various matters of common interest" of which the Los Angeles job was only one.

"At no time," wrote Marchand, "did I indicate any knowledge of the government's intentions with regard to the Canada Council. Being fully aware of the content of your conversation of the same day with Council chairperson Maureen Forrester, to whom you had clearly said that no decision had been taken by the government, how could I, or anyone for that matter, have made the statements Mr. Porteous attributes to me?" The government denied Porteous's intended dismissal and the department referred all further inquiries to the PMO. This was technically correct, since the Cabinet had not passed the order-in-council, the official instrument.

But the fat was in the fire. Because it was unlikely that Marchand had called Porteous without instructions from the minister, the director's side of the case seemed all the more believable. Editorialists across the country condemned the Tories for their attempts to politicize the arts. Even the kindest of them called for an explanation and a full statement on cultural policy. Others, led by the *Globe and Mail*, demanded a non-partisan replacement as a demonstration of a hands-off approach. Prominent members of the arts community were up in arms again. Even members of Masse's task forces joined the public protest. Quebec editorialists, however, took a milder view: Masse was well regarded in French Canada and Quebec artists did not have an equal fear of American cultural influences. As long as Quebec artists were allowed the freedom to do their work, the way the money was handed out did not interest them.

Realists agreed that as far as his job was concerned, Porteous might as well have poured gasoline on himself and struck a match. But the protest might save the Canada Council and the arm's-length relationship. Curtis Barlow, the president of the Canadian Conference of the Arts, complained that the arts community had had no success in gaining Masse's ear. Despite the minister's denials, some claimed that he had privately admitted his wish to take over the allocation of operating grants to arts bodies. The arts community, therefore, decided to focus its lobbying efforts on Brian Mulroney, hoping that he would force Marcel Masse to leave the Canada Council alone.

Since Masse had gone to spend a holiday at his home in the south of France, he did not respond to Porteous's charge. He left his defence to the prime minister and Lubor Zink of the *Toronto*

Sun. An extreme right-winger, Zink believed that Porteous was part of the "collectivist regimentation of Canada and government control of the arts." Brian Mulroney called Maureen Forrester after Porteous's news conference to reassure her about the government's intentions to make changes to the council only after consulting her.

Throughout the summer, the search went on for a replacement for Timothy Porteous, but the director's press conference and the resulting uproar scuppered any plans for a quick succession. Obviously, the clamour would start again if no credible replacement were to be found. Porteous, a lame duck, languished in official limbo.

But Forrester was consulted both about the candidates for director and about proposed new board members. She took a tough stand and warned of trouble ahead if the government did not respect the arm's-length relationship and continued making grants through the Department of Communications. At the beginning of September, the government announced the appointment of Peter Roberts, the former Canadian ambassador to the Soviet Union, to head the Council. Hidden on the back pages of the press was the firing of Timothy Porteous.

* * *

The fracas following the November cuts and the Porteous *cause célèbre* taught Masse a great deal about getting his own way and navigating the political shoals of cultural policy. His task forces on various aspects of Canadian culture co-opted some potential opponents, deferred potentially contentious questions, and developed policies. The strategy worked and many former critics began to temper their opposition to the minister. The task force on broadcasting was co-chaired by Professor Florian Sauvageau of Laval University and Gerald Caplan, former secretary of the federal New Democratic Party, a group long known for its support of the public broadcasting system. Caplan had joined the Friends of Public Broadcasting in their protest a few months earlier and accepted the appointment because of his conviction that the Conservative government had a commitment to "broadcasting as part of public property." The task force on the film industry set up during the first week of September was largely composed of the private film producers who had long been pressed for a greater slice of the pie.

The task forces gave the minister some breathing space which Masse used to find an issue that redeemed himself to the arts community. He chose publishing.

* * *

When it came to power in September 1984, the Conservative government did not apply the provisions of Bill C-15 to cultural industries. This legislation established Investment Canada, which succeeded the Foreign Investment Review Agency, and was designed to encourage rather than prevent foreign investment. Investment Canada, however, was still required to screen take-overs of industries related to the country's cultural heritage or national identity.

The English-language publishing industry in Canada suffers from endemic problems. There are three different types of publishers: Canadian-owned houses; agencies, which do not publish books themselves but distribute either domestic or foreign titles; and the subsidiaries of foreign firms that publish Canadian authors as well as distribute their parent firm's products.

Although the industry has been exceptionally successful at getting government money by waving the banner of cultural nationalism and rallying the troops, it is also particularly vulnerable to foreign takeovers. In the early 1970s, the sale of Ryerson Press and Gage to American publishing interests led to federal and provincial assistance programs to support Canadian-owned firms. Cultural nationalists could put forward cogent reasons for protection, since many Canadian subsidiaries of American firms were set up merely to flog the products of the parent company. The Association of Canadian Publishers delighted in pointing out that 90 percent of books by Canadian authors were published by Canadian-owned firms.

Even the Tories' decision to exempt the cultural industries from Bill C-15 did not quite satisfy the publishers. They called for mandatory screening and for a precise definition of the exemption for cultural industries—particularly for publishers. The question was more than academic, since Gulf and Western was proposing to take over Prentice-Hall Canada as part of its purchase of the American parent firm.

Before he left for his summer holidays in 1985, Masse had tried to redeem his image which had been tarnished by the Porteous affair. On July 7, he became the champion of all good causes. Emerging from a priorities and planning committee meeting in Baie-Comeau, he nailed his nationalist colours to the masthead. Less than 20 percent of book publishing was in Canadian hands, he said, as he proclaimed a series of new policies to protect the industry from excessive foreign control. Protection for publishing was a perfect prescription for the raucous authors who had been castigating the Minister of Communications. Fifty percent Canadian ownership, no less—such was the minister's aim. Masse told reporters that the government would not look favourably on any attempt to expand foreign ownership in publishing. Joint ventures were all right—one should not make the Americans too nervous. Unfortunately, some acute observers noted that while Masse's statements sounded well, they did not alter the existing arrangement.

By the fall of 1985, the question of the proposed Gulf and Western takeover of Prentice-Hall Canada had been hanging fire for more than eight months and no consensus had emerged. Masse had stated in July that he would allow such indirect acquisitions if the deals did not lessen competition and if the applicant agreed to sell control of the business to Canadians within two years. A Canadian group, which included former Liberal Cabinet minister Roy MacLaren and the owners of Key Porter Books had expressed an interest in Prentice-Hall and this seemed to strengthen the minister's hand. At the end of the first week in September, a newspaper leak reported that Investment Canada opposed the acquisition of Prentice-Hall Canada by Gulf and Western. The Cabinet was to review the decision in six months and only the Cabinet could reverse the agency's position.

Obviously, the situation complicated the government's life. A negative decision would signal to foreign investors that the country was not open for business as the Tories had claimed. Gulf and Western began to make harsh noises in Washington and the question threatened Canada's bona fides in any freer trade discussions. In the House of Commons, the prime minister affirmed that "there are cards that shall never be disposed of, or touched. These deal with our national sovereignty, our independence, and our cultural integrity.'' The Prentice-Hall takeover had become a test of the government's resolve, and Masse epitomized the determination to retain control of the cultural industries. Margaret Atwood commented that ''Marcel Masse, who until recently was seen by the Anglocults as only a slight improvement on Darth Vader, has suddenly emerged—due to his stand on cultural sovereignty vis-a-vis the publishing and film industries—as a veritable Man from Glad.''

Masse's resignation from the Cabinet on September 25 did nothing to diminish his growing stature as the defender of the artists' virtue. Rick Salutin, the playwright, who just a few days before had read to the minister a list of artists' demands, commented: ''I hope his successor will fight the cultural sovereignty question like he did. Masse was fighting the good fight on that one.'' (The sour notes came from the Canada Council, where Franz Kraemer, the music officer, remarked, apropos of Masse's difficulties: ''It couldn't have happened to a nicer man.'')

Two days after Masse quit, Sinclair Stevens reinforced the ex-minister's role as the champion of Canadian culture. The Minister of Regional Industrial Expansion announced that the Cabinet had approved the takeover of Canadian-owned Classics bookstores by the British-controlled W. H. Smith. This left Coles Book Stores, a subsidiary of Southam's, as the only Canadian-owned chain. As the villain of the piece, Stevens provoked criticism from the Opposition in the House of Commons, from book trade representatives, and from members of a Canadian group, forestalled in their efforts to prepare a competing bid. The decision, perceived as the omen of things to come, provoked the cultural nationalists to lament Masse's departure even louder.

While Masse remained on the sidelines, the issues did not. Benoît Bouchard, the acting Minister of Communications, seemed clothed in the spirit of his predecessor. He affirmed the active role of the government: it should preserve cultural sovereignty and protect publishing and broadcasting by keeping these industries out of any free trade negotiations. Both the Canadian ambassador to Washington, Allan Gotlieb, and his American counterpart in Ottawa, Thomas Niles, reported the United States' unhappiness with this approach. Then the Tories began to use cultural sovereignty to shepherd through Bill C-20. The measure, broadened by Conservative backbenchers in committee, gave the Cabinet the ability to provide policy directives to the CRTC. Because the Tory MPs portrayed the bill as a safeguard for cultural sovereignty, this threat to the arm's-length relationship received little publicity. Although still on the benches, Masse coached his temporary replacement to great effect.

Masse's wanderings in the wilderness ended on November 28, when he re-entered the House of Commons cleared of any wrongdoing. His return to the Cabinet occurred just when the government seemed ready to renege on Mulroney's pledge and to use the cultural industries as negotiating tools in freer trade negotiations. The Secretary of State for External Affairs, Joe Clark, had said as much. But Masse soon made it clear to the press that his own views had not changed; he sent Francis Fox and James Marsh, the editor of the *Canadian Encyclopedia*, as emissaries to the provincial capitals. David Peterson quickly took a strong stand supporting Masse's position.

Within a few days of his resuming the reins, the report of Masse's task force on film threatened to spark a confrontation between cultural nationalists and Hollywood. The report took as its theme the thesis that Canadians must own and control the cultural industries and the means of mass communication in order to affirm both cultural and political sovereignty. The task force strongly recommended that Investment Canada ensure greater Canadian control of film distribution operations. It was hardly music to the ears of Gulf and Western, the company that owned Paramount Pictures and was thereby a major Canadian film distributor. Foreign domination of film distribution remained an important reason for the chronic undercapitalization of film companies and the difficulties in financing Canadian feature films. The report urged fiscal incentives to encourage private investment in production, distribution, and export as well as a feature film fund with an annual budget of $60 million.

Federal support for the film industry became one of Marcel Masse's pet projects. Since 1983, when the Canadian Film Development Corporation changed its name to Telefilm Canada, it had administered the Canadian Broadcast Program Development Fund to provide incentives to independent film producers to make television programs rather than feature films. A film producer had to secure a letter of intent from a Canadian broadcaster guaranteeing the appearance of the film on prime-time television. The fund stimulated more than a thousand hours of Canadian programming and encouraged twice as much money from other areas to be devoted to Canadian productions.

But the production of feature films still languished and the 1985 task force recommended direct government participation to overcome the disadvantages of a small domestic market so close to the United States. Further tax incentives would encourage private investment in Canadian-owned film and video production, distribution, and export companies. An aggressive export policy could give Canadian producers access to other revenue and a feature film fund of $60 million would support the creation and marketing of Canadian films from their development through to their distribution. In March 1986, the meeting of federal and provincial ministers discussed the report which Masse had endorsed.

But it was publishing policy and not the film industry that was seen as the acid test of the government's commitment to promoting and protecting Canadian culture. Writers like Margaret Atwood trooped from one ministerial office to another to lobby for cultural sovereignty and for limits on the operations of subsidiaries. During the first months of 1986, that meant trying to stop the government from allowing Gulf and Western to take over Prentice-Hall Canada. Government policy required Gulf and Western to turn over its acquisition to Canadians within two years and the American firm had until the end of January 1986 to prepare a strategy.

The auguries were mixed but not unfavourable to the lobbyists. But the extreme nationalists could not point to unanimous support from the Association of Canadian Publishers, which represented the Canadian-owned firms. Some were uncomfortable that the government was trying to impose its will retroactively on a takeover that had occurred in December 1984—half a year before Masse announced his publishing policy. Others felt that the important point lay in Canadian authors' ability to get published and not in the ownership of the publishing house per se. The motive, however, might have had nothing to do with publishing itself but might indicate the message that the Mulroney government wanted to send to the United States about Canada's willingness to negotiate freer trade. The White House and the American embassy in Ottawa put forward this side of the argument as they pressed the Conservative government to approve the deal.

In a speech to the Canadian Book Publishers' Council at the end of January, Masse reiterated his commitment to the Baie-Comeau announcement. He made it clear that he did not want Canada to be treated as part of the American market. The publishers' group, which represented the bulk of the non-Canadian firms, was not too impressed with what they felt was a policy of expropriation that would not create more Canadian books.

By the beginning of February, Masse began to pass the buck on the Prentice-Hall case. The question, he told reporters, was in the hands of Industry Minister Sinclair Stevens. In mid-March, just before Brian Mulroney was due to visit Washington for his second summit with President Reagan, the Cabinet approved the takeover. Gulf and Western, however, had to sell one of its Canadian subsidiaries. This was Ginn and Company, a textbook company and the smallest of Gulf's Canadian holdings. In addition, Simon and Schuster, another Gulf and Western subsidiary, agreed to retain a Canadian distributor and agreed to promote the works of at least ten Canadian authors through its international distribution network. "We won," declared Stevens, somewhat illogically.

The compromise met with approval in Washington, although the United States government still objected to Masse's publishing policy. "We don't believe there is a relationship between the promotion of Canadian culture and assets which are foreign-owned," commented Harvey Bale, an American trade official.

The decision received more wholehearted approval from Canadians because the buy-back of Ginn made the takeover more palatable to the nationalist Association of Canadian Publishers, which was already cooperating with the Department of Communications to devise a new publishing policy. To the federal-provincial meeting at the beginning of March, Masse had proposed a joint textbook program with an emphasis on buying Canadian books.

By early April, the department sent out a draft of a comprehensive plan which posited that cultural sovereignty, including the economic and financial control of the means of distribution, required a publishing sector with a normal level of participation by Canadians who had access to a domestic market and who were capable of financial self-sufficiency. Given certain factors (the maintenance of foreign investment policy, the protection of the market, and industrial development support), the rationalization of cultural support, along with federal and provincial initiatives, would free publishers from dependence on grants, and free government funds to support purely cultural pursuits. The Canadian Book Publishing Development Program of $7 million administered by the Department of Communications was being spent on cultural rather than on industrial support.

The department had come to feel that grants and incentives were ineffective without structural measures that would give Canadians access to the domestic market. It was prepared to shift the funds for cultural support from the book publishing program to the Canada Council. By releasing money to the Canada Council, the department felt that unprofitable but culturally significant titles would get increased government support.

The ministry, however, wanted to keep control of the industrial elements of publishing. Self-sufficiency could be better maintained by keeping the foreign investment policy that Masse had announced in July. A proposed Canadian cultural investment bank, the equivalent of the Federal Business Development Bank, would, along with tax incentives, improve publishers' access to financing. Since the future of the publishers' postal subsidy was in doubt, the department sought replacements for it. Among them, a likely choice was strengthening a buy-Canadian policy for libraries and schools and joint funding with the provinces to finance textbook publishing.

* * *

By the spring of 1986, Marcel Masse had charmed the culture vultures right out of the trees. In the middle of a government freeze on spending, he had been able to pry $2.2 million from the federal treasury. And to prove he held no grudges, he gave it to the Canada Council, his old adversary, to reduce the deficits of arts organizations. This one-shot donation was an important attempt to dispel fears that the minister was seeking to subvert the council's power and independence.

This impressive display of the minister's political clout was followed within the month by the budget presented by Finance Minister Michael Wilson. The arts community reeled when Wilson announced that federal support for cultural activities would rise by $375 million over five years. (The new $33 million feature film fund to be administered by Telefilm Canada, which partly implemented the film task force's recommendation, the $13 million book publishing development program, and a $5 million grant for the recording industry were all part of it.) This largesse was all the more astonishing, considering the leaks to the press which indicated that the Nielsen task force was going to recommend cutting back on government involvement in the arts and that the budget would be tough for them to swallow.

Would this have happened without the querulous and clamorous cultural sector? Even the provincial ministers were purring at the federal-provincial conference in Montreal during the first week of March. The conference agreed to establish two committees to study ways of ensuring that Canadian films and books gained better access to the Canadian market. This came about although the provinces could not agree on specific buy-Canadian rules nor on using provincial licensing to strengthen Canadian film distribution. But that was for later, and for now Marcel Masse could bask in his accomplishments.

Part Three
Getting on with the Americans

Chapter Eleven
Mulroney's Canada
on the World Stage

Foreign policy is not a subject that has absorbed Canadians in recent years. Under Pierre Trudeau, the country turned its back on the world to concentrate on the struggles between Ottawa and Quebec City. Trudeau had discarded the Canadian foreign policy that Mike Pearson, the "helpful fixer," had built up and maintained, and his interests and talents (aside from regular appearances at Commonwealth and summit meetings) were largely taken up with domestic affairs.

Brian Mulroney was different. He too had to apply his undoubted skills as a negotiator to federal-provincial concerns, but he was also lured by the glamour of the world stage. It was understandably flattering for him to be seen talking as an equal with the likes of Reagan and Thatcher, to be listened to respectfully at summits. Even if Mulroney was new to it, foreign relations had its obvious attractions and its payoffs at home.

To handle the details and the day-to-day questions, Mulroney gave the post of Secretary of State for External Affairs to Joe Clark and that of Minister of National Defence to Robert Coates. As it turned out, neither was especially adroit, and both caused the prime minister more than their fair share of problems.

* * *

To the surprise of many (and particularly those who had joked that he would become high commissioner in Lusaka), Joe Clark, forty-five years old, was named to the portfolio of Secretary of State for External Affairs. It was a generous gesture by a new prime minister to the man he had driven from the leadership of the Conservative party a year earlier. It was also a shrewd move. Generosity to an opponent can backfire, but often it can turn a rival into an ally. A cooperative Clark within the Cabinet was far better than a conniving former prime minister and party leader in exile. The image of John Turner, returning to power a decade after storming out of the Trudeau Cabinet, must have been very much in Mulroney's mind. Moreover, Clark was an experienced politician in a government and caucus that was full of brand-new MPs and ministers. He was too young to be a wise old head, but he had substantial ability and some experience in foreign affairs. These traits made Clark a good choice for the sometimes difficult Department of External Affairs, especially as Mulroney himself had no experience and few fixed views in that area. Clark was also a better choice than Sinclair Stevens, although Stevens had been foreign policy critic in opposition. External Affairs officials and many Canadians interested in foreign policy, who were frightened by Stevens's slasher image, all breathed much easier.

Clark was a moderate man, someone whose behaviour under continuous assault in opposition had won him the public admiration that had always been denied him as prime minister and in his own party. He started off well with his senior officials by telling them that while he was glad they were pleased that he was their minister, he knew it was really just because they had been spared Stevens.

Although Clark was at the helm at External Affairs, he was not to have a free rein in foreign policy. Mulroney did not set up the Cabinet committee on foreign and defence policy, a committee that had been a fixture of government for years. By tradition, the chairman of this committee was the Secretary of State for External Affairs, and that might have been too much power in the hands of an old rival. Instead, Clark and the Minister of National Defence, Robert Coates, were given seats on the priorities and planning committee, the key directing body of ministers. Clark was hardly excluded from a share of real power; but he did not have as much as he might have anticipated.

Clark was sometimes less than surefooted in his new post. For example, he forbade officials in his department to talk to reporters without prior approval. Off-the-record briefings were a departmental tradition and Clark's penchant for secrecy, even though it was shared by the prime minister and those around him, was jarring. It was also unenforceable and self-defeating. The root of it was Clark's deep mistrust of the "intellectually arrogant" (as they were characterized by a Clark aide) officials in his department, an attitude widely believed to be fueled by his wife, Maureen.

The Under-Secretary of State for External Affairs, Marcel Massé (not to be confused with the Minister of Communications), had been appointed Clerk of the Privy Council during Clark's brief stint as prime minister. But at External Affairs five years later, their relationship simply didn't work. "Every time we asked for something," one of Clark's key political aides said, "we were just told no. Massé had gotten very bureaucratic and was giving bad advice."

More problems occurred through sheer sloppiness. A commentary sent on tape by Clark's office to a radio station contained unerased sections of the minister's own dictation. There were no state secrets of any importance on the tape, but the oversight suggested that no one was properly minding the store. On another occasion, Clark, on the advice of his department, told Parliament that no threats had been made against the Turkish Embassy before terrorists attacked the building and killed a security guard. Later, an embarrassed and furious Clark had to admit that he had been misinformed by his officials. Later still, the external affairs minister told the House of Commons that Canada had not been invited to participate in Star Wars—only to discover that an announcement to that effect had just been made at a NATO meeting in Luxembourg. The Canadian ambassador to NATO, the official who should have informed Ottawa of the invitation, had not done so, obeying his instructions from Erik Nielsen, by that time the Minister of National Defence. The contretemps wasn't Clark's fault, any more than the other errors had been, but the recurring troubles all suggested that he had less than a firm grip on his portfolio. The minister's political image also suffered when his brother, a Calgary lawyer, received government legal work. Patronage, the Mulroney government's biggest problem, had even tarnished old squeaky-clean Joe Clark.

Mulroney himself could also twist the knife on occasion, as he did late in November 1984, when Clark made a speech in which he referred to the way a "very powerful elite" of journalists and bureaucrats was out to "get" the new government. The prime minister exploded at the choice of words, and his aides made sure the press learned of his anger. The next spring, when President Reagan slapped a ban on trade with Nicaragua and failed to inform Canada in advance, Clark's instant response was to deplore the lack of consultation and to express regret at the move. Two days later in Bonn, West Germany, however, the prime minister, with a red-faced and nervously smiling Clark at his side, said that he was "not at all" unhappy about the lack of notice. "Why would they call us up to tell us something or ask our advice when they knew our answer in advance?" Mulroney said, effectively cutting the ground out from under his minister's feet. "What do you do?" asked one of Clark's political aides. "Get mad and upset? I don't know if it was important enough to resign over." Perhaps not, but it did suggest that the policy of the government was not entirely clear in the minds of the prime minister and the external affairs minister.

The "poor Joe" image that had dogged Clark as party leader and prime minister seemed ineradicable. Inevitably, that affected the minister's standing with his own officials, and the gaffes, some of which resulted from the inefficiency of officials, increased Clark's problems. Clark remembered all too well the difficulties that Flora MacDonald, external affairs minister in his short-lived government, had had with the mandarins in the Pearson Building. They had their own agenda and sometimes, if it didn't coincide with the government's, the bureaucrats would not budge. Clark was determined that this would not happen to him. The "elitist" officials in the department had to be brought to heel. This meant, for example, that the minister's staff was made large and powerful; it meant that briefings by officials were few and that communications between the under-secretary and the minister infrequent. The department itself had been forced by the Trudeau government to incorporate many of the trade officials of the old Department of Industry, Trade and Commerce. That had cramped External's style and hurt its self-esteem, and the process of digestion was still going on in a department that still considered trade an unsuitable occupation for gentlemen. Worse yet, it had made the External Affairs bureaucracy, which had not been efficient since O. D.

Skelton set the pattern in the late 1920s, more cumbersome than ever with three deputy ministers under the under-secretary.

If Clark was less than happy with his officials, the popular reaction to his green paper on foreign policy, *Competitiveness and Security: Directions for Canada's International Relations*, did little to make him feel easier. Released on May 14, 1985 (just before the Wilson budget slashed Canadian foreign aid spending), the paper posed a series of fifty-two questions on subjects ranging from defence to foreign aid to human rights. Excluded from these questions were the "cornerstones" of Canadian policy, such as Canadian membership in NATO and the United Nations and participation in the defence of North America. Few people disagreed with these cornerstones, but the method employed in the paper seemed evasive. Critics were quick to note that the decisions on free trade with the United States and on Canadian participation in Star Wars research would likely be made before any foreign policy review was complete. Moreover, those areas were seen to be in the hands of the PMO, along with most other Canada-United States questions. Similarly, the sections on collective defence in the review were toned down to banality, largely because the Department of National Defence under Erik Nielsen was doing its own review of policy. As deputy prime minister, Nielsen had enormous clout with Mulroney, far more than Clark. If the green paper was intended to give control of foreign policy back to External Affairs, it had not succeeded. Jeffrey Simpson in the *Globe and Mail* called the exercise "a relentless restatement of the obvious," merely another indication that the Mulroney government was affected by political uncertainty bordering on fear. That might have been the unkindest cut of all for Joe Clark.

By the end of the first year and a half of the Tory government, Clark's stature had not risen noticeably. The government spokesman on the important questions was invariably Mulroney himself. The prime minister basked in the glow of his friendship with Reagan and association with the powerful at the Bonn summit and the Commonwealth heads of government meeting. Poor Joe bore the brunt of the criticism. It was not that he was shut out of power—the Cabinet committee on foreign and defence policy was re-established on July 5, 1985, with Clark as the chairman—so much as that he seemed dogged by bad luck, unable to escape from under the little black cloud that followed him everywhere. Nor was Mulroney deliberately scuttling Clark's efforts to run his department well. After all, Mulroney would suffer if External Affairs looked inept. The prime minister had ample opportunity to castigate Clark in private for his errors while preserving the appearance of cordiality in public. In fact, Clark's aides (if not Mulroney's) spoke feelingly about how highly the prime minister valued their minister, seeing him as one of the few competent ministers at the Cabinet table, one of the few *simpatico* red Tories in a ministry that was skewed well to the right. Nevertheless, Clark had not done terribly well in External Affairs. He had not increased his own prestige in the Cabinet or the country, and he had not given a lead strong enough to enhance his officials' prestige at the committee meetings that really run Canada. Intelligence, ability, and a concern for the Third World did not seem to be sufficient. Luck also played a part in politics, and Joe Clark had none.

* * *

With traditional support in the Maritimes and British Columbia, especially among voters of Anglo-Saxon origin, the Progressive Conservative party in and out of office has always portrayed itself as the advocate of a stronger Canadian military presence. In World Wars I and II, Tories called for conscription and total war, catchphrases that had sunk them for generations in Quebec and with the ethnic communities. John Diefenbaker overcame the liabilities of the past in 1957 and 1958, but he soon forfeited much traditional Conservative support and gravely weakened the party, in the eyes of some of those who had voted for him in 1958, with his equivocal stand on nuclear weapons. The Tories regained some strength by the vigour of their opposition to Paul Hellyer's unification of the armed forces in the 1960s, but their interest in defence questions had seemed minimal during the Trudeau years, except for their general complaints that the Liberal government had allowed the Canadian military to slide toward obsolescence.

The charge was all too true. The subject of defence always seemed slightly embarrassing to Trudeau. Armed forces personnel had shrunk to 82,000 by the end of the regime. Equipment was old and falling apart. By the 1980s, Canada's allies in North

America and Europe were more than slightly annoyed by the weakness of Canada's armed forces.

The problem was most severe for the navy. Many of its twenty-three warships were reaching the point at which it was dangerous to put to sea; only four were less than twenty years old. Some of the electronics aboard the ships were so outdated that they still relied on vacuum tubes, unobtainable except in Eastern Europe. Although the Liberals had launched a six-frigate building program in 1977, the construction period stretched into the far-distant future. By the 1990s, even with the new frigates, the navy would have only ten ships fit to fight.

The air force was in slightly better shape, with new CF-18 fighters coming into service, although its air transport capabilities were sadly deficient. At the same time, the condition of the radar lines in northern Canada had become bad enough to irritate the United States government, which feared attack by the Soviet Union over the North Pole by ICBMs and cruise missiles.

The army was short of modern equipment as well, understrength in Leopard I tanks, almost immobile, and all but defenceless against attacking aircraft. Like all the services, the army had too few men to carry out all its missions. Late in the 1970s, the Liberal government had finally told NATO that it would increase defence spending by 3 percent above inflation each year, a vow that was faithfully kept. Even so, the deficiencies of fifteen years could not be repaired overnight.

In opposition, Mulroney had promised to increase the strength of the forces to 92,000 and his defence critic, Harvie Andre, had said that his party, if elected, would increase spending on defence by 4 percent a year. Mulroney upped the ante to 6 percent and during the election campaign, he proposed a $190 million program, including the recruiting of 2200 servicemen and women in one year, distinctive new uniforms for each of the services, and an increase in capital spending. What the Conservatives would do once they came to power remained to be seen.

* * *

The man put in charge of the Department of National Defence by Mulroney was Robert Coates. A fifty-six-year-old lawyer who had represented the Nova Scotia riding of Cumberland-Colchester since his first election to Parliament in 1957, Coates had written a conspiracy-thesis book about the ouster of Diefenbaker, dramatically entitled *The Night of the Knives*. He had not been in the forefront of those supporting Joe Clark as leader, however, and after the election defeat in 1980, Coates became one of Clark's most vocal opponents in caucus and an early Mulroney loyalist. An inveterate traveller to right-wing regimes, Coates vigorously supported the governments of Taiwan, South Africa, and South Korea. His reputation with External Affairs officers who had to look after him during these travels was not high.

Why Coates got the defence portfolio remains uncertain. Mulroney presumably had to reward some of his right-wing caucus supporters, and Coates probably was less dangerous than some of the others. Coates, however, had ideas of his own. In particular, he wanted to overcome what he saw as the civilian and military bureaucracy's resistance to change. This got him into difficulty at once: before long, the minister's staff was fighting what one aide called an "internal guerilla war—the bureaucracy can make a minister look like an ass very easily and you can't fight back." That was bad enough, but tension between two key members on Coates's personal staff made the problem worse than it had to be. J. Duncan Edmonds, an Ottawa business consultant, was Coates's senior policy adviser and Rick Logan was his political chief of staff. Logan had worked for Coates in opposition and had relayed political scuttlebutt to the Mulroney camp during the anti-Clark struggle. He was to be the focus for many of his minister's subsequent problems. His interference with military decisions was bitterly resented by senior officers at National Defence Headquarters, and his influence on Coates angered Edmonds (who resigned in January 1985). The hallmark of a leader, one general said, is picking good staff people, and Coates failed dismally here.

One of Coates's first acts on taking office was to summon the Chief of the Defence Staff, General G. C. E. Theriault, to discuss new uniforms for the forces. That involved him in a fight at once. Then Coates drew hostile fire when he emerged from a meeting with American Secretary of Defense Casper Weinberger to say that "national defence is a special priority of the Mulroney government." Defence spending was not a universally popular subject in Canada. There was even more criticism after Coates suggested in Winnipeg that the peace movement was in sad shape, which, as he put it, "is only right and proper." He added that in his home province, officials knew how to handle protesters—they threw them in jail. "That was not his most felicitous remark," the prime minister said.

More significantly, Coates won a place on the policy and priorities committee of Cabinet, becoming the first defence minister in years to be at the centre of power. He also launched a study of defence policy, promising to release a green paper in February 1985 and to follow it up with a white paper later in the year. He also promised that Canada would increase the size of its forces in NATO and add six frigates to the navy at a cost of $4.5 billion.

Coates, however, was aware of the financial problems facing the government. As he said in London during a European tour in October 1984, major defence commitments (estimated at $10 billion over the next decade) had to wait until "there is some kind of financial read of just how desperate the financial situation is at home." How desperate it was became clear in November when Finance Minister Michael Wilson cut defence spending to $9.37 billion, a drop of $154 million from the 1985-86 budget of Marc Lalonde. For the first time since 1979, Canada would not meet its commitment to increase defence spending by the promised 3 percent. The reduction was, in fact, more severe, for along with the cut, the additional $190 million Mulroney had promised during the campaign disappeared. "It hurts to say it," one departmental official said grimly, "but we probably would have done better under the Liberals." That setback at the Cabinet table should have sobered Coates—it certainly sobered his officers at defence headquarters—but his statements did not change noticeably in the following weeks. At the beginning of 1985, he was arguing that a defence build-up would help economic recovery, and calling for thousands more regulars and tens of thousands of reservists.

Coates's most important venture was new uniforms for the military, something that the party had promised to satisfy the Tories' civilian constituency, not to meet military demands. Estimates placed the cost between $36 million and $100 million, a large sum when capital spending was much more urgent. Nonetheless, Coates persisted, running into opposition from the Chief of the Defence Staff, who was already frustrated at having to deal with the minister through his political chief of staff and furious at spending money on a nonessential item when the forces had aircraft that could not fly because of a dearth of spare parts. At best, the proposal evoked a tepid response from servicemen, most of whom had worn the green uniform for their entire careers. The public, however, was unquestionably enthusiastic about new uniforms. During the 1985 military tattoo in Ottawa, naval participants appeared in old-style uniforms and the crowd roared. One spectator yelled, "Fuck you, Hellyer," a jab at the Liberal defence minister who had unified the forces, and a shout that evoked huge cheers from the crowd.

The "Coates of many colours" were shown publicly on February 7, 1985. The navy's featured dark blue winter dress and summer whites and the air force's a handsome light blue all year round. The army retained the green winter uniform but received tan summer dress. Rank badges remained the same for all three forces, one sign that unification was not yet out of style. The cost estimate issued at the fashion show was $55.6 million for the new service dress.

As it turned out, the new uniforms were Coates's swan song. On February 12, the Ottawa *Citizen* revealed that Coates, Logan, and one other aide had visited Tiffany's, a sleazy bar with strippers and pornographic films in Lahr, West Germany, on a late November trip to the Canadian Forces base there. According to the newspaper, the minister had spent about "two hours drinking and chatting at the bar with one of the strippers," while his two aides "disappeared with two other women to another part of the establishment." The *Citizen* also suggested that the bar visit might have posed a security risk by opening Coates to blackmail. Certainly that was the view of the most senior civil servants in the Privy Council Office, although Coates sued the newspaper for libel.

The next day should have been one for Tory celebrations in the House, because of the off-shore energy deal that Pat Carney, the Minister of Energy, Mines and Resources, had negotiated with Newfoundland. However, the House fell silent when Coates announced his resignation, which had apparently been asked for by Mulroney and offered by Coates. The prime minister told the country that he had learned of the allegations on January 22, investigated them, and "assured myself that at no time and in no circumstances was the national security of Canada compromised in any way." Why then had Coates resigned? Mulroney said only that the minister's judgement had been poor. No clear answer was forthcoming. Some people suggested that Coates had stepped down to spare his family embarrassment or because he had belatedly realized that he was unable to handle the defence job and had left at the first opportunity. According to rumours, Coates had talked with the deputy prime minister, Erik Nielsen, who, when Coates said that he was thinking of resigning, said, "Good."

Equally puzzling was the source of the Tiffany's tale. The *Citizen* noted that Logan, who resigned with Coates, had bragged about the incident when the minister's party returned to Canada. Others suggested that senior officers, unhappy with Coates's style and his lack of clout in the Cabinet, had seized the opportunity to oust him, or, most likely of all, that Duncan Edmonds, who had resigned on January 17, had tipped off Gordon Osbaldeston, the Clerk of the Privy Council, about the events in Lahr. The one certainty is that few, if any, tears were shed at National Defence Headquarters when Coates departed for the back benches. The affair hurt the government, particularly since Solicitor General Elmer MacKay was under fire at the same time for his conversations with Richard Hatfield, the New Brunswick Tory premier, who was in difficulties on a marijuana possession charge.

In Coates's place, as acting minister, came Joe Clark. Clark would have been less than human if he had not relished the turn of events that sent him to replace Coates, not least because the two men disliked each other. But Clark's appointment was only temporary and, although speculation about a permanent replacement focused on Harvie Andre, the Minister of Supply and Services, and Allan McKinnon, defence minister in the 1979-80 government, Mulroney confounded everyone and delighted the Department of National Defence by selecting Erik Nielsen, the deputy prime minister, for the post. (Andre later became Associate Minister of National Defence, with responsibility for day-to-day operations.)

Without a doubt, Nielsen was one of the most powerful ministers in the Mulroney government. An RCAF aircrew officer during World War II with a Distinguished Flying Cross to his credit, a lawyer first elected to Parliament in 1958 from the Yukon, Nielsen, sixty-one, had established his reputation in the scandal sessions of 1964, 1965, and 1966. A fierce Diefenbaker supporter, a ferocious Grit-hater, Nielsen had uncovered scandals right and left and had destroyed the careers of three Pearson government ministers: Guy Favreau, Maurice Lamontagne, and René Tremblay. All were francophones, and in the atmosphere of the 1960s, that was enough to win Nielsen the reputation of being unsympathetic to Quebec and its aspirations. The distinguishing factor in Nielsen's long years in the House was loyalty—once Stanfield succeeded Diefenbaker, he had the Yukon MP's full support, as did Clark when he took over. Now Mulroney had his devotion, and Nielsen, the man who enforced caucus and Cabinet discipline, the man who headed the task forces looking at ways to save money in all departments and agencies, the vice-chairman of Cabinet's most powerful committee, the priorities and planning committee, and a member of all other Cabinet committees, was now also Minister of National Defence.

For the officers of the department, this was the best choice imaginable. Instead of a weak minister with a tendency to go off half-cocked, they now had potentially the most powerful peacetime minister since Brooke Claxton held the portfolio before and after the Korean War. With the department in need of equipment and hungry for a bigger slice of the budget pie, officers openly said that this was their chance, possibly their last chance, to create a modern military force. As important, Nielsen was one minister who could counter Clark's external affairs department and possibly make the case for Canadian participation in and endorsement of Star Wars research.

One sign that the service chiefs might be right came at once when Nielsen, on March 11, just two weeks after his appointment, announced that Canada would send an additional 1200 troops to serve with the brigade group in NATO. The additional cost per year would amount to $100 million. The new defence minister got the credit, even though the idea had come from Derek Burney, the organizer of the Quebec City summit of March 1985. Burney had simply wanted a little extra frosting on the summit cake to please Reagan, and the military was astonished. Soon afterwards, Nielsen tabled an outline of the $7 billion Canada-United States overhaul of the Arctic radar warning system with Canada's share being just over 10 percent. The agreement to upgrade the North Warning System was signed at the summit. Before long, National Defence's new and powerful budget muscle was alarming other departments. It was seventh heaven at National Defence Headquarters on Laurier Avenue.

However, senior officers soon began to suggest that Nielsen really had no clear goal to achieve at Defence, that there was neither plan nor policy. In part, this attitude was a direct result of Nielsen's penchant for secrecy and for keeping officers working in one area isolated from others in different areas. If there was a plan, only the minister would know all the details—a foolish way to proceed in a large organization. The certainty was that Nielsen's white paper, like the green paper Coates had got under way, was nowhere in evidence. Initially scheduled for release in late 1985, the paper was rescued from cancellation in the spring of 1986 and handed to a surprised Harvie Andre by the prime minister. As his responsibility for the department increased, Andre seemed prepared to devote more time to the white paper than Nielsen. However, most of those working on the white paper predicted that, if and when it did appear, either it would recommend only minor tinkering with present commitments or it would recommend cuts. If Nielsen and Andre could not protect the vital commitments and deliver enough money for the Canadian Forces to carry out their missions, the disillusionment among serving officers would be very great indeed.

What made the doubters at National Defence even more unhappy was that Nielsen was proving more trouble-prone than they had expected. There was consternation in December 1985, when the minister defended his department's refusal to release the titles of eight agreements with the United States on a list presented to a parliamentary committee; this was followed by embarrassment when someone remembered that the full titles had been made public by the Trudeau government five years earlier.

More important, at the end of January 1986, a reporter for the *Toronto Star* discovered an interview Nielsen had taped in 1973. In the transcript, which had been available in the Public Archives for years, Nielsen admitted to having eavesdropped on Liberal caucuses during the 1960s. This was old news, events that had taken place during the most disgraceful era of Parliament and something that could and should have been explained away with a simple apology. Unfortunately, Nielsen and Mulroney exacerbated the situation by refusing to apologize and arguing in legalese. The opposition, eager to get at Nielsen, one of the most unpopular members in the House, walked out in protest at the Tory stonewalling. Not until four days later did Nielsen issue a quasi-apology: "I apologize to those who believe that proprieties were violated," the minister said. John Crosbie, the Minister of Justice, also had to eat humble pie for his too-enthusiastic defence of his colleague. It was a minor but revealing incident that demonstrated the eagerness of the opposition and the press to attack Nielsen, showed that Mulroney's instincts were far from infallible, and demonstrated that Nielsen's toughness could be a liability.

By the spring of 1986, observers were betting that Nielsen would retire early. The budget, issued on February 26, increased the odds that his departure would come soon. Although the icy defence minister dutifully applauded Wilson's speech in the House, the results were disastrous for the armed forces. Instead of the 6 percent increase in defence spending that Mulroney had promised, the increase for the 1986-87 year was to be only 2.75 percent and, in the following years, 2.5 percent. In effect, National Defence would lose $285 million over the next two years. Officials, noting that capital expenditure programs on the books included a low-level air defence system for the country's NATO troops, the modernization of four old Tribal Class destroyers into air defence ships, new rifles (at $925 each), and the North Warning System, conceded that one or more simply had to be deferred.

By the end of March 1986, the ship refits had been approved at $1.4 billion, a decision that virtually guaranteed that the LLAD system for the NATO forces would proceed very slowly. (In April, the government did announce that Litton Systems had won the LLAD competition, as well as the ship refit contract, but no final papers were signed. The opposition argued that the P.E.I. provincial election and Litton's promise to locate a radar plant in Charlottetown had helped determine the choice. If the Mulroney government was trying to help its friends on the Island, the effort failed on April 22, when Joe Ghiz's Liberals swept into power.

The contract was duly removed from P.E.I.) The forces did get the go-ahead to increase their strength by 1752 persons and to raise the NATO troop strength by 970; 1062 civilian employees were to be cut.

What had happened, it was clear, was that Erik Nielsen had lost the battle of the budget to Michael Wilson. Insiders suggested that Nielsen must have concurred in the decision, such was his influence with Mulroney. Whatever the sequence of events, Canada's promises to its allies and Mulroney's promises to the country had been tossed in the discard. Erik Nielsen, National Defence's first minister in years with clout, had not lived up to expectations.

Chapter Twelve
Star Wars, the *Polar Sea*, and Acid Rain

The Mulroney government's first goal on taking power was to create better relations with the United States. Under Pierre Trudeau, the relationship had grown strained and the small fissures that inevitably exist between two neighbouring countries had developed into gaping chasms. The cerebral Trudeau had had little in common with Nixon, Ford, Carter, or Reagan, and he had sometimes failed to conceal his contempt for the lesser men who ruled the strongest power on earth. Personalities mattered, but there were great issues at stake between Canada and the United States too, questions of trade, superpower diplomacy, and defence. There were the National Energy Program, the discriminatory provisions directed at advertisers on border television stations, and environmental problems such as acid rain.

Mulroney wanted to do better than his predecessor. Before coming to power, the new prime minister had never shown much interest in questions of foreign policy. He knew the United States well, however; as chief executive officer of the Iron Ore Company of Canada, an American subsidiary, he had rubbed shoulders with businessmen like those surrounding President Reagan. Mulroney spoke business-talk, and he had convinced himself that he could deal with the Americans. The jocularity, the back-slapping blarney and storytelling that were the staples of the prime minister's sometimes overpowering charm could, he was sure, work in Washington as well as in Ottawa.

There were reasons for this hope. Mulroney was convinced that American investment was necessary to galvanize the Canadian economy, and he feared that investors would stay away in droves if the air between Ottawa and Washington was as foul with abuse as it had been under the Liberals. He knew—if he did not quite understand—the sensitivity of nationalistic Canadians to American investment and the power of Reagan's America, but he believed that these, like all problems, could be managed. He could see benefits for his country and government from friendliness with the Reagan administration. Part of Mulroney's optimism was probably a by-product of his all-too-obvious desire to be seen to be sharing confidences with the great and powerful. But most of it undoubtedly sprang from Mulroney's conviction that he could bargain effectively with Reagan, a task he had set himself even before the September 1984 election and which he pursued with intensity after it.

Mulroney and Reagan's shared Irish heritage gave the two men, each the intellectual peer of the other, something to talk about and they soon established a genuine rapport with each other. The two men, the septuagenarian movie-actor-turned-president and the much younger lawyer and former branch-plant executive, liked each other, even if Brian Mulroney's beliefs did not, as some Canadians had feared, make him the Reagan of the North.

But charm alone was not enough when dealing with the White House, the Department of State, Congress, and the hundreds of agencies that had an interest in the trans-border relationship. Before he had been in office very long, the prime minister found that the United States administration was aggressive and determined to get its own way. Some issues could be managed, but decisions had to be taken too. And very often those decisions were harder to make than Mulroney had anticipated before he came to power.

* * *

Canada shares the continent with a superpower and that simple fact of geography governs almost every aspect of Canadian life. For almost fifty years, that propinquity has played a vital role in Canadian defence. Ever since Franklin Roosevelt and Mackenzie King signed the Ogdensburg Agreement in 1940, the two countries have cooperated formally and wholeheartedly in defending North America. The wartime arrangement was followed in the Cold War years by a host of additional agreements for joint training, for cooperation in industrial mobilization, for radar warning lines, and for common air defence under NORAD (the North American Air Defence Agreement). The men and women of each country's armed forces have worked well together, the professional Canadians benefiting from exposure to the superior technology of the Americans.

At the political level, however, troubles have been more frequent. Touchy Canadian politicians have always resented getting their orders from the Pentagon and the utter insensitivity to Canadian sovereignty occasionally shown by American officers. The latter has been a recurring complaint since World War II and the era of the "Army of Occupation" that built the Alaska Highway through the Northwest. During the furor over Canadian acceptance of nuclear weapons in 1962-63, defence questions nearly paralysed all relations between Ottawa and Washington. But the nuclear debate demonstrated that the Canadian public sometimes perceived defence as important enough to override nationalist concerns and that it viewed Washington as the leader and the guarantor of Canadian and western security. The fall of Diefenbaker and the election results in 1963 showed that Canadians wanted to cooperate with the Americans, and no government after 1963 was bold enough to oppose Washington on issues of fundamental continental security. Trudeau might have cut troop strength in NATO, but he did not lead Canada out of NORAD, and he accepted the testing of cruise missiles over Canada early in the 1980s.

For Brian Mulroney, a man without any background in foreign policy or defence, Canada's relations with the United States in an era of Star Wars must have seemed bewildering. President Reagan's call for a Strategic Defense Initiative in March 1983 had Buck Rogers overtones to it, but the proposed defence system against intercontinental ballistic missiles (which some saw as profoundly destabilizing to the system of deterrence that had preserved a precarious peace) also carried serious implications for arms control, east-west relations, and the future of the western alliance. The money involved was staggering— Reagan initially directed $26 billion to research.

When Mulroney took over, he had to confront the question of Canada's role in SDI. Would the country be asked to participate in the research and, if so, should it? Would the Americans link the

Canadian reaction to SDI to policy in other areas? For example, what were the implications for Mulroney's efforts to build closer relations to the United States if Canada said no? Could a refusal to participate in Star Wars affect free trade if the government decided to seek it? Would any of the radars, lasers, and missiles that could make up SDI have to be stationed in Canada? Did Canada's continued participation in NORAD have any implications for SDI? And, given the high rate of unemployment in Canada, would participation in SDI create jobs? All of those questions remained unanswered as Mulroney settled into office in the fall of 1984. None could be easily answered, and the government's initial handling of the question suggested the degree of uncertainty it felt.

In December 1984, Joe Clark hinted at a NATO meeting in Brussels that there were divisions in the Cabinet over Star Wars. This was a reference to the differences between his Department of External Affairs and the Department of National Defence, led at the time by Robert Coates. Coates did not hesitate to proclaim that Canada would benefit economically if it could get major SDI research contracts. For his part, Clark stated the obvious: the defence minister was "more enthusiastic" than he was about SDI. But if there were serious divisions, the prime minister overlooked them when he said that Canada had not been invited to participate and would continue its policy of pressing "incessantly for the elimination of all instruments that damage the cause of peace."

A few days later, on December 23, Mulroney (showing his red Tory streak) noted that he was "less than enthusiastic" about participating in the "militarization of space." But in January 1985, after the Soviet Union agreed to resume discussions on arms control with Washington (a step that SDI supporters hailed as demonstrating the potency of their weapon system), the government line began to change. Joe Clark told Parliament on January 20 that although SDI was "highly hypothetical," nonetheless, "in the light of significant Soviet advances in ballistic missile defence research in recent years and deployment of an actual ballistic missile defence system, it is only prudent that the West keep abreast of the feasibility of such projects." Knowledgeable Canadian officials privately supported SDI research, justifying their stance by pointing out that since the United States was going ahead with it anyway, it was a waste of time to oppose the inevitable. They added, however, that the Americans were ahead in virtually every area of anti-missile defence now and for the foreseeable future and that close study of Reagan's statements on SDI suggested that even the American president knew this. Nonetheless, that this was indeed the new Canadian line became certain when the prime minister defended SDI by saying that the proposal "merits the approval of an ally while negotiations between the superpowers were under way." Did that mean Canadian participation? No, Joe Clark said on February 5, "there is no plan, current, pending, or anticipated, that would have the government of Canada involved in any way in the Strategic Defense Initiative." The critics on the opposition benches, led by Pauline Jewett of the NDP and Lloyd Axworthy of the Liberals (who sounded much more militant in the cause of peace as an opposition MP than he had as a Cabinet minister), quickly reacted when they learned of the discussions with the United States about the North Warning System. This had to be connected to SDI, they said fearfully. In fact, the modernization plan was directed against Soviet cruise missiles. Robert Coates, in any case, was ready for the critics: "There is no current or projected plan regarding replacement of the [thirty-year old] DEW [Distant Early Warning] line" that would involve Canada "in any aspect of U.S. strategic defence initiatives." However, defence officials argued that the radar upgrading would strengthen sovereignty: the system was to be run and manned by Canadians, an improvement over the heavy American involvement in the DEW line.

In February 1985, MPs learned that a sentence that had put strong barriers in the way of Canadian participation in ballistic missile defence systems had been deleted from the NORAD treaty in 1981. Shortly thereafter, Paul Nitze, one of the American "arms control ambassadors," told reporters in Ottawa that he could not rule out using the North Warning System as a component of SDI. "That remains to be seen," Nitze said. "This is a research program that hasn't yet resulted in the development of specific systems." That was true enough, but what disturbed some Canadians was that some components of the projected SDI, such as the Airborne Optical System, the Terminal Imaging Radar, and the High Altitude Endo-Atmospheric Defense Interceptor, might have to be based in

Canada. The next day, both External Affairs and the State Department called the press reports of Nitze's remarks misleading, adding that the two countries "have not discussed any expansion of the North Warning System into an anti-ballistic missile defence system and no such discussions are planned."

If that sounded clear, it wasn't. Almost simultaneously, Richard Burt, the American Assistant Secretary of State for Canadian Affairs, told the press that the new warning system in the Arctic was designed to meet the missile threat. Upon learning that this contradicted Canadian statements, Burt, scrambling, said that he had been in error. The confusion deepened at the Quebec City summit on March 17 when, after the agreement on the North Warning System was signed, American Defense Secretary Casper Weinberger said on television that his government might some day want to put weapons in Canada as part of a joint upgrading of air defences. Reagan also referred to possible Canadian involvement in SDI. Clearly no one in either Washington or in Ottawa knew what was happening, and if the American tactic was to pressure Canada and to mobilize Canadian opinion, it was not working.

Erik Nielsen had been Minister of National Defence for only a short time since Robert Coates's self-immolation, but he was already sounding much like his predecessor. He did his bit to help the country out of its confusion by telling a parliamentary committee a few days after the Quebec summit that all the "options are open" on SDI. Joe Clark said much the same thing to the committee, adding that no invitation to participate had been received from the United States and that no decision would be made until such an invitation was offered. On March 23, the prime minister helped out by saying that his government would consider participating if asked, if there were possibilities for job creation.

Two days later, Fred Iklé, the American Under-Secretary of Defense for Policy, said flatly that Canada had been invited to participate as part of a "continuing process" of negotiations over shared defence systems. Joe Clark categorically denied any invitation: "Mr. Iklé," he insisted, "was wrong." But Clark looked foolish when reports from Europe the same day (where Erik Nielsen was attending a NATO meeting) made it absolutely clear that a formal invitation, asking for a response within sixty days, had just been received. Clark had been let down by Nielsen, who had failed to inform Ottawa of the American invitation, and by the bureaucracy at External Affairs, which had not delivered the message.

What had happened, NATO insiders said later, was that Weinberger decided to release the invitation to the NATO allies only on the air journey to Europe, thereby catching everyone off guard. The Norwegians, for example, told the press they had not been invited, only to discover that their reporters had the text of the letter. In other words, Clark's embarrassment sprang from the bureaucracy's failure to communicate with Ottawa, and, more crucially, from Weinberger's sloppiness—something of which Canadian officials, unimpressed with Weinberger's intelligence and his grasp of the issues, were sharply critical.

The fact that the Americans had made an offer did not mean that Canada was going to take a role in SDI. A few days later, Mulroney told a Baie-Comeau press conference that it was one thing to support American research. "It is another—quite another—to be invited to participate actively in a project where you are not the big player, where you don't set the thrust, and where you have no control over the parameters." What Canada would do, the prime minister declared, "will be in the interests of Canada as a sovereign nation, a loyal ally, and as a believer in freedom. Those are the criteria upon which the decision will be made."

In this confused atmosphere, Mulroney finally did the sensible thing. On April 19, on the suggestion of Gordon Osbaldeston, the Clerk of the Privy Council, he named Arthur Kroeger to head a study of possible Canadian participation in Star Wars research. Clark told the press that the government needed more information and that Kroeger was to "take a hard look at its strategic implications, its scientific implications, its economic implications, so that the government of Canada will be in a position to judge knowledgeably whether Canadians would want to become involved in the research." The issue could now simmer on the back burner for a few months, and the government could deflect all questions by advising everyone to wait for Kroeger.

Kroeger was worth waiting for. A deputy minister since 1974, he had begun his career as a foreign service officer in External Affairs, where he made himself an expert on defence. After serving as the Treasury Board's watchdog on defence spending, he became deputy minister of Indian Affairs and Northern Development in 1974, deputy minister of Transport in 1979, and deputy minister in Economic and Regional Development. He had stage-managed Mulroney's National Economic Conference in March 1985, and he had helped to ensure that the much-maligned conference was, if not a great success, at least not a disaster. (After his SDI stint, Kroeger would become Sinclair Stevens's deputy in the Department of Regional Industrial Expansion late in 1985.)

Kroeger talked first to officials in National Defence to help him with his SDI task. Then he went to Washington and Europe to find out if Canada would be expected to pay a share of Star Wars' costs in order to get some of the research contracts. His job was also to estimate the number and the value of the contracts Canada might receive.

He quickly found the answers. Although Reagan's proposed $26 billion for SDI research sounded like a vast sum, the numbers were inflated. In the first place, the five-year SDI research plan amounted only to about 15 percent of the United States' research budget over that period. Nor was it all new money. The Pentagon had sponsored anti-missile research for almost three decades at huge cost. In other words, only about $10 billion over five years was new money, and even that smaller figure was so large that Department of Defense officers claimed that they were not quite sure how to spend the money. (One External Affairs official commented drily that he was sure the Pentagon would find a way.) Nor could Canada expect to get much in even the best of circumstances. The American military was protectionist and Canada had never received more than scraps from the great barbecue: ordinarily only 0.66 percent of American procurement is spent in Canada. In the SDI-induced confusion in Washington, no one could tell Kroeger how much Canada might get from SDI research, so he simply applied the 0.66 percent to the $26 billion and divided by five years. The resulting figure—just over $30 million a year—was a relatively small sum. Canada could say no to SDI without losing anything much in terms of jobs or dollars.

But more than dollars were involved. Reagan had tied his place in history to SDI and the dream of removing the nuclear threat from the world (or at least from the United States). Given this hope and the state of the bilateral relationship, Canada could not simply dismiss SDI as a chimera. Here too, Kroeger discovered that matters were not quite what they seemed. Weinberger had promised large contracts to his NATO allies in March; but in Washington, Pentagon officers quickly pointed out that, really, they didn't need any help, thank you. If any research contracts were to go to Canada, they could be handled easily enough under the existing web of agreements and committees. Nor was Canada asked to put up any money of its own (although any offers would be gratefully received). In June, officials said that if the Canadian government did not want to participate officially, no one would be upset so long as no barriers were placed in the way of private contracts. The Americans, one official close to Kroeger said, were so embarrassed by their inability to deliver on Weinberger's grandiose promise (and by the unwillingness of most of their allies to participate) that they actually expressed relief that Canada might permit its companies to bid.

The lines of the Kroeger report were thus fairly clear by the beginning of June, although the report itself was not handed to the prime minister until the end of the month. There was little money to be made from SDI and little to be lost in terms of Canadian-American relations by giving a governmental ''no thanks'' to the American invitation. Kroeger's report laid out the issues (avoiding any recommendations in the best official Ottawa style) in two papers, a five-page one for the planning and priorities committee of Cabinet, and a twenty-page one for Mulroney's staff. The text of both remains secret.

In the meantime, Joe Clark had grown concerned about public opinion on SDI. A genuine populist, Clark truly believed that Canadian foreign policy would be improved if the people had a say and if the widespread belief that foreign policy was elitist could be countered. Other than through opinion polls (which in July 1985 showed 53 percent in favour of participation in SDI research), how could this be achieved?

The government answer was to create a parliamentary committee on international relations, jointly chaired by Tom Hockin, an MP from London, Ontario, and a former political science professor at York University; and by Senator Jacques Flynn, one-time minister in the Diefenbaker and Clark governments. The committee was asked to report by August 23 with recommendations on SDI and free trade, the two major issues of Canada-United States relations. Hockin was the effective head of the committee. Long interested in foreign policy, and the author of important articles on the subject, Hockin had desperately wanted the job to show that he was Cabinet material.

To Hockin, the problem posed by SDI was not primarily one of bilateral relations. Nor was the fear of making Reagan unhappy very important. The real difficulty facing the Mulroney government, he believed, lay with the Canadian people: could they trust the Tories to defend Canadian national interests? With that as his concern, Hockin and the committee toured the country, astonished by the interest that SDI and free trade aroused. Aerospace industry spokesmen promised to create 50,000 jobs if SDI research were encouraged. Supporters of the Americans and NATO urged Canada to do its bit. Peace groups sent representatives too, and the anti-Americanism that is never far below the ordinarily placid exterior of most Canadians surfaced in denunciations of Reagan and all his works. What was important, however, was that people came from hundreds of miles away to say their piece for five minutes. Hockin opened the doors wide and allowed ordinary men and women to walk in off the street to give their opinions. It was all very refreshing—and a smart move by the government.

It was, however, difficult to manage. Hockin encouraged the Liberals, themselves badly split, to write the basic report on free trade, but the SDI issue required more delicate handling. If the Tories on the committee said yes to direct government participation in SDI, the opposition would be certain to shout that Mulroney had issued his orders, even though Hockin was adamant that he had been left entirely free to manage the committee. If the government members said no, then the opposition was equally certain to claim credit. As it was, the Conservative MPs and senators were almost evenly split on the merits of SDI research, and in the circumstances, Hockin did the best he could, producing a report right on his deadline that said the committee had too little information to make a firm judgement. That suggested, the report said, an interim no to direct government participation in SDI. That was the best course in political terms, one that meshed neatly with Kroeger's report.

Thus, by the end of August, Mulroney had the basis of a decision. He was greatly assisted by the summer's *Polar Sea* incident, which had led Canadians all across the country to take a dim view of Washington's intentions and which had forced the government to emphasize sovereignty. Now, if the prime minister said no to SDI, much of the criticism that was sure to fall on the government when he announced his decision to seek free trade negotiations with the United States later in September could be dissipated. Moreover, Mulroney was well aware of polls by Decima Research, the party's opinion sounding machine, that demonstrated that peace issues continued to be important to Canadians. What could be more peaceful than to say no to SDI research?

On September 7, after full discussions in Cabinet and caucus, Mulroney announced that his government "has concluded that Canada's own policies and priorities do not warrant a government-to-government effort in support of SDI research." On the other hand, he said, private companies would have no barriers placed in their way if they sought contracts.

Mulroney's decision was immediately applauded by peace groups, most of them hitherto critical of government policy. Even the opposition beamed—and tried to take the credit: "It's a great victory for us," said Jean Chrétien, the Liberal party's foreign affairs critic. Not even Washington was upset. A White House spokesman said the president, called by Mulroney to be informed of the decision, had thanked Mulroney for the "opportunity to work with Canadian private corporations." Mulroney had escaped with some credit from an issue that had bedevilled the government for months. The credit for his policy really belonged to Arthur Kroeger and Tom Hockin, however.

Equally important in all this, from the government's point of view, was the fact that Canadian industrial interests were not hurt by the SDI decision. Despite all the lobbying by the aerospace industry before the Hockin committee and in ministerial offices, as late as November 1985 not a single Canadian company had even expressed interest in securing SDI work. Four months later, General Abrahamson, the head of the SDI organization in Washington, could still say that no Canadian company had yet submitted a serious proposal for SDI research. Canada, it seemed, would have clean hands.

* * *

The same process of hesitation and recovery that had character-ized the Tories' reaction to SDI occurred when the United States decided to send its Coast Guard icebreaker *Polar Sea* through the Northwest Passage.

Even if Canadians rarely venture north of the populated strip of Canada that hugs the border, the North has a special place in their minds and hearts. The Canadian and American governments overlooked this fact during the *Polar Sea* affair and the Americans were apparently astonished by the outcry. The Mulroney govern-ment, no less stunned, recovered and managed to turn initial irresolution into a strong policy response.

In 1985, the United States Coast Guard decided to send the icebreaker *Polar Sea* from Thule, Greenland, through the North-west Passage to the Beaufort Sea and Alaska. The voyage was planned to begin on August 1. Although its mission in the North was less than clear—unspecified research for the United States Navy—American officials justified their choice of route by insisting it would save time and fuel. That was a reasonable explanation; however, Canada claimed the Northwest Passage as its internal waters, and the United States did not seek permission before deciding on the route. Washington's reasons were simple: in Ameri-can eyes, the Passage was an international strait through which any nation had the right of innocent passage, a matter of impor-tance to the Americans with their global interests. But if the Americans had not asked for permission, neither had Canada demanded it. As a senior legal officer in the Department of Exter-nal Affairs explained: ''We are not in the business of preventing ships from using the Passage, and no single voyage will affect our legal position.''

The United States Coast Guard had been planning the voyage for some time, and it had told the Canadian Coast Guard of its plans early in 1985. One researcher who read the State Depart-ment file on the *Polar Sea* affair noted that the Coast Guard had not even been aware of problems over sovereignty and had simply planned its voyage and passed word to its Canadian sister service as a courtesy. Perhaps the informality of it all explained why the Canadian Coast Guard failed to tell the Department of External Affairs. Not until early May did the department learn that the *Polar Sea* was coming, and even then the information came from a reporter. On May 13, Ottawa told its embassy in Washington to make "discreet, low-level enquiries" about the Reagan administration's intentions. Discussions ensued, but only at low bureaucratic levels, in part at least because the Ottawa bureaucracy could not work out a strong common position. Both Ottawa and Washington hoped to keep controversy to a minimum.

They agreed to disagree on the status of the Passage, while concentrating on American compliance with the environmental standards Canada had put in place with the Arctic Waters Pollution Prevention Act after the oil tanker *Manhattan* had used the Passage in 1969. The tanker had not had Canadian permission for its trip, but it did have Canadian representatives on board and the ship had been able to complete its voyage only with the aid of a Canadian icebreaker.

Both countries agreed that the *Polar Sea* would also have Canadian officials aboard and that the voyage could proceed without prejudice to either's claims, should the matter ever go to the International Court of Justice. Again, that was a reasonable position, except that use of the Passage without permission could be construed as weakening the Canadian claims of sovereignty. On the other hand, since the Americans had never before accepted the legality of the Arctic Waters Pollution Prevention Act (to do so would have been a nod in the direction of Canadian sovereignty), a tit-for-tat was situation developing; neither would give up much in terms of international law.

Although these behind-the-scenes talks were going on, the plans for the *Polar Sea* voyage were unknown in Canada until Franklyn Griffiths of the University of Toronto wrote an article about them in the *Globe and Mail* on June 13, 1985. To Griffiths, although there was no reason to deny passage to a nonpolluting vessel, the country "faces the prospect of having to save face by granting permission whether or not it has been sought." That was the issue in a nutshell. For the Tory government, the danger lay in arousing Canadians' fears that the warmth of Mulroney's courtship of Reagan and the increasing military cooperation with the United States (especially in the North) had begun to compromise Canadian sovereignty. Even those who took a calmer view of the situation than did the militant nationalists were troubled: what was the advantage of clinging to Washington if Reagan were trying to seize the Arctic? "The Americans," Jean Chrétien said, "are using their friendship with Mulroney to take away a piece of Canada."

That was what worried many people, and in late July the *Polar Sea* issue blew into a major storm. Critics in the press charged the government with pussyfooting, a charge that appeared to be justified when the government "authorized" the voyage on July 31. The authorization was questionable, because the *Polar Sea*, according to naval experts, was a vessel prone to hazardous oil spills and was considered by some to be unsafe for high Arctic use. (The Americans did give categoric assurances to Canada about safety and promised to accept full responsibility for cleaning up any oil spills.)

Christopher Young of the Ottawa *Citizen*, the most vitriolic critic of government policy, angrily suggested that the Americans realized full well that they could do anything they wanted with Mulroney now, so eager was he for good relations. The *Polar Sea* incident, he said, "shows that sucking up doesn't pay."

But what precisely was Canada to do? The Americans could be told that they could not sail the Passage, but how could Canada stop them if they went ahead? The claims could be tested in the International Court, but even though Canadian specialists in international law believed that Canada could win such a case, American experts were just as strong in their views of the justice of their own case. In other words, everything might be lost in court. There was also the possibility of Mulroney using his vaunted special relationship with Reagan to get the Americans to back off. Whether this channel was tried is not known, but Joe Clark did telephone Secretary of State George Schultz to talk about the *Polar Sea*. He was astonished to discover that Schultz had never heard of the affair. In any case, nothing resulted from Ottawa's attempts to press the matter at high levels.

Under the circumstances, international lawyers said, Canada should declare the Passage internal waters and enclose it by establishing territorial waters around the Arctic islands. (This meant plotting straight baselines from headland to headland, and measuring the territorial sea outward from those lines.) The lawyers urged the government to move ahead quickly, because "the longer we wait to draw the baselines, the less credible our claim becomes." That was probably true, but as the *Globe and Mail* noted on August 2, Canada had to back up legal sovereignty with technological sovereignty by establishing a full range of land- and sea-based services to ensure that control was actual and effective. In the attenuated condition of the armed forces (the major exercise of sovereignty was sixteen Aurora long-range air patrol missions a year over the ice) and in a period of budget restraint, technological sovereignty might be hard to achieve.

The whole Canadian position had to be reconsidered. That was the message that B. M. Mawhinney of the legal division of External Affairs gave to the nation on August 1, just as the *Polar Sea* began its journey. Promising an "intensive review" of sovereignty in the Arctic, Mawhinney said it was still too soon to determine if Canada's claims should be tested in the court or through negotiation with the United States. That was only common sense, although Mawhinney's political masters in the Prime Minister's Office, who had thus far been unusually silent on the issue, apparently complained bitterly to External Affairs about his remarks.

The prime minister, holidaying at Harrington Lake in the Gatineau, remained uncharacteristically invisible as the storm built. The staff in Joe Clark's office explained that Clark had been in Asia when the issue first arose, that he was bone-tired from the past months of strain, and that he had erred initially by listening to the legal technicalities and letting them take precedence over the public response. Gerald Morris of the University of Toronto law school was blunter. "We have come out looking like a bunch of clowns," he said. "I think the way this has been handled has been a farce, a fiasco." No one, not Mulroney nor Clark nor the officials at External Affairs, had thus far emerged with any credit whatsoever.

Morris suggested that the United States government, aware that in the past Canada had not always seen eye-to-eye with Washington on military questions in the Arctic, was asserting its right of access. Senior officers at External Affairs were inclined to agree. "They were testing our sovereignty," one said.

Evidently, one point had escaped consideration in Washington. If the Northwest Passage were international, as the Americans claimed, then what was there to prevent the USSR using it? Paul Robinson, then the American ambassador to Canada, as poorly briefed on this issue as on others, told the press in Ottawa that although the Passage was international, Washington would be upset if the Russians used it. "We're saying it's international water. We have other security concerns that would naturally involve the Soviet Union."

The USSR had already declared the Northeast Passage internal waters and, according to a Soviet embassy official, his government supported the Canadian claim. "Whether it is the Northwest Passage or the Northeast Passage doesn't matter. Our position is based on the provisions of international law. The waters around islands belonging to a country are the internal waters of that country."

For its part, the State Department in Washington argued, "Our position is the same in regard to the Northwest and Northeast passages." The difference was that the United States, in public at least, was not trying to run its ships through Soviet waters, presumably because the USSR would take steps to stop any such attempt (although the Russians did not react militarily when United States Navy ships entered territorial waters in the Black Sea in March 1986). This, the *Globe and Mail* said, "is a predatory policy, one based on respect for a rival superpower and contempt for a feckless friend. Is Canada indefinitely to allow a bully to kick ice in its face?"

Perhaps the answer was yes. On August 21, Joe Clark said that the government had decided not to go to the International Court. "From a legal perspective," he said, "we are better to respond to a challenge to our jurisdiction rather than . . . cast doubt on our claims by taking the case there ourselves." That was weak, and the Ottawa *Citizen* drew the obvious conclusion: "Canada's decision means . . . the government is afraid it would lose the case." Maybe that was why the next day Mulroney made the toughest statement yet. Any suggestion that the Arctic waters did not belong to Canada would be "an unfriendly act," Mulroney said. "It is

ours. We assert sovereignty over it and even though we were left
with few instruments by the previous government, we shall assert
our sovereignty over it.'' That same month, the priorities and
planning committee of the Cabinet, at a meeting in Vancouver,
declared the protection of Canadian sovereignty a priority of the
government.

On September 10, while the new American ambassador, Thomas
Niles, was admitting that Washington had botched the *Polar Sea*
affair, Clark outlined a tough new policy in a speech in Parliament. Effective January 1, 1986, straight baselines around the
outer perimeter of the Arctic archipelago would take effect. At the
same time, legislation to extend criminal and civil law to the
off-shore Arctic would be put before the House of Commons (this
occurred in April 1986) and ''immediate'' talks with the United
States on ''cooperation in Arctic waters,'' on ''the basis of full
respect for Canadian sovereignty'' would be sought. Clark also
announced that Canada's military presence in the North would be
strengthened and that the government would build a Polar Class 8
icebreaker to exercise ''more effective control over our Arctic
waters.'' That was a good stand, however long overdue. For its
part, the United States government expressed ''regret'' over the
Canadian statement.

The military steps necessary to put Clark's policy into effect
were not undertaken immediately. Officers and officials at National
Defence Headquarters were quick to argue that the real threat was
in Europe and that resources deployed in the North were resources
wasted. The generals and admirals were also indifferent to the
proposed icebreaker (a huge vessel of 38,000 tons, estimated to
cost $500 million to $900 million), particularly if the money had
to come from their budget.

The idea of building such a ship had been mooted for years, but
the strong public response to the American incursion as well as
Mulroney's growing concern about his image of indecisiveness
had led to a perceived need for action. Hence the decision to build
the icebreaker, even though Harvie Andre, the Associate Minister
of National Defence, told a parliamentary committee that there
was little military utility in one. ''It is not a particularly good
weapons platform,'' he said. ''The threat in the Arctic is not
naval, it is air [based] . . . .So other than the flag-carrier aspect, it

is not the most useful way for the defence department to spend its money.'' Andre obviously feared that if National Defence had to pay for the icebreaker, the re-equipment of four destroyers would be struck off the budget. Sovereignty was not the top priority for his department, whatever the Cabinet said. National Defence officials and officers evidently believed that Canada gained more by being a good ally abroad than by defending the ice against its friends.

External Affairs disagreed. In a secret Cabinet paper on Canadian sovereignty dated October 10, 1985 which was leaked to *Maclean's*, the department encroached on National Defence's turf by calling for $4 billion worth of defence measures in the North, including the icebreaker, four nuclear submarines capable of operating for long periods under Arctic ice, a satellite to watch the area, and the installation of submarine sound detection systems. The paper recommended that no additional money be provided for these systems; everything had to be allocated from existing budgets. That precipitated a bitter fight between Clark at External Affairs and Nielsen and Andre at National Defence.

Until the Defence white paper appeared, however, the outcome remained uncertain. In typical Mulroney government style, the February 1986 budget postponed a decision, and the estimates for the polar icebreaker were eliminated entirely. No one would say if that was a final decision. Presumably the fight in Cabinet and between departments would continue. The only certainty was that public opinion would compel Canada to maintain a stronger presence in the Arctic. ''Use the Arctic or lose it'' was the message, and the electorate was sure to punish any government that weakened Canada's sovereignty in the North.

* * *

Canadians not only want to preserve their sovereignty over their territory, they also want to protect that land from the damage done by acid rain. The unspoiled lakes and forests of the near north are a part of the Canadian heritage, scenery that has been enshrined in the paintings of the Group of Seven and in the writing of countless novelists and poets. More to the point, perhaps, hundreds of thousands of tourists come to Canada each year to fish and swim in the lakes and thousands make their livelihood from this tourist traffic. Hundreds of thousands more (mainly from the vocal, letter-writing middle class) own cottages on small lakes in the Laurentians or Muskoka. Those Canadians have watched their investments dwindle as their lakes acidified and died.

Characteristically, Canadians pointed the finger at the Americans for this problem. As most people saw it, the great coal-burning utilities and steel plants of Pennsylvania and Ohio poured their filthy fumes into the sky and the prevailing winds carried the pollution into Canada. That was true as far as it went, but few people realized that at least half of the acid rain that falls on Canada is produced in this country, and a huge quantity of it comes from one source—INCO's Sudbury nickel refinery, with its enormous smokestack. Until recently the clean-up efforts in Canada have been half-hearted at best, as governments at every level preferred to keep up employment rather than press nervous corporations to take the expensive measures necessary to rid their smokestacks of pollutants. But Canadian governments at least recognized that acid rain was a problem, and in the latter years of the Trudeau government, efforts were made to begin correcting the neglect of generations. In 1982, the Liberal government announced its intention to enforce a 25 percent cut in sulphur dioxide emissions, and promised a further 25 percent cut if the Americans agreed to halve their emissions. The Americans, however, refused to be pressured, and the most the Reagan administration would do was to fund further research on acid rain. Frustrated, the Canadians decided to reduce acid rain on their own. The costs, which were substantial, were to be borne by consumers, in part by increasing electricity bills by 2 to 5 percent.

What Brian Mulroney thought about environmental questions when he came to power was unclear at best. As the president of the Iron Ore Company, he had worked for a branch plant of one of the great American polluting industries. The ecological efforts of his company in northern Quebec were not exemplary, and the Baie-Comeau area, Mulroney's birthplace, was a textbook example of how a beautiful natural region could be despoiled by lack of environmental concern. Nor did his first choice for Minister of the Environment suggest that he had much interest in conservation. Suzanne Blais-Grenier, a well-educated but brand-new MP from Montreal, quickly got into trouble by supporting budget cuts in her department that would have gutted the Canadian Wildlife Service and much environmentally sensitive research. She seemed to support logging in national parks and she had a gift for annoying the concerned citizens and environmental activists who had helped John Roberts, one of her Liberal predecessors, persuade the Trudeau government to move faster on environmental issues. At the beginning of March 1985, however, Blais-Grenier announced tough new vehicle emission standards and financial aid to help smelters modernize their anti-pollution controls and cut sulphur dioxide emissions in half over the next ten years.

That was progress, and it was more than merely cosmetic. However, the Mulroney government had as its top priority the securing of better relations with Ronald Reagan's America. Free trade was the goal, and too much squawking about acid rain might interfere with the march toward negotiations. Moreover, Reagan did not believe that acid rain was a problem. Indeed, the president (possibly citing his *Reader's Digest* clipping files) seemed to think that trees caused pollution. All that Reagan was willing to consider was more research to determine if acid rain actually existed. Nor was there overwhelming support in Congress for action. Representatives from the northern states, seeing their lakes and forests destroyed, were sensitive to the problem, but congressmen from the Sunbelt cared not a whit about the problem.

Thus the Canadians had a dilemma on their hands. To make matters worse, Mulroney, in a fit of enthusiasm of the sort that sometimes left his staff reeling, declared that acid rain deserved to be at the very top of the agenda for his first meeting with Reagan in Quebec City in March 1985. As everyone realized, the preparatory work for the Shamrock Summit would determine the final communiqué, and the simple fact was that American officials had little interest in committing their government to spending anything on acid rain. On the other hand, Mulroney had to get something from Reagan on this score, or else his government would be painted as one that was willing to give the Americans whatever they wanted on foreign investment, say, or on new warning systems in the North, but was unable to get any concessions in return. The best that anyone could hope for under the circumstances was a commitment that looked good on paper, cost little, and did not embarrass either Reagan or Mulroney.

And, *mirabile dictu*, that is precisely what emerged from Quebec City. The two leaders, just before they appeared on stage to sing "When Irish Eyes Are Smiling," announced that each was naming a high-profile envoy to study acid rain. William Davis, the former premier of Ontario, was Mulroney's choice and Drew Lewis, the Secretary of Transportation in Reagan's first-term cabinet, was the president's. Lewis and Davis (serving for $1 a year) were to report on their efforts to "pursue consultation," to "enhance cooperation," to "pursue means," and to "identify efforts" on acid rain. The suggestion of envoys, first raised in Ottawa by Ambassador Paul Robinson, had apparently been carried to Washington by Fred Doucet of the Prime Minister's Office and put forward in a White House meeting with Michael Deaver, Reagan's deputy chief of staff, on February 28, 1985. Deaver apparently wanted a smooth summit and supported the idea of envoys as a way of being cooperative.

(Deaver was later hired by the Canadian government as a lobbyist and his actions in helping the envoy idea win acceptance in the White House became a central and critical point in an investigation of his activities by the General Accounting Office in Washington in the spring of 1986, to determine if he violated the conflict of interest law.)

Mulroney hyperbolically claimed that the appointments had "broken the deadlock" between the two governments. "We did not work a miracle, but we did take a significant step forward." Perhaps, but the American officials were quick to say that while the agreement on envoys represented the president's recognition of the "commonality" of the problem, Reagan still had a "basic view" that more research was necessary before action was taken. These comments took the gloss off the ebullient Mulroney's blarney and fed the scepticism of environmental activists.

"Envoys are better than nothing," the executive coordinator of the Canadian Coalition on Acid Rain said, "but our experience in Washington is that the president is still the problem." Peter Hurley added (accurately) that Bill Davis "is not known as a leader on the environment." Public enthusiasm was tepid at best, and the general view seemed to be that Reagan had bought one year during which he had to do very little. Nor was there any certainty that, if the Davis-Lewis report recommended active measures, Reagan would accept them.

No one expected the envoys' report to amount to much. And it didn't. On January 8, 1986, Lewis and Davis released a bland thirty-three-page document that recommended that the United States spend $5 billion on pollution-control technology (half the money to be provided by the government and half by industry), but failed to set any targets for actual reductions in sulphur dioxide emissions. The report suggested the voluntary development of technology, did not recommend mandatory enforcement of emission standards, and described acid rain only as a ''serious environmental problem'' and a ''serious transboundary problem.''

Bland had been acceptable in Ontario during Davis's long tenure, but it had not worked on Secretary Lewis. Indeed, Davis admitted with unusual frankness that he had relied heavily on Secretary Lewis's advice on what ''stands a chance of acceptance'' by the American administration. Davis called this ''realistic thinking.'' ''I may be naive,''the former premier said, ''but I sense, from Mr. Lewis, that [the recommendations] will pass.'' Lewis told reporters there was a fair chance Reagan might accept the report. But the difficulty now lay with Congress and the polluters themselves. ''The problem is to what degree we can solve the problem and at the same time not create great social and economic unrest in the area that would be most adversely affected by any action we take . . . I think it's going to be very, very difficult. This is no cakewalk.''

It was no call to action either. The House of Commons special committee on acid rain was not impressed by Lewis and Davis's efforts. The report, the committee said bluntly, ''has implicitly treated current environmental damage as trivial or zero. This ignores what is already known about the whole range of damage . . . and it treats too lightly the potential irreversibility of some damage to the environment.'' Even worse, the major polluters in the United States endorsed the report. The National Coal Association, for example, smugly welcomed the idea that polluters might be given funding to develop anti-pollution technology.

By March 1986, just before the second Reagan-Mulroney summit, there had been no progress involving the appropriation of new money to battle pollution. Not even the $2.5 billion recommended in the January report was at all certain—or seemed even likely—to get Reagan's support in a Washington that was struggling to come to terms with new deficit-cutting strategies. An attempt in January to get congressional action on acid rain went nowhere. Moreover, congressional supporters charged that Canadian efforts in support of the Davis-Lewis report were hurting their attempts to get legislation with teeth. Henry Waxman, chairman of the health and environment sub-committee of the House of Representatives, told Ambassador Allan Gotlieb that Canadian anti-pollution lobbying was a "betrayal," and that he expected that Reagan, even if he endorsed the envoys' report, would not spend more than the $400 million left in already appropriated monies from 1970s anti-pollution legislation. Other congressmen were more caustic. "Your government is getting hung out to dry by its socks. And the sad thing is, it doesn't seem to realize it."

It is difficult to cope with Congress at the best of times, but with Reagan's indifference to the subject and with his still-impressive mastery over Congress, there seemed some reason to believe that Johnny Canuck had been hornswoggled yet again by Uncle Sam. (Reagan negotiates like the Soviets, said one admiring White House aide. "What's mine is mine. What's yours is negotiable.")

Certainly Mulroney was doing his best to ensure that the Americans realized how important acid rain was to Canada—and to the credibility of the prime minister's policy of being pleasant and accommodating to the United States. Acid rain remained at the top of the agenda, he told the *New York Times* in an interview before the 1986 summit. "I mean, it's killing an important part of our environment. And just as surely as summer follows spring, it will ruin the environment unless we act. And Canada cannot act by itself." (When the *Times* then asked if Mulroney needed some concession on acid rain to be credible in Canada, Mulroney airily replied, "Oh no, I am credible with Canadians no matter what.") Mulroney's new environment minister, Thomas McMillan, was pragmatic about the situation. The Tory government had shown its "bona fides in Canada-U.S. relations" over the last eighteen months. "Now is the time for the payoff."

The payoff came, but it had little money attached. "I'm pleased to say that I fully endorse [it]," Reagan said of the envoys' report at the close of the two-day summit. Mulroney was effusive: "It's written right here," he crowed, bragging about what he called Reagan's "full and unequivocal" endorsement of the fight against acid rain. It was a ''major departure'' for an administration that had hitherto failed to recognize the existence of the problem. True, but Reagan had not firmly committed himself to persuade Congress to provide money for the war on acid rain. ''Although we do not now have all the funds,'' a White House spokesman said, ''the administration will seek to provide in the future the funding recommended in the joint report.''

If Mulroney was thrilled at his success and if the *Globe and Mail* hailed him for getting Reagan to take the first step, his foes at home were unimpressed and unappeased. Liberal environment critic Charles Caccia summed up the response in the House of Commons by noting, ''We are still downwind from those 26 million tonnes of sulphur dioxide and there will not be one milligram of reduction in the next five years, no matter what the claims.'' The Tory front bench lamely replied that the Reagan announcement was ''an important first step,'' and Mulroney himself, after his return to Ottawa, seemed to be suddenly aware that he had got very little beyond a scrap of paper from the president. The next month, American energy secretary John Herrington confirmed this: the program was ''more modest'' than the administration had hitherto indicated, he told a House of Representatives sub-committee—and there were no budget proposals to raise Reagan's promised $5 billion. Sulphur dioxide was going to keep on pouring over the border, and Reagan had once again effectively delayed action. Brian Mulroney had got nothing for his summitry.

The difficulties that Mulroney had encountered in dealing with the United States should have provided a cautionary note. But the prime minister had even grander dreams for the relationship. He wanted to solidify the trade and economic links between the two countries into a binding form that would, he believed, guarantee Canadian prosperity for the future. The goal was free trade.

Chapter Thirteen
The Great Free Trade Gamble

The world of the 1980s is an increasingly protectionist place. Canada had watched as the Japanese effectively manoeuvered to keep whatever goods they chose out of their booming market and the European Common Market did the same. But as long as Canadian goods could be sold in the United States, all this could be tolerated. The Americans, however, watching their corporations flee the high-cost North American labour market for Korea, Taiwan, or Singapore, and watching the Japanese take over and dominate completely whole sectors of the automobile and appliance markets, were increasingly alarmed. The huge American trade deficit each year confirmed the damage, even if the extraordinarily high value of the American dollar was largely responsible for this. Inevitably, congressmen began demanding protection for their constituents, and they began to get it—despite President Reagan's professed belief in a freer trading world.

The impact on Canada of the growing trend toward high tariffs in Washington was worrying. With Europe and Japan closed to much of Canada's exports of manufactured goods, how could Canada survive if the American market became protectionist? To Prime Minister Mulroney and his government, this situation, admittedly one with potentially disastrous consequences, had to be faced. And to the Tories, the way to deal with it was to seek guaranteed access to the great market to the south.

Mulroney's drive for free trade with the United States unquestionably ranks as the major initiative of the Conservative government. It is a gamble. It poses great risks. It offers possible benefits. And the outcome of this push for a new trading relationship with the Americans will undoubtedly determine the electoral success or failure of Brian Mulroney's government—and the way it will be viewed by history.

* * *

Polls can be dangerous and misleading, and nothing illustrates this better than the free trade issue. In June 1984, before Mulroney's Conservatives came to power, opinion surveys by Environics Research Group Ltd., published in the *Globe and Mail*, showed that 78 percent of a national sample supported the idea of free trade with the United States and only 17 percent disagreed. The next June, 65 percent remained in favour and 30 percent disagreed. So strong were the numbers, so positive the response, that the prime minister and his party could be forgiven for assuming that Canadians were prepared for a shift in policy. At the very least, the people seemed receptive, ready to be persuaded that a closer relationship with the Americans in terms of trade and tariffs was in their interest.

On September 26, 1985, therefore, Prime Minister Mulroney announced in the House of Commons that he had spoken that day to President Reagan in Washington "to express Canada's interests in pursuing a new trade agreement between our two countries." There was, Mulroney said, support for free trade among the provincial premiers and from important sectors of the business community, and that was heartening. But Mulroney said that he was aware of the concerns that many Canadians had expressed about closer economic relations with the United States, and he promised that "political sovereignty, our system of social programs, our commitment to fight regional disparities, our unique cultural identity, our special linguistic character—these are the essence of Canada. They are not at issue in these negotiations." Moreover, the prime minister said, he had told Reagan that Canada wanted to negotiate "the broadest possible package of mutually beneficial reductions in tariff and non-tariff barriers between the two countries." It was a good statement, a careful statement, one made to the cheers of the government benches and in the expectation that the country was ready to move ahead.

In September 1985, the country did seem ready. But over the

course of the next six or seven months, the polls began to show a massive decline in support for free trade, the government began to get itself into difficulties with the provinces on the ways in which the negotiations with Washington would be conducted, and Ontario and Quebec expressed serious reservations about the fate of their manufacturing and agricultural industries under a new trade regime. Moreover, Reagan was slow to get the United States ready, and Congress seemed prepared to hold back its permission for the administration to negotiate unless and until Canada showed a willingness to resolve some outstanding trade problems. The issue of free trade soon showed every sign of becoming a political quagmire.

For the Progressive Conservative government, the implications were serious indeed. The government had tied its fate to the successful negotiation of a free trade treaty with the United States. In their first lacklustre year in office, the Tories had lurched and staggered. Cutbacks in social programs and attempts to reduce the deficit were positive changes in the eyes of some in the business community and many editorial writers, but program changes often hurt ordinary voters and rile countless special interest groups, including the provincial governments. The Tories' fears of activist government and the prime minister's regrettable inability to take hard decisions also created an urgent necessity for forceful action in at least one area. And what better area than trade with the United States, Canada's largest customer?

But something went wrong on the road to a treaty with the United States. Somehow the optimism of September 1985, the certainty that free trade could be the key to Mulroney's re-election in 1988, turned into the nagging concern that free trade would be extremely difficult to negotiate in the first place, and even then might be rejected by the people.

*　*　*

Free trade was an issue burdened with the full weight of history. Under a variety of names—reciprocity, unrestricted reciprocity, commercial union, and customs union—it had at once beguiled and ensnared Canadian governments for almost a century and a half. In the 1840s merchants in Montreal had been disturbed enough by the disappearance of the trade preferences they had hitherto received in the British market to call for annexation; as a result, the British had secured reciprocity with the United States, largely as a way to keep Canada within the Empire. The Reciprocity Treaty of 1854 that resulted was widely believed to have ushered in good times in the Canadas, and even if the figures did not quite support that interpretation, certainly the abrogation of the treaty by the Americans at the end of the Civil War brought difficult times—and helped to spur Confederation.

The new dominion looked repeatedly to Washington for another trade treaty, both Conservatives and Liberals trying to establish the reciprocity that could bring prosperity back. But Washington remained uninterested until in 1911 Sir Wilfrid Laurier's Liberal government, anxious to hold on to support from the West, finally negotiated an agreement that covered natural products. The Conservatives denounced the French-Canadian Laurier for selling out the Empire, and Ontario businessmen put up millions to ''bust the damn thing,'' which they saw as the thin edge of a wedge that would eliminate the National Policy of high tariffs under which they thrived. Bust it they did, and Laurier lost the 1911 election. Reciprocity was out.

Not until 1935 did Canada and the United States sign another trade treaty, one that merely reduced tariffs on a large number of items. Even so, relations between the two countries were getting closer: World War I had pushed them together, and World War II forced Canada into a defensive and economic alliance with the new superpower to the south. In the years after 1945, as Europe lay in ruins, prey to Communism, Ottawa looked south once again. In 1947 and 1948, the Mackenzie King Liberal government secretly negotiated a massive trade agreement with Washington, one that provided for a virtual customs union and that allowed for a long transition period to let Canadian industry adjust to open competition. It might have been a good deal in the circumstances of 1948, but Mackenzie King, fearful of the Tory opposition, remembering 1911 (when he himself had lost his seat in the Commons), and unwilling to fight a major campaign at the end of his long career, got cold feet and cancelled the arrangement.

But if free trade was dead in 1948, the process of continental integration continued without check as the Americans made heavy investments in Canada and as Canada's trade options diminished. A sectoral arrangement, the Defence Production Sharing Agreement, negotiated by the Diefenbaker government in 1959, put special rules in place to govern defence purchases, an attempt to get the Pentagon to buy more in Canada so as to balance the books put into the red by Canadian acquisition of American aircraft and missiles.

The Auto Pact of 1964 attempted to achieve a similar state of affairs. This agreement guaranteed increased jobs in the Canadian auto industry and for a time gave Canada's trade balance a healthy fillip (so much so that President Lyndon Johnson actually complained to the Canadian ambassador, "You screwed us on the Auto Pact"). But there were good years and bad ones for Canada under the pact's terms. Despite the jobs they created, the Auto Pact and the Defence Production Sharing Agreement, as Stephen Clarkson wrote, "generated technologically dependent, managerially backward and economically weak industries that provide a cautionary rather than exemplary experience."

By the beginning of the 1970s, therefore, the Trudeau government, anxious to avoid further integration and not happy with the status quo, had trumpeted its Third Option of diversifying trade (and orienting foreign policy generally) away from the United States. But the Third Option proved to be a dismal failure in the face of geography, economics, and the reluctance of the Europeans and Japanese to buy anything other than raw materials from Canada.

Complete free trade may have been killed in 1864, in 1911, and in 1948, but hardy perennial that it is, it was destined to be resurrected in the uncertain circumstances of the 1980s. The Third Option had failed—what now? The first sign that free trade might be seen as an answer to Canada's economic problems came in 1982 when a Senate committee recommended the elimination of all tariffs between Canada and its neighbour. The Trudeau government rejected that idea, but later in the year it began negotiations with Washington on sectoral free trade. Instead of letting down all the barriers, sectoral approaches looked only at free trade in certain defined economic areas. The problem here was obvious: each country wanted free trade only where it could make gains at the other's expense. The modern and efficient Canadian steel industry, for example, was enthusiastic about free trade in specialty steel products where it was far stronger than the decayed and rusting industries in Pennsylvania and Ohio. For their part, the Americans looked to free trade in data services, a direct threat to the nascent (some said stillborn) Canadian computer industry. In other words, in every trade agreement someone gained and someone else lost, and that was as true of a sectoral agreement as of a sweeping pact.

But in the Canadian situation of the mid-1980s, the call for free trade, full or sectoral, with the Americans was surprising. The simple fact was that, thanks to the General Agreement on Tariffs and Trade and especially to the Tokyo round of talks in 1979, some 85 percent of Canadian manufactured goods going south already entered or would soon enter the United States free of duty. In other words, Canada would make relatively few additional gains in a treaty with the United States. That was all the more important because almost four-fifths of Canada's trade—about $150 billion a year—was with the United States and Canada's overall trade surplus depended heavily on its $20 billion credit in trade with the United States. On the other hand, only between 60 and 65 percent of American manufactures came into Canada without duty. Under the GATT rules, free trade was defined as a situation in which 80 percent of trade was free of tariffs. In other words, American access to Canadian markets was certain to increase in the event of free trade. Canadian industry, sure to be faced with tough competition from the American plants with their longer production runs and economies of scale, stood to lose most. But, as the supporters of free trade said, only those "Darwinian" industries that were lean, competitive, and ready to fight for international markets, deserved to survive. That was small comfort for the unfit—and for all the workers who depended on weaker industries for their jobs.

Why then did anyone in Canada want free trade? The reason lay in the protectionist mood in Congress and in the United States generally. The days when the manufactured goods of America were prized all round the world were long past. Japanese radios, television sets, and automobiles were cheaper and often better made than American products, a state of affairs with catastrophic implications for employment in Pittsburgh, New York, Cleveland, and hundreds of other cities. The United States, still the richest power on earth, had developed a huge trade deficit (in 1985 alone it was $120 billion) that was a constant drain on the economy. In those circumstances, the response in Congress was simple and direct: raise the tariff and hit back at every country that seemed to be taking advantage of the United States.

That attitude posed problems for Canadian manufacturers, such as lumber producers and meat packers. What they wanted was guaranteed access to the richest market in the world. To get that, they needed exemption from both legislative and administrative import sanctions in order to make the costly investments necessary to compete with and in the United States. The problem was serious. The countervail legislation with which Congress had armed the administration's trade officials permitted American industries to secure tariff protection by claiming that foreign producers benefited unfairly from subsidies of their own. ''Buy American'' legislation at federal and state levels, bans on foreign carriers in inland waterways, and a multiplicity of other protective devices barred or hampered Canadian exporters trying to crack the United States market. If a free trade treaty could overcome American countervail legislation and legislative and administrative non-tariff barriers, then it could win support in Canada.

In 1984, the trade issue had already become a staple of the financial pages, but it was not a major public concern until November, when Donald S. Macdonald, former Liberal finance minister and chairman of the Royal Commission on the Economic Union and Development Prospects for Canada, entered the debate. Speaking to reporters at a conference on Canadian-American relations in Harriman, New York, Macdonald noted that ''many Canadians are nervous about the prospect of putting in jeopardy that perhaps rather fragile structure of national sovereignty that was built in a country called Canada . . .'' Although he conceded that those fears deserved to be addressed, Macdonald (tipping his hand on the Royal Commission's major recommendation) said that Canada had to take a ''leap of faith . . . at some point Canadians are going to have to be bold and say, yes, we will do that.'' That statement, whether it was made with the Mulroney government's foreknowledge or not, was certainly something the Tories accepted.

The debate on free trade was now on the front pages. Economists were enthusiastically in favour, a *Financial Post* survey showing 84 percent popular support for free trade (but only 25 percent rating the chances of negotiating an actual treaty at better than 50 percent). The leaders of the economists' bandwagon were at Queen's University, where Richard Lipsey presided; his department weighed in with its prognostications, almost all of which looked to a permanent boom if free trade came about. The macroeconomists' computer calculations showed an increase of up to 7 percent in the gross national product under free trade and growth in employment and manufacturing. No one really believed all that, and senior bureaucrats in Ottawa did not trouble to hide their scorn when growth projections of that sort were bandied about. "It's all macro, macro, macro," one said, "when the world is micro, micro, micro." In other words, the big picture is less important than the thousands of little pictures that make up the economy.

The key player on Canadian trade relations with the United States was obviously Brian Mulroney. During his race for the Conservative leadership in 1983, while John Crosbie was calling for free trade, Mulroney had denounced the very idea of "opening the floodgates to the Americans," as a delusion that could endanger Canadian sovereignty. But during the 1984 election campaign, although he devoted most of his efforts to denouncing the sins of the Grits and although the Conservative campaign handbook said not a word about the subject, the Tory leader indicated that he now favoured a more open border with the United States. Even so, Mulroney called only for "fair trade, not free trade."

As prime minister, Mulroney appointed James Kelleher as Minister for International Trade. Kelleher, fifty-five, was a corporate labour lawyer from Sault Ste. Marie who had worked for Algoma Steel. Although he had been a Mulroney supporter since the 1976 party convention, he was a freshman MP and, as his civil servants quickly discovered, a lightweight intellectually and within the Cabinet. Kelleher was fated to be the lightning rod for free trade, given ample room by Joe Clark, to whom he reported. Some of Clark's aides talked about the freedom their minister gave the lawyer from the Soo, noting that Kelleher had more than enough rope to hang himself if free trade did not succeed, but not enough to seize all the credit if it should turn out to be a winner. Clark himself chaired the Cabinet sub-committee watching over the trade issue, something that made good sense considering how intimately trade was involved with the whole question of Canadian-American relations.

Also very much in the picture was Sinclair Stevens, the Minister of Regional Industrial Expansion, a department cobbled together out of parts of the old departments of Industry, Trade and Commerce and Regional Economic Expansion. DRIE had lost responsibility for trade to External Affairs, a loss still keenly felt by senior officials. Stevens, aggressive and ambitious, was ready to listen to his officials' concerns that trade was obviously of importance to the country's regions and to industrial sectors over which DRIE keeps watch. Stevens was a wild card in the free trade game, and one of his senior officials described the Minister of Protection, as some called him, standing on the shore, waving his handkerchief as the great free trade ship left harbour, just like the *Titanic*, on the way to disaster. That same official, however, argued that Stevens was genuinely concerned about protecting Canadian access to the American market and believed that a trade negotiation was the only way to achieve this. Perhaps Stevens was just confused.

Another minister to be considered was Michael Wilson in Finance, the best chance, one senior trade official noted, for a sensible policy that would combine multilateralism and free trade negotiations. The problem was, this same bureaucrat noted, that Wilson had been damaged politically by his defeat on social welfare universality early in the government's term (although his 1986 budget revived him).

The final key player on free trade was Fred Doucet, the official in the Prime Minister's Office with the responsibility for this issue (and others affecting Canada-United States relations, such as acid rain). Doucet was a charter member of Mulroney's St. FX gang, a holder of a PhD and, before Mulroney became leader of the party in 1983, the development officer at his alma mater. Mulroney had recruited him to be chief of staff in the Office of the Leader of the Opposition, a position in which Doucet was a notable failure because of his inability to get along with others in the party's election machinery. Nothing if not loyal, however, Mulroney had placed his old friend in the PMO and given him important responsibilities. Rapidly building an office-wall collection of photographs showing himself and his boss with world leaders, Doucet was probably the wrong man in the wrong place. Public servants sympathetic to Mulroney had tried to warn the prime minister about Doucet's inability to understand how policy was formed, but they could not get through to him. What effect this would have on free trade—to say nothing of the future of the government—was uncertain.

The task for the government, once most of its players were in place, was to offer a token of Canada's goodwill toward the United States and American investors. In December 1984, Mulroney told a New York business audience that his "message was clear here and around the world. Canada is open for business again." That unfortunate phrase (stolen from Premier Grant Devine of Saskatchewan), one that readily offended nationalists disturbed by the government's increasingly pro-American policies, was Mulroney's way of characterizing the removal of many of the restrictions on investment that the Liberals' Foreign Investment Review Agency had supposedly enforced. FIRA, toothless as it had become, was soon replaced by Investment Canada, an agency with the mandate to seek investors.

The same month, Kelleher made the rounds of the provincial capitals to study the premiers' moods. Provincial cooperation was essential to reduce non-tariff barriers—for example, the Liquor Control Board of Ontario levied substantial charges on American wines in its (futile) efforts to encourage oenophiles to drink the Ontario product. However, none of the provinces, not even those most enthusiastic about free trade with the United States, seemed willing to face reality. "It may be," said one researcher from the Canada West Foundation, "that the provinces think they'll not have to face the inconsistencies, at least not in their political lifetime." Certainly the Americans took the provincial barriers seriously; the liquor boards' discriminatory pricing policies headed their list of grievances with Canada. On the other hand, Ontario, as the province with most to gain by the freeing of trade within Canada, was in favour of removing non-tariff barriers, even if it did not wholeheartedly support free trade.

In January, Trade Minister Kelleher's discussion paper on ways to "secure and enhance market access" appeared. The words "free trade," presumably deemed to carry too heavy a historical weight, did not appear, but in a paper that canvassed the options (maintenance of the status quo, sectoral arrangements, a comprehensive pact, or a framework arrangement to set up institutional mechanisms for further talks), the government indicated its choice: "a comprehensive agreement which provided for the removal of tariffs and non-tariff barriers on substantially all bilateral trade" with the United States. The sectoral approach was forgotten, and Mulroney's Canada began to seek a full-fledged and comprehensive agreement.

That stance was confirmed when the first ministers met in Regina in February 1985. While Frank Miller of Ontario and Peter Lougheed of Alberta sparred over free trade, the prime minister stood slightly above the fray. He was in favour of prudence on the trade issue, he said, "because I believe in it. But there's another side of this coin. This is the old Canadian tradition of being terrified by shibboleths. You throw off a slogan in this country and you scare the hell out of half the people whether it's relevant or not . . . Free trade is one of them. It conjures up all kinds of scarecrows and myths and problems, and what I think we have to do is try to depoliticize some of it . . . If we're going to get into this kind of discussion," Mulroney said, "we have to do it with maturity and with an understanding that all of the people intervening in the debate are trying to be helpful. Free trade is all in the eyes of the beholder." Vague as it sounded, it certainly did not mean that the government was against free trade, although Mulroney clearly preferred a different, less emotive label.

The next scene took place in Quebec City when Mulroney met with President Reagan on St. Patrick's Day, March 17, 1985. The "Shamrock Summit," as it was calculatingly called, featured the two leaders and their wives on stage at a gala performance singing "When Irish Eyes Are Smiling," arguably the most mawkish and embarrassing moment in Canada's long history of relations with the United States.

Nonetheless, the Quebec meeting speeded up the move toward free trade. Although White House sources suggested before the meeting that the two countries were on the verge of a "blockbuster" agreement ("something truly big in the trade area"), the immediate results were less spectacular. Instead, Reagan and Mulroney agreed to ''halt protectionism.'' The president assured his new friend that ''he would use all of his energies to pre-empt any move that would put Canada in peril from protectionism.'' The summit and the warm relationship Mulroney had cemented with Reagan apparently eliminated any remaining doubts about the free trade idea that might have been lingering in the prime minister's mind.

The president and the prime minister also asked Ambassador William Brock, the American trade representative, and James Kelleher to establish within six months ''a bilateral mechanism to chart all possible ways to reduce and eliminate existing barriers to trade.'' The leaders also issued a declaration promising action within a year to reduce tariff barriers, to simplify regulations interfering with trade, and to eliminate barriers interfering with high-tech trade, among other items. The declaration, for some reason best known to External Affairs, quickly became a classi-fied document and virtually disappeared. Even so, officials in the United States were jubilant. ''We want to come up with the broad-est possible concept,'' said William Merkin, the Canadian expert and deputy assistant trade representative in the office of Ambassa-dor Brock.

But as Canadians should have known, the limit of American attention on Canada was always brief. Within a few days of the summit, Brock had been transformed into the Secretary of Labor in Reagan's cabinet, thus throwing the Quebec agreements and their timetable into disarray. Any new trade representative would need time to master the Canadian dossier; and no possible succes-sor was likely to have Brock's political savvy in dealing with an increasingly protectionist Congress. His successor, Clayton Yuetter, a blunt Nebraskan who had worked on trade matters between 1975 and 1977, was nominated by Reagan to the post on April 3. He was, White House spokesman Larry Speakes said, ''as good a replacement as could be found,'' something less than wholehearted approbation. Yuetter began by calling the American relationship with Japan, smaller in dollar terms than the link with Canada, ''the most important political and economic relationship by far.'' That did not augur well for Mulroney.

Reports from Washington were also gloomy. First, there was

the utter unpredictability of Congress in a pre-election session, unpredictability that increased as every representative felt obliged to introduce protectionist bills to take care of the workers in his or her district and as the list of major legislation (including tax reform) lengthened. Free trade with Canada simply was not high on the list of priorities. As Canadian Ambassador Allan Gotlieb noted, "Reagan would not have a snowball's chance in hell of getting a loosening [of tariffs] through Congress now."

Second, the very procedures demanded by American law posed difficulties. Canada (and any other nation) had to request trade negotiations, but, before they could begin, President Reagan had to obtain the assent of the Senate finance committee and the House of Representatives ways and means committee. Under the so-called "fast-track" procedure, Congress had sixty legislative days in which to hold hearings and to respond before formal talks could begin, and it still retained the right to approve the final treaty. That was not very encouraging, considering the way fishing treaties, negotiated by officials from both countries, had been turned back by the Senate, ever responsive to regional interests.

Third and perhaps most important, there was the Japanese problem. Given the $37 billion American trade deficit with Japan and their virtual inability to crack the Japanese market, the Americans were fixated on trade with Asia. Yuetter's almost instinctive comment on his appointment made this clear. Canada remained a vague problem, despite the larger total trade north and south in North America (and Canada's huge trade surplus with the United States).

Finally, there was the GATT. Washington's primary goal had always been a major multilateral negotiation to lower tariff barriers, to tackle the problem of non-tariff barriers, and to cover services, the area the Americans dominated. For the Reagan administration, bilateral negotiations were largely a device to encourage the multilateral laggards to get in step, in part at least by threatening to give Canada a special position that could hurt European or Japanese interests. In other words, Canada might simply be a stalking horse for the Americans. Moreover, merely talking about free trade with the United States worried Canada's other trading partners, especially the British, the Japanese, and the West Europeans. On the other hand, if the call for early multilateral negotiations (endorsed by ministers attending meetings of the Organisation for Economic Co-operation and Development in Paris in April, but stalled at the Bonn Summit in May 1985) were to succeed, then Canada might find itself trying to negotiate a special arrangement with the United States in the context of a hectic, protracted, worldwide negotiation. In the past, Canadian teams had produced satisfactory results in such circumstances; but this was no guarantee for a repeat performance.

The Mulroney government also faced difficulties on the domestic front. In Ontario, the election of a Liberal government under David Peterson in May changed the political equation. The provincial Tories, although they were dubious about the potential impact of free trade on the province's manufacturers, might have been expected to respond to ties of party loyalty. But the Grits, dependent on support from the Ontario NDP to retain power, were certain to be less cooperative (although Peterson, who talked harshly about free trade in public, was said by Ottawa officials, and even by those of his own bureaucracy, to be tooting a different horn in private). Later in 1985, the election of Robert Bourassa's Liberals in Quebec would swell the ranks of the doubters. A central Canadian lobby, the perennial bugbear of Western politicians, was taking shape.

Some federal ministers also urged caution, notably Sinclair Stevens, and a substantial number of bureaucrats questioned free trade's supposed benefits. Organized labour was hostile. Women lobbyists were beginning to say that female workers, concentrated in low-paying jobs in weak industries, would suffer most in any free trade arrangement. Even business groups were starting to sound more restrained. The Business Council on National Issues talked about the necessity of gradual trade liberalization. The Canadian Chamber of Commerce called for a comprehensive approach to trade liberalization and urged caution in pursuing freer trade with the United States. And the Canadian Manufacturers' Association was calling on Ottawa to make a careful analysis of benefits and losses, something that Ottawa was slow to do. This was surprising in view of the fact that the business groups had supported free trade from the first. In fact, as Carol Goar of the *Toronto Star* reported on October 26, 1985, Ambassador Paul Robinson had first broached the idea of free trade when Trudeau was in power to the Canadian Chamber of Commerce and subsequently to the Business Council on National Issues and the Canadian Manufacturers' Association. Initial enthusiasm had dwindled, however, as the consequences for some of their members became clearer.

Another group was also beginning to express concern: the cultural industries. Marcel Masse, the Minister of Communications, had firmly declared that the protection of cultural sovereignty was his top priority, but in September 1985 Masse chose to resign while the RCMP investigated irregularities in his election campaign financing. That alarmed cultural nationalists, and their concern did not cease when Masse was cleared and returned to the ministry. The cultural community, with its ready access to the media, was worried about takeovers in the publishing industry, cable television advertising, control of motion picture cinemas and distribution, and a host of other issues. Most of the arts community was nationalistic, fearful that if Canadian manufacturers said jobs would be lost if they were not protected, then cultural sovereignty would be quick to be sacrificed at the bargaining table. Certainly, Canadian ownership of publishing industries was a matter for negotiation. Film would also be on the table, or so Joe Clark told Parliament on November 5.

A secret External Affairs document, "Canadian Sovereignty," which was prepared for Cabinet on October 10, was leaked to *Maclean's* and published on November 11. The document suggested using cultural programs as "trade-offs" in the negotiations if the government, by mounting a massive public relations campaign, could convince Canadians that their identity would flourish in an economy strengthened by free trade. Denunciations of the Tories as "assimilated Americans" were already beginning.

Other critics of the government's free trade ideas argued that Mulroney was making a historic change in Canadian policy in response to a temporary protectionist mood in the United States. What would happen if three years down the road the American dollar dropped in value, the Canadian dollar rose, and trade conditions around the world eased? What would happen, they asked, if Canada, having made the changes in its economy that free trade demanded, suddenly found that the Americans had changed direction? And what would happen if the United States threatened to abrogate the trade arrangements unless Canada supported American positions on foreign policy issues? Those kinds of concerns were usually pooh-poohed (although Joe Clark was said by those close to him to be particularly concerned about the latter point), but they were the sorts of questions Ottawa—and Canadians generally—had to consider. Once in place, free trade would be hard to dismantle, and Canada's bargaining position with Washington might well be weaker after free trade was in effect than before.

As 1985 wore on, however, Mulroney had some things in his favour. The pressure for free trade from the Western premiers and, to a lesser extent, from the eastern provinces continued when the premiers met at St. John's in late August. Major business leaders continued to press the government on the issue, and Richard Lipsey of Queen's University produced a book for the C. D. Howe Institute again calling for a full free trade arrangement. A parliamentary committee, steered by London MP Tom Hockin, produced a nearly unanimous report in favour of free trade, provided that such sensitive areas as communications and cultural and social policies were excluded.

The American ambassador, Paul Robinson, a rough-talking businessman and Reagan campaign contributor, was gone by early September, replaced by a smoother diplomat, Thomas Niles. That could only help. And Decima Research, the Tory party's pollsters, reported in late summer that 80 percent of the country favoured closer ties with the United States, up from 60 percent who had felt that way only three years before. Two-thirds of the public expressed general support for the idea of free trade, which most saw as meaning more jobs. (Later polls done for the Shoe Manufacturers' Association of Canada, one of the industries threatened by free trade, showed that 66 percent of the population preferred import quotas to protect jobs in Canada, even if higher prices were the result. The public, in other words, remained confused and volatile on the trade issue.)

Most important, on September 5, the Macdonald Royal Commission on the Economic Union and Development Prospects for Canada produced its massive $20 million report. As Donald Macdonald had indicated ten months earlier, the commission's major recommendation was for free trade. ''The day of the apologetic

Canadian is gone,'' the report argued, ''and there is no reason to suppose that our present confidence will be undermined by an arrangement designed only to secure a continuing exchange of goods and services with the United States.'' Moreover, the commission called for an end to the rigid support systems that had protected Canadian trade for decades. In effect, Canada was to rely on ''the flexibility of markets and policies which facilitate competition and adjustment.'' Macdonald also urged that an office of the special trade negotiator be established to take over the responsibility for negotiation from the gaggle of competing departments, and he explicitly rejected a customs union or common market. Free trade, à la Macdonald, involved only the free flow of goods and services across the border, each nation retaining an independent approach to taxes and import regulations and the flow of investment capital and people. The Commission recognized that some plants might be forced to close as a consequence of free trade and that many men and women would lose jobs. Overall, however, Macdonald argued that the benefits would outweigh those losses in every region of the country.

For Mulroney, more than a little battered on the trade question, the report was a boon. For one thing, the commissioner and all of his colleagues were Liberal appointees—Mulroney himself had earlier called them ''a bunch of Grits''—one factor certain to dampen some of the opposition fire on free trade. Moreover, the commission's report and the dozens of research studies that accompanied it provided a body of data and a reasoned framework for the debate. ''The timing couldn't be better,'' said one senior bureaucrat to the *Financial Post*. ''You are looking today at a Conservative Cabinet of forty ministers, deeply stunned by a full summer of criticism . . . .''

Emboldened by the Macdonald report, the Cabinet decided to act on free trade. According to senior officials, however, when the Cabinet made its decision, the ministers had not looked in detail at the papers prepared by the departments concerned or at the analytical materials, especially estimates on job losses (or gains), the geographic effects, or the sectoral effects. It was incredible, one External Affairs official agreed, that the Tories didn't seem to remember 1911. The only explanation suggested was that when ''the PM says move, we move.'' The government, this official said, was going into a hailstorm, unaware of the costs that free trade could force on the protected sectors of the economy. Perhaps that was the reason why the prime minister gave Joe Clark ultimate responsibility for the coming trade initiative. Was Mulroney saddling his old rival with the potential blame? Or was it that the Secretary of State for External Affairs was one of the very few competent members of the Cabinet? Probably both contained a grain of truth.

On September 26, Mulroney finally told the country that he was seeking talks with the United States on free trade. The announcement had been delayed by Tunagate and by the troubles that engulfed Marcel Masse, but at last it was out. The Tories wanted to negotiate a new economic order in North America.

* * *

There were serious organizational and political problems still ahead of the Mulroney government before it could begin negotiations with Washington. The cooperation of the provinces was one such problem. Whereas all except Ontario (and Quebec after its government changed in December) were supportive, nonetheless all the premiers wanted a voice in the coming negotiations. Free trade was a good thing, in other words, only insofar as it did not clash with Saskatchewan's or Nova Scotia's special interests. For example, Mulroney was well aware that provincial non-tariff barriers were a major interest of the Americans, and some would unquestionably have to be sacrificed if free trade came into effect. But which ones? He also knew that Premier Peterson of Ontario was worried about the possibility that the Auto Pact might be on the table in the negotiations. If it were, did this mean that the province that was home to most of Canadian auto production had to have a seat at the table or a veto?

On October 11, Mulroney said that he was looking for ''a mechanism where a senior official of the various provinces would be present during the negotiation to make sure that their input and cooperation were there . . . . If we were to have negotiations,'' Mulroney added, ''it would be with an almost daily consultation process with the parties involved. Otherwise it would lead to absolutely nothing.'' That sounded as if the Canadian trade delegation would need a large hall in which to hold meetings; it was also a recipe for confusion. Just how a trade negotiator would cope with the babel of voices was unclear.

The choice of a trade negotiator was still uncertain. Through October and into November 1985, no evident progress was made in securing someone to manage the negotiations. While Reagan continued cautious soundings with Congress (the president did not request congressional authority to negotiate a trade agreement with Canada until December 10), Mulroney's government seemed to be spinning its wheels. "The sooner a negotiator is chosen," one official said, "the better. He will have to assemble a strong-sized, good team, and galvanize this government." On November 8, Mulroney finally found a man for the job in Simon Reisman.

Reisman, sixty-six, a blunt, abrasive, old-style Ottawa mandarin (of a sort), had worked in the Department of Finance since his return from military service in 1946. He had been on the fringes of the free trade negotiations of 1947-48, and he had negotiated the Auto Pact of 1965. As deputy finance minister for John Turner (to whom he had acted as an adviser during the 1984 election), he had bashed heads in the bureaucracy to help his minister get his way. Reisman's political connections helped disarm the Liberals, who could criticize the appointment only in a muted way. Reisman was also a good choice for a scapegoat if Mulroney needed one later on in the process.

Moreover, Reisman was a committed free trader. As far back as 1961, he had told friends that free trade was inevitable and necessary and need not threaten Canadian sovereignty. Whether he would accept the reality that free trade was fundamentally a political question, subject to all the variables of the prime minister's political calculus, was dubious at best.

On the other hand, as an Ottawa consultant/lobbyist since his retirement from the public service in 1975, Reisman was an advocate of the Great Recycling and Northern Development Canal project, a device to turn James Bay into a freshwater lake, divert rivers, and sell water to the United States. The plan called for the Americans to put up the capital and pay for the water. Reisman had suggested that water could be Canada's trump card in any trade talks. By itself, this connection made Reisman suspect to many nationalists (and others) to whom water resources were sacrosanct. With Reisman in charge of the free trade negotiations, those fears would only increase. Reisman himself downplayed them: "If I thought for a moment that there was any threat to Canada as a nation, to Canada's independence, Canada's ability to decide its own course, its own style of life, its own radio, television, books, then I wouldn't be in this for a moment."

Before long, Reisman was putting his office together (with $800,000 for redecoration and equipment and $958,000 a year for rent of office space one floor down from the Rideau Club—lunch arrangements were *so* important). With a staff of eighty-four—not, knowledgeable critics argued, the "best and brightest" bureaucrats in the public service—Reisman had assistance and a $10-million-a-year budget that dwarfed that of his counterparts in Washington, where as late as February 1986, precisely one American officer was gathering data on United States objectives and aims. Responsible to a sub-committee of the priorities and planning committee of the Cabinet, Reisman (given the sensitivity of the free trade issue and its centrality to the government's future) had ready access to Mulroney. The trade negotiator also managed to persuade his political masters to put Sylvia Ostry, hitherto the country's highest-ranking trade bureaucrat, under his control with a mandate to handle multilateral negotiations under GATT. Reisman was now the master of all trade, and if he disliked Ostry (and he did not hesitate to criticize her to his aides for her ideas and even her clothes), it was still better to have her under his control.

Arrogant, tough, hard-driving, Reisman initially had things very much his way. Moreover, he could make as much use as he wished of the International Trade Advisory Committee, a group of thirty-nine private-sector advisers headed by Walter Light of Northern Telecom, and fourteen advisory panels set up to represent individual industries in such areas as agriculture, fishing, mining, energy, chemicals, and automobiles. Light's blue-ribbon committee had clout, especially since Light had a high profile and abrasive style. He urged his colleagues not to "rationalize, rubber stamp, or otherwise endorse government positions," and added the obvious: "There won't be any lid on my mouth." There was potential for difficulty there as well.

Even so, with great speed, Reisman had carved out a substantial empire for himself, one that if skilfully managed could provide invaluable assistance during the negotiations. But only a master juggler could keep all those balls in the air, and by the first months of 1986 observers were already beginning to speculate that Reisman would not stay until the long negotiations with the United States were completed. The intractable difficulties in dealing with the provinces and their varied interests, and the overriding problem of taking instruction from a weakly led government and from confused PMO officials, all lent credence to the speculation.

The criticism of free trade continued. Premier Peterson's government argued that free trade would cost jobs—281,000 in Ontario alone, or so a study (prepared by American consultants!) suggested in late November, just prior to the First Ministers' Conference at Halifax. (Later studies for a legislative committee argued that the results of free trade would be at worst neutral for Ontario employment.) The federal government countered by attacking the credibility of the Ontario study and by suggesting that its own investigations showed that without free trade, up to 146,000 jobs might be sacrificed. All that the charges and countercharges demonstrated was that the data was incomplete, misleading, and prey to tendentious use. Indeed, Ottawa's slowness in gathering credible data was all too clear.

The First Ministers' Conference, to the astonishment of many, agreed on "the principle of full provincial participation" in the trade negotiations and on the need for a ninety-day period in which to reach agreement on a joint database, on trade objectives, on the obstacles the Americans might put in the way of achieving those objectives, and on just how the provinces would participate. The bargaining between provincial and federal officials on the participation issue, however, was bitter. Moreover, Premier Peterson, making a brilliant debut, lectured the prime minister in his closing remarks: "What we said . . . is that full participation is not just consultation. The bottom line is that the negotiating team will take instructions from the first ministers. Without the agreement of this group," Peterson added, "I can't imagine any agreement going forward." The premiers of Alberta and British Columbia tended to agree. Even so, the exact definition of "full provincial participation" remained unclear. In December, James Kelleher said flatly, "There will be only one negotiator at the table—the federal government."

At meeting after meeting in the months ahead, promised data was not presented (Ottawa blamed Peterson's government) and each side's conception of the other's role remained confused. By the beginning of March, Alberta's new premier, Don Getty, anxious to be seen to be as tough as his predecessor and pressed on by the leading business interests of his province, was leading a nine-province drive (with only Richard Hatfield's New Brunswick dissenting) to get full information on the Reisman negotiating strategy and a guarantee that the battle plan would constantly be checked with the provinces during the bargaining.

Some officials argued that the war with the premiers had to be escalated. In March 1986, Alan Nymark, the assistant chief trade negotiator in Reisman's office, prepared a major strategy document called "Federal-Provincial Cooperation in Free Trade Negotiations" for Clark and Kelleher to present to the trade sub-committee of the priorities and planning committee. Prepared in extraordinary secrecy and not (as is the norm) circulated in advance of the sub-committee meeting, Nymark's document posed three options: to accept Premier Getty's eight-point plan; to have Ottawa pass legislation declaring all free trade arrangements exclusively a matter of federal jurisdiction; or to arrange a "cooperative" approach.

The first two options were dismissed out of hand, as the author intended they should be, and the ministers, to everyone's surprise, accepted the cooperative approach. The surprise was occasioned by the fact that, despite the label, the cooperative approach was confrontationist. In this option, Ottawa was always to have the controlling hand in the free trade negotiations and although there was to be consultation with the provinces (including a first ministers' meeting, if this could not be avoided), Ottawa was to make the decisions. Moreover, Reisman was to be the sole negotiator, responsible only to Ottawa. He would decide who sat at the table and who participated in negotiations, and would merely "report" to the provinces. The sub-committee also agreed that Ottawa would submit any items in the trade agreement that fell within provincial jurisdiction to the provinces, but the federal government would reserve the right to make a final decision on proceeding with them. Finally, in terms of implementing any trade agreement with the United States, the federal government declared itself ready only to make every effort to ensure provincial compliance, something that might not satisfy the Americans. The hard line of Nymark's paper was accepted at once by the federal ministers, who were struggling to recover the ground that Ottawa had lost to the provincial capitals since the Halifax meeting. In one sense, their haste was surprising, if only because Privy Council Office officials, aware that the document was rough (not to say crude), had confidently expected that several meetings would be needed, giving them time to smooth out the rough edges. Those were sure to strike sparks in the provincial capitals, there being little indication of federal willingness to cooperate in the position paper. Ontario and Quebec, for example, groping toward the formation of an alliance on trade questions, were certain to be furious, and the Maritimes, the perennial weak sisters of Confederation, would become even more frightened that any deal with Washington would be at their expense. Whether the "cooperative" approach could be sold to Premiers Getty, Peterson, Bourassa, and their supporters was doubtful at best. The palmy days of federal-provincial cooperation were over.

The confusion over the role of the provincial governments, the concern over culture, and the growing campaign against free trade by labour and nationalist groups, organized by February into a Coalition Against Free Trade, all combined to weaken the government. (The one political plus for the Tories was that John Turner's Liberals, divided on this issue and with their force sapped by Donald Macdonald's conversion into free trade's biggest booster, were no better placed, arguing for both multilateral negotiations and discussions with the United States. In other words, the Grits stood for multilateralism and free trade and the Tories for free trade and multilateralism.)

The polls reflected the confusion. In November 1985, after Mulroney's announcement that Canada sought negotiations, 58 percent favoured free trade (down 7 percent since June and 20 percent since April 1984), and 31 percent opposed it. In February 1986, 54 percent favoured free trade and 35 percent opposed it. Those who gave strong support to the idea had fallen from 46 percent in the first survey to 20 percent in the last. In Ontario, support for free trade had fallen by thirty-three points and in Quebec by nineteen since April 1984. Moreover, although early surveys found only age differences among those offering opinions, the February 1985 sounding showed that union members, blue-collar workers, and low-income and older Canadians were those most disturbed by the prospect.

The Mulroney government, on this issue as on others, was losing ground, a condition not helped at all by the Reagan administration's decision at the beginning of 1986 to slap a 6.85 percent duty on Canadian groundfish imports in response to the cries of New England fishermen and in retaliation for Ottawa's subsidies to its fishermen. Ominously included among those subsidies (in American reckoning) was unemployment insurance. In March, however, the Commerce Department ruled that this was not a subsidy that should be countered with penalty duties, and the duty imposed at the beginning of the year was lowered to 5.82 percent. The Commerce Department, while giving unemployment insurance its stamp of approval, had identified fifty-four federal and provincial programs that, in its view, could be countered by import penalties; that was the reason for its duty.

There were serious implications for other industries. Were Canadian social programs and regional measures to stimulate industry to be on the bargaining table (as reports from Washington argued they should be)? If so, what would Nova Scotia, for example, say about that? And if Canadian social programs and regional assistance programs had to be brought into line with American ideas to secure markets for Canadian goods in the United States, was that a price the Canadian people would pay? Washington reports suggested that the administration was stiffening its overall trade posture and beginning to build a case for an internationally agreed "right of establishment" for multinational enterprises. Did that mean that every multinational in any and all circumstances could set up in Canada? That was an issue certain to be resisted by any Canadian government, even Mulroney's that was "open for business." If the policies of the two countries had to harmonize on such questions, in the jargon of the day, who would make the concessions? Did anyone in Canada really believe that the United States would adjust its policies to bring them into line with Canada's? Did this mean that Canadian policies would have to be changed to give Washington "the level playing field" it wanted? If so, the odds against free trade were lengthening.

More significantly, Washington was getting annoyed at the frustrating and disturbing Canadian course on the issue. Trade officials there were looking for a payout on a Canadian trade deal and were worried about the public haggling between the provinces and Ottawa. Yuetter told a congressional committee on February 19 that "our position is that all of Canada must be bound by any agreements that are reached," adding that "it would be imperative for the government of Canada" to work out matters with the provinces "before sitting down to negotiate with us." The American trade representative stated baldly, "We will insist on that." At the same time, he said that his government was disturbed at the growing number of subjects that Canada wanted to exclude from the negotiations, a commonly held view in Washington. "First it was going to be free trade, then it was free trade except for culture, then culture and provincial exclusions, and now it's agriculture," one of Yuetter's officials said.

At the root of Washington's concerns was doubt about the prime minister's toughness and ability to deal with the provinces and free trade critics. Moreover, the Americans said, if Canada insisted on excluding contentious subjects from the talks, then American interest groups would do the same thing (and by spring they were doing just that and causing squabbles between Yuetter and Treasury Secretary James Baker). The only result, they feared, would be to narrow talks to a strictly limited agenda. One Washington trade consultant, Edward Nef, summed it up; "I don't think anyone down here really knows what the Canadian position really is any more."

Those representatives and senators who thought they understood that position were unhappy with it, particularly the Pacific Northwesterners, who were furious at what Canada's lumber exports (which held 31 percent of the American softwood market) were doing to their constituents. Led by Senators Packwood and Baucus, two members of the Senate finance committee who had a crucial role to play in clearing Reagan's request for trade negotiations through the Senate, the lumber representatives had forced "high-level" talks between the two countries on lumber, stirring fears in Ottawa and in British Columbia's lumber towns that Canada was being blackmailed into concessions as a price for the free trade talks. Among the American demands were a reforestation tax on lumber exports, a revamped system of fixing the value of crown land timber, an introduction of the American system of "auctions" to raise prices, and a mill tax that would increase costs to lumber producers. American sources said Canada had "no alternative" but to accept some or all of those options. The Americans wanted higher prices, and the senators, fifteen of whom spoke in the Senate on February 26 about the industry's problems (twenty-five more sent written comments), were pressing hard for a resolution of the issue on American terms. Baucus even threatened to block Reagan's call for trade negotiations unless Canada modified its tree-cutting practices. Similar tactics and protests were under way in the House of Representatives' ways and means committee, where the chairman was pressing for tougher countervailing duty decisions, something directed squarely at Canadian lumber exports. The ways and means committee, however, decided to forgo the opportunity for hearings on the Canadian trade request, in effect giving approval for the administration to proceed. The Senate remained to be heard from.

The American senators and representatives could not be blamed for using whatever leverage they had to advance their constituents' interests. But the administration could be faulted. Reagan, a free trader by conviction but evidently not one in a hurry to conclude a pact with Canada, had been slow to negotiate. And Reagan did not name a trade negotiator to begin preparatory work until March 1986, when his choice fell upon Peter Murphy, a thirty-seven-year-old ambassador-level bargainer. Murphy had won his spurs as chief textile negotiator between 1981 and 1983. Tough, cool, and quiet, he would make an interesting contrast with the older, explosive Reisman. The president also omitted free trade from his State of the Union address in February 1986, offering only a brief mention of it in his legislative "wish list" for the year. The truth was that free trade had not caught the imagination of the American public nor of American industry. Predictions now were for long-drawn-out negotiations, extending, some suggested, for up to five or six years—a timetable that must have horrified Mulroney, who was hoping to use free trade as a big card in his re-election drive, scheduled for 1988.

The free trade issue was high on the agenda at the second Reagan-Mulroney meeting in mid-March 1986, but it was overshadowed first by the emphasis placed on acid rain and then by the publicity generated when Sondra Gotlieb, the wife of the Canadian ambassador in Washington, slapped her social secretary in full view of guests at a dinner at the embassy in honour of Vice-President George Bush. Overshadowed or not, the trade issue drew positive comments from Reagan and Mulroney in their public statements, and perhaps most important, Tip O'Neill, the Speaker of the House, opened a meeting between members of the congressional foreign relations committee and the prime minister with the prediction that Congress would approve the negotiations in April. "I hope we'll have the political courage and stamina to see the talks through to their conclusion," he said. Mulroney used the occasion to argue against preconditions on the talks, and he referred specifically to the softwood lumber problem. A meeting with senators was also said to be productive, although the prime minister could not have been pleased to be referred to as "Prime Minister Muldoon" by Rhode Island's Claiborne Pell. ("Senator Smell's" malapropism threatened to replace Myron Baloney as the favourite moniker for Mulroney.)

Despite the bumblings and grumblings of the senators, no one—and certainly not the Reagan administration or the Canadian embassy—was prepared for what happened. On April 11, ten of the twenty members of the Senate finance committee pledged to vote to refuse the Reagan administration's request for "fast-track" free trade talks with Canada. "It is my prediction," Senator Packwood said, "that if we were voting today the committee would turn the administration down." Observers agreed that Canada, despite the lumber problem, was almost an inadvertent victim of senatorial rage. Packwood's committee was preoccupied with the global trade picture, the budget, and taxes, and the senators were furious at the way they were being treated by the White House. The free trade request, relatively unimportant in American eyes but sensitive nonetheless, just happened by at the right time to be sideswiped.

Ottawa was appalled at the prospect that the committee could block the fast-track approach and most of the government's future prospects. The fast-track route gave the Senate only one crack—a simple approve or reject vote—at the final free trade package, something that was absolutely critical to Canada. Otherwise, every senator could pick out the one clause that hurt his or her constituents and demand alterations.

Nevertheless, it was hard to see what Ottawa could do to rectify matters. Opposition MPs, cheered at the prospect that the senators might, as some put it, save Canada from itself, pressed Mulroney to withdraw the free trade initiative, only to be answered with a curt, "The answer is no." "These things happen," Mulroney said the next day. "We still intend to proceed." In Washington, the administration persuaded the senators to delay their vote until April 22 (and then, when a majority could not be found, until April 23), allowing time for full-scale lobbying of the committee members. Yuetter and Gotlieb led the lobbyists, followed by other administration and embassy officials and, on April 21, by Reagan himself. In Canada, Trade Minister Kelleher added to the pressure by stating, "We still expect the president to honour that commitment. [The president] knows as well as we do that failure to do so will raise doubts in Canada and elsewhere about Washington's credibility and its commitment to liberalizing trade."

One way out of the senatorial dilemma might have been to give the senators and their specific concerns a greater voice in the negotiating process, an idea that was floated in the days preceding the finance committee vote. Indeed, according to Carol Goar of the *Toronto Star*, Secretary of State Schultz called Joe Clark on April 22 to ask if Canada could live with a resolution that set out the senators' "wish list" for the talks. That wish list included the elimination of subsidies on Canadian exports to the United States, an undertaking by the provinces to abide by any trade agreement, and a suggestion that some American non-tariff barriers be declared off-limits in the bargaining. Although there were divided counsels among the officials and politicians, the Canadians in the end said no. The prime minister in particular was not amused: "The position of the government of Canada is that we shall not accept any preconditions," he told Parliament. That seemed to close off that approach as far as Ottawa was concerned, but reality now suggested that the Senate had won itself a greater say in all trade negotiations. (For example, when an American negotiator said that the Senate would not buy a specific proposal, after the events of April 1986 how could Ottawa's bargainers hope to refute such a claim? Reisman had an answer: "I'm not going to give up one damn thing by virtue of the fact that the Senate has had a debate or that the senator has had a debate or that there will be individual items that arise during the course of it,'' he told the *Globe and Mail*'s Christopher Waddell. ''Be clear about that. In fact, if anything, it has made me more resolute than ever.'')

When the Senate finance committee finally voted on the Reagan request for authority to negotiate with Canada, on the afternoon of April 23, the result was a ten-ten draw on a motion to give the president authority to negotiate until January 3, 1988. Under Senate rules, that constituted approval, and Mulroney's free trade initiative was still alive. The result had been achieved only through concentrated presidential pressure on Hawaiian Democrat Sparky Matsunaga, who switched his vote at the last moment. What the price was for Matsunaga's support, and that of other senators who had switched sides earlier, was not clear. Oregon's Packwood noted that he expected to receive a letter from Reagan confirming the president's pledge to resolve the lumber issue quickly—and separately from the free trade negotiations. Canadian officials from the prime minister on down maintained that this was impossible or unlikely, or both. Reagan was also expected to send another letter, pledging close consultation with the Senate during the negotiations.

There was certain to be trouble ahead with the Congress, especially if the negotiations did not conclude before the president's bargaining authority expired in January 1988—and almost no one in either country expected the negotiations to finish that quickly. Senator Danforth of Missouri, one of those who had refused to alter his negative vote, sounded angry when he said that ''we are going to be watching these negotiations like eagles; we will be watching very, very closely what is being done.'' He added, ''I serve notice now that this senator does not have to go along. I will be very, very hard to please when the administration comes back to us for approval of what they've negotiated.'' Danforth was not alone in holding that view.

The Mulroney government was obviously relieved but still shaken by the result in Washington. Both Mulroney and Reisman told reporters that it was far from certain that the negotiations would produce a treaty that would satisfy Canadians. Canadians had seen a sample of senatorial capriciousness in action, and the press was generally cautious. The public, Jeffrey Simpson said in the *Globe and Mail*, "will be exceedingly sensitive to anything that smacks of excessive concessions." Mulroney had to be as aware of that as anyone, but at the very least his government's political agenda had survived, more or less intact.

With both sides stating that the negotiations would begin on May 21, 1986, all that remained for Ottawa to do now was to get the role of the provinces sorted out. The hard-line federal position was all set to be tried, but after the April follies in the Senate, perhaps there was some merit in keeping provincial discontent as a counter to that of the senators. Reagan could not give Canada too many concessions because the senators would object; Mulroney in turn could not concede too much because Toronto and Halifax and Edmonton would shriek. Suddenly the provinces had become a wild card that might be of use in the negotiations—and if the negotiations failed, then Mulroney, if he played his hand correctly, could blame the Liberal governments in Toronto and Quebec City. He also had the option, in the event of a breakdown in negotiations with Washington, to blame the Americans. That would involve a fast switch in policy, but an anti-American stance was, after all, very much in the Tory tradition.

There was a long road ahead on free trade, but Mulroney had managed to get the Americans to the bargaining table. That was an achievement. But what the result might be economically for Canada (and politically for Mulroney) was no clearer in the spring of 1986 than it had been in September 1985. The difficulty was that the Tories, by mid-1986, had little going for them other than free trade as the next general election drew nearer. True, the economy was stronger and unemployment was down, but interest rates were still higher than in the United States, and the collapse in oil and wheat prices had poleaxed the Alberta economy. The dollar was weak—a blow to every Canadian travelling to the States or Europe—and provincial harmony, gracefully achieved earlier by Mulroney's giving the premiers almost everything they wanted, was inevitably beginning to fragment. Without free trade as the main plank in their election platform, what else would the Mulroney Tories have to offer in 1988? And if that was so, would better relations with the Americans force the Canadian government into taking any deal rather than the best deal? "The last thing we want," one senior official said, "is a deal at any price. We will push the bilateral negotiation as far as we can, and then decide whether it is worth trying to conclude or not." That was undoubtedly the intent, but whether talks could be broken off without a sweeping agreement after the government had invested so much of its prestige in them was another question.

The one certainty was that in this area as in so many others, Mulroney had managed to turn his huge and unassailable majority into a position of weakness with remarkable speed.

Chapter Fourteen
Conclusion

We began this book by referring to the meteoric rise and precipitous fall of the Diefenbaker government in the period 1958 to 1962. As of mid-1986, there are already signs that history is about to repeat itself. Most of the public opinion polls published since the turn of the year show the Liberals either neck-and-neck with the Tories or ahead. The Conservatives continue their domination of federal politics in the West, but the polls show a slip in their popularity even there. In Quebec, they are already far behind the Liberals and do not enjoy much more support than they did in the pre-Mulroney era. What is of great long-term significance is the decline of Tory support at the provincial level. Conservatives have been replaced by Liberals in Prince Edward Island and Ontario; Liberals have regained power in Quebec and have won seats in the legislatures of Manitoba and Alberta. In Alberta, the NDP scored a breakthrough in the May provincial election, winning sixteen seats, and the once-invincible Tories suddenly look vulnerable. In Saskatchewan, Conservative premier Grant Devine was on the verge of calling an election early in 1986, but is holding off in the face of certain defeat by the NDP.

The trends in provincial politics bode ill for the federal Tories. In Canadian politics there is a definite long-term pattern that exists because the Canadian people, in their wisdom, have built a system of checks and balances by voting for one party in provincial elections and for another in federal elections. What usually happens is that long-term political change begins at the provincial level, as voters begin to defeat governments of the same political stripe as the government in Ottawa. Finally the federal government falls, is replaced by the opposition, and the cycle begins all over again. It happened under Trudeau, and it is happening under Mulroney. The fall of the central power bastion is sometimes delayed for many years, as was the case under Trudeau, but fall it usually does. And when the federal government proves itself to be less competent than normal, the transition speeds up. If this is now happening, it is further evidence pointing to a one-term Tory government.

If Mulroney goes the way of Diefenbaker, his four years or so in power will have served only one enduring national purpose—it will have given the Liberals the rest and rejuvenation they so badly needed. This too has become a pattern in Canadian politics—the Liberals, in this century, have come and gone in cyclical fashion. The cycle generally goes like this: a strong leader emerges; the strong leader begins to dominate the party; party policy and party organization are neglected; the leader, for one reason or another, is rendered ineffective; party popularity plummets; defeat follows; the party, in opposition, renews itself and is able to regain power, usually with a new leader. The pattern began with Wilfrid Laurier, party leader from 1887 to 1919 and prime minister from 1896 to 1911, and was repeated with Louis St-Laurent, leader from 1948 to 1958, and prime minister from 1948 until 1957, and with Trudeau, leader and prime minister from 1968 until 1984, with a brief spell as opposition leader during the Clark interregnum of 1979-80. William Lyon Mackenzie King, who led the Liberals from 1919 to 1948, was defeated at the start of the Depression, but was re-elected in 1935 and managed to avoid defeat thereafter by allowing young Turks in the party to reform its structure and platform in the closing months of World War II. So far, there has been almost no reform or rebuilding of the Liberal party under Turner.

Mulroney did not lead his party to victory in order to set the stage for several more decades of Liberal rule. Why then is the pattern beginning to repeat itself? Why is there talk of a one-term Conservative government? Part of the explanation must be that the government, for the most part, has done a bad job of governing. Scandal and misadventure have followed scandal and misadventure and it seems as if a week cannot go by without some further story of a conflict of interest, a ministerial indiscretion, or a judgement that seems to fly in the face of common sense. To this must be added the government's almost complete lack of direction, a shortage of talent in the Cabinet (especially from French Canada), and major policy errors in almost every sphere from culture to banking to social policy.

The Tories came to power with the idea that government was already too big, too active, and too involved. They had no intention of launching major new governmental initiatives, because they believed that the government was already doing more than enough. In fact, they wanted to dismantle, to withdraw, to back away. They talked of deregulation, of privatization, of re-examining social policy, of dismantling the National Energy Program, and so on. They had and have no major new policies to put into place. They did not and do not believe in pro-active government. Their primary intention, therefore, was to cut the size of government and then manage it smoothly and efficiently. These are not unworthy objectives, especially since the welfare state has become so firmly entrenched and the government has so much control over the economic system. The problem lies not in the objectives, but in the execution. Each governmental stumble shows that the Conservatives are not doing the most important thing they sought to do—make government work better than it has in the recent past.

Many of the misadventures that have plagued the government happened because of inexperience and because any first-time Cabinet is bound to contain people who should not be there. But there is more to it than that. This government seemed very sure of its direction when it was first elected, but it lost its way shortly after that. The only area in which it can be said to have delivered what it promised was in energy. It has reneged on its defence promises. It bungled its re-examination of social policy and failed to make any important changes to that policy. It has, so far, done little about privatization except to sell one unprofitable company—de Havilland—and dispose of a number of others that are too small to matter. And so it goes.

Many of the difficulties the Conservatives have had must be laid at the door of the prime minister. Almost from the beginning of his tenure, he has acted as if the government were in imminent danger of defeat, as if he were the leader of a minority government. He has the largest absolute majority in Canadian history, but his decisions are the decisions of a politically frightened man. He governs by the polls in a constant search for popularity. He presented Canadians with an image of self-assured strength, but he has governed like a man unable to find his way.

Mulroney is not completely different in his constant attention to the polls from those who came before him. When politicians discovered pollsters in the 1940s, the nature of politics began to change. Politicians once made policy and policy decisions and then checked the polls to see how the public reacted. Now, before making decisions, they check the polls to see how the public may react. But Mulroney ties himself to the polls more tightly than Trudeau ever did because the Tories have become the traditional "out" party of Canadian politics at the federal level and he fears that history will repeat itself. Long-term Tory strategy is to displace the Liberals as the new majority party, dominating politics in the next decades as the Liberals have dominated it since the end of World War I. These concerns have led Mulroney to an unending search for the middle ground on every issue and yet he has usually satisfied no one. He and his government have governed by the polls and have backed off on almost every major decision they have had to make. They want to be loved more than respected. This is a formula for political disaster, and will be self-defeating in the long run.

Mulroney dominates the Cabinet and there are no other ministers who approach him in power or authority. Time after time it was he who determined the particular course of one minister or another. He made the final decision to bail out the Western banks, for example, and he made the final decision both to go with the de-indexation of the OAS and to back off from that decision. Michael Wilson is still finance minister because he bent to Mulroney's will. That obviously suited both him and the prime minister.

Even though the government is largely to blame for its own growing unpopularity, Canadians are no longer sure of what they want from government and make demands on it that it cannot possibly fulfil. They want fiscal responsibility without cutbacks. They want strength as well as flexibility. They want to protect Canadian culture but they also want unlimited access to American movies, television, books, and magazines. They despise weak leaders and rebel against strong ones. Any government that allows them to determine its political direction will end up chasing its own tail.

Take the entire issue of governmental involvement in the Canadian economy, for example. It may be reasonable for the government to take steps to help guard Canadians from the economic consequences of unemployment, sickness, and retirement. But does the welfare state have to extend to profitable corporations? Should unprofitable transportation and communication services be subsidized by the government? Should inefficient or unprofitable publishers be protected by legislation? Canadians as a whole answer "yes, but . . . " or "no, but . . . " to almost all of these questions. Canadians must decide what role the government ought to be playing in Canada's economic, social, and cultural life. A government that is unwilling to incur the wrath of one sector of the voters or another will always be strictly limited in its options.

We could point to many decisions this government has made that show this most clearly, but we believe that the battle over Mulroney's "sacred trust" offers the best example. The policy paper Wilson introduced to the Canadian people on November 8, 1984—*A New Direction for Canada*—asked Canadians to think about their government's social welfare policies to decide if the basic assumptions of those policies were still valid and the objectives still desirable. It was a good start. But what happened then? The official opposition did its job—it opposed the government— and many Canadians reacted negatively, especially those most directly affected. All that was normal; what else did Wilson and Mulroney expect?

Caught between public opposition and its own internal contradictions, the government began to back down and in the end there was no "new direction for Canada" in the social welfare area. That would have been acceptable if it had resulted from a great national debate, but it did not. It resulted from a loss of political will. There, in that story, are the two elements we have been pointing to; a people who don't want to think about life after government and a government that doesn't want to think about life after defeat.

When the Conservatives were elected in September 1984, they were given a mandate to do things differently from the way Trudeau had done them. Trudeau, and no one else, had set the political agenda in Canada from 1968 to 1984, and although some Canadians might have agreed with many of Trudeau's objectives, they grew to resent his methods. Mulroney promised an end to confrontation and he delivered. But he also promised competence, efficiency, and a re-examination of the role of government in society. All of this has been much slower in coming. The Tories believe that if unemployment drops and economic performance improves in the next few years, they will overcome the setbacks that have beset them since September 1984. They may be right, although economic recovery may have little to do with domestic policies. But if they do not soon demonstrate a much greater capacity to make decisions, to take action, and to manage well, the economic improvement they seek may elude them. Improving the climate for business is as much an exercise in psychology as it is in economics and finance; how can business people and investors feel confident about a country that is badly governed?

If this government does not soon begin to project an image of self-confidence and direction, an image based on competence and good management, the electorate will surely snatch Mulroney's "sacred trust" away.

Afterword

On Monday, June 30, 1986, after this manuscript was completed, Brian Mulroney announced a major Cabinet shuffle. In effect, the first half of the Tories' term in office had drawn to a close. There was no coincidence in the timing. A few days before, opinion polls had confirmed that the Conservatives were trailing the Liberals everywhere but in the West (and even there, the Tories had slipped badly). The months of scandal, misadventure, and indecision had taken their toll and Mulroney had shuffled the deck to try to find a winning hand.

The prime minister set about repairing the government's tarnished credibility and indicated some new directions and strengthened priorities. The most important signal came from the departure of Erik Nielsen, the deputy prime minister, who moved to the back benches—likely at his own request. As Mulroney's enforcer, Nielsen had taken most of the flak for the government's stumbling and errors during the first twenty months. He must have been tired of the press's bitter attacks on his stonewalling. His departure went unlamented. Insiders, however, predicted that the government would be hard pressed to find someone else who could force Mulroney to make decisions.

In contrast to Nielsen, the new deputy, Don Mazankowski, had proven to be a popular figure on both sides of the House of Commons. Mazankowski immediately began setting a new style. He moved the office of the deputy prime minister from an obscure ninth-floor location on Sparks Street to a suite down the hall from Mulroney in the Langevin Block. It seemed that Mazankowski would be a force to be reckoned with in setting policy and that he would probably take a higher public profile than his predecessor.

In line with his desire to make Quebec into an enduring Tory stronghold, Mulroney moved to shore up Cabinet representation in the province. In large measure, the changes indicated a preoccupation with Montreal, the provincial economy, and patronage. The weaker Quebec ministers were out—the press no longer had the perils of Andrée Champagne to regale the public with. Power accrued to the Montreal area with the appointments of Monique Landry, Gerry Weiner, and Jean Charest. To meet criticism that Quebec ministers had no say in economic decisions, Mulroney made Pierre Cadieux the Minister of Labour and promoted Michel Côté and Benoît Bouchard into the important economic portfolios of Regional Industrial Expansion and Employment and Immigration, respectively.

Patronage had much to do with Marcel Masse's move from Communications to Energy, Mines and Resources. While the shift put another Quebecker into an important post, energy was not the hot potato in 1986 that Pat Carney had inherited in 1984. Masse would have time to untangle the Conservative party's affairs in Quebec and to straighten out the charges of kickbacks to MPs and outright graft that had resulted in criminal charges being laid against a Quebec backbencher. The demotion of Roch LaSalle was the other side of the coin. The long-time Tory MP had lost the struggle to control the party's provincial machine and was too close to the unsavoury side of the Quebec situation.

Monique Vézina took over as Minister of Supply and Services. She had performed well in her apprenticeship, doling out contracts for the Canadian International Development Agency. No doubt Mulroney hoped that she could award the vast contracts that went with her new job without attracting undue criticism.

Mulroney reinforced the conclusion that he depended on the free trade gamble to win re-election. The tough and successful Pat Carney took over responsibility for the critical negotiations with the United States. By putting Carney on the firing line, the prime minister introduced yet another strong personality into a situation already replete with them. Would Carney and Joe Clark be able to overcome the tension inherent in their junior/senior ministerial relationship? Carney's initiatives would have to pass Clark's scrutiny. Moreover, could she bend Simon Reisman to her will? Mulroney gambled that she could.

The Cabinet changes did not indicate any change in the government's conservative fiscal and financial agenda. Michael Wilson stayed at the Department of Finance. Although Barbara McDougall did not get the reward she had earned for her role in the banks affair, she took over a new position as Minister for Privatization. This seemed to indicate that Mulroney still attached some importance to moving in this particular area.

As with any exercise in cabinet making, there were surprises and disappointments. The unexpected choice of Flora MacDonald, the nationalist red Tory from Kingston, as Minister of Communications, was likely dictated by the need to find a place for a figure with a strong following in the party. Perrin Beatty's promotion to the Department of National Defence elevated one of the government's youngest and brightest lights. It must have been a disappointment to the former associate minister, Harvie Andre, who had been considered Nielsen's most likely successor in the defence portfolio. Almost certainly, the change meant that the defence white paper would be delayed yet again.

The new Cabinet image was better, no doubt of that. To Quebec, Mulroney could show that French Canada had a say in looking after the country's purse. To the West, this might be alarming, but Mulroney could point to Mazankowski. To satisfy Ontarians, the prime minister could cite Beatty and Wilson. David Crombie's new post as Minister for Multiculturalism was also designed to placate Toronto voters, Even Newfoundland, with John Crosbie as Minister of Transport, had its opportunity to get more money from the government.

But image was not the whole problem. Canadians had voted for change in 1984, and they had trusted Brian Mulroney to begin the process. But for all his pious pronouncements, Mulroney had demonstrated from the start of the regime that old-style patronage remained a critical component of his politics, and Canadians soon realized that the revolution of September 4, 1984, had merely substituted one set of faces for another on the government's Jetstars and in luxury hotels in New York and Paris. That destroyed trust, and every misadventure and policy flipflop since the first days, no matter how unctuously Mulroney tried to present them as part of a natural learning process, reinforced the public's perceptions. The result is that the Conservative government has apparently lost much of its credibility, well before the halfway point in its mandate, and only the almost equal mistrust of John Turner's Liberals has prevented an even worse showing in the polls.

The root of the problem is Brian Mulroney. One of the authors of this book attended a sober academic conference in the spring of 1986. He was astonished to discover that every time Mulroney's name was mentioned, conferees snickered. Twenty-five years ago, John Diefenbaker drew similar responses, and such earned contempt ultimately brought the Chief down. After less than two years in power, Brian Mulroney already faces the same popular (and academic) response, and in a very real sense, he is on the verge of becoming a liability to the party he led out of the wilderness.

The government still has time to turn around volatile public opinion. John Turner clearly has no firm policy direction, and such as he has flies in the face of his previous positions. Broadbent, while personally popular, remains a permanent minority leader. Getting rid of Nielsen may help the government, and some of the Cabinet shifts seem to have put the right people into the proper spots. The prime minister's failure to provide good government and effective leadership is not as easily remedied. The Canadian people wanted Brian Mulroney to lead them and thus far he has not done so. If he can, they may still follow; if he cannot, they will likely turn back with some reluctance to the Liberals. If that happens, the Mulroney government will join John Diefenbaker's as just another Conservative aberration in Canada's Liberal century.